Education in Emerging Indian Society

Education in Emerging Indian Society

Dr Madhumita Sharma

MD PUBLICATIONS PVT LTD
NEW DELHI
www.mdppl.com

Published by :

MD Publications Pvt Ltd
"MD House", 11, Darya Ganj,
New Delhi-110 002
Phone : +91-11-41563325 (Customer Service)
+91-11-41562846 (Editorial)
E-mail (orders) : order@mdppl.com
Website : www.mdppl.com

ISBN : 978-81-7533-222-5

Published and Printed by Mr. Pranav Gupta on behalf of MD Publications Pvt Ltd at Printext, New Delhi.

PREFACE

Education in India has a history stretching back to the ancient urban centres of learning at Taxila and Nalanda. Western education became ingrained into Indian society with the establishment of the British Raj. Historically, Indian education has been elitist. Traditional Hindu education was tailored to the needs of Brahman boys who were taught to read and write by a Brahman teacher. During Mughal rule (1526-1858), Muslim education was similarly elitist, although its orientation reflected economic factors rather than those of caste background. Under British company and crown rule (1757-1947), official education policies reinforced the preexisting elitist tendencies of South Asian education.

The present educational system of India is an implantation of British rulers. Wood's Dispatch of 1854 laid the foundation of present system of education in India. Before the advent of British in India, education system was private one. With the introduction of Wood's Dispatch known as Magna Carta of Indian education, the whole scenario changed. The main purpose of it was to prepare Indian Clerks for running local administration. Under it the means of school education were the vernacular languages while the higher education, was granted in English only. British government started giving funds to indigenous schools in need of help and thus slowly some of the schools became government-aided.

Post primary education has traditionally catered to the interests of the higher and upwardly mobile castes. Despite substantial increases in the spread of middle schools and high schools' growth in enrollment, secondary schooling is necessary for those bent on social status and mobility through acquisition of an office job. Though still by and large, the higher education in India is controlled by the government and is highly subsidized, in the recent years, private sector is making successful forays in the realm of higher Indian education, particularly in professional courses. This development can make, and is already making higher Indian education in engineering, medical, management, etc. unaffordable for many Indian students.

India has made huge progress in terms of increasing primary education attendance rate and expanding literacy to approximately two thirds of the population. However, education is still far behind developing countries such as China or Thailand. Most children never attend secondary schools. An optimistic estimate is that only one in five job-seekers in India have ever had any sort of vocational training. It presents a historical overview of education in Modern India from its colonial beginning in 1757 through the birth of an Independent India in 1947 till the early years of the new millennium as well as the developments and the changes that have taken place in education in our country in the early years of the new millennium following globalisation.

I am very grateful to Mr. Pranav Gupta, Director of MD Publications Pvt Ltd, New Delhi, for his kind cooperation and support for this book.

Dr Madhumita Sharma

Contents

1

Indian Society

Indian society is multifaceted to an extent perhaps unknown in any other of the world's great civilizations. Virtually no generalization made about Indian society is valid for all of the nation's multifarious groups. Compre-hending the complexities of Indian social structure has challenged scholars and other observers over many decades. The ethnic and linguistic diversity of Indian civilization is more like the diversity of an area as variable as Europe than like that of any other single nation-state. Living within the embrace of the Indian nation are vast numbers of different regional, social, and economic groups, each with different cultural practices. Particularly noteworthy are differences between social structures in the north and the south, especially in the realm of kinship systems.

Throughout the country, religious differences can be significant, especially between the Hindu majority and the large Muslim minority; and other Indian groups—Budd-hists, Christians, Jains, Jews, Parsis, Sikhs, and practitioners of tribal religions—all pride themselves on being unlike members of other faiths.

Access to wealth and power varies considerably, and vast differences in socioeconomic status are evident everywhere. The poor and the wealthy live side by side in urban and rural areas. It is common in city life to see a prosperous, well-fed man or woman chauffeured in a fine car pass gaunt street dwellers huddled beneath burlap shelters along the roadway.

In many villages, solid cement houses of landowners rise not far from the flimsy thatched shacks of landless laborers. Even when not so obvious, distinctions of class are found in almost every settlement in India.

Urban-rural differences can be immense in the Indian Society. Nearly 74 percent of India's population dwells in villages, with agriculture providing support for most of these rural residents. In villages, mud-plastered walls ornamented with traditional designs, dusty lanes, herds of grazing cattle, and the songs of birds at sunset provide typical settings for the social lives of most Indians. In India's great cities, however, millions of people live amidst cacophony—roaring vehicles, surging crowds, jammed apartment buildings, busy commercial establishments, loudspeakers blaring movie tunes—while breathing the poisons of industrial and automotive pollution. Gender distinctions are pronounced. The behavior expected of men and women can be quite different, especially in villages, but also in urban centers. Prescribed ideal gender roles help shape the actions of both sexes as they move between family and the world outside the home.

Crosscutting and pervading all of these differences of region, language, wealth, status, religion, urbanity, and gender is the special feature of Indian society that has received most attention from observers: caste. The people of India belong to thousands of castes and caste like groups—hierarchically ordered, named groups into which members are born. Caste members are expected to marry within the group and follow caste rules pertaining to diet, avoidance of ritual pollution, and many other aspects of life. Given the vast diversity of Indian society, any observation must be tempered with the understanding that it cannot apply to all Indians. Still, certain themes or underlying principles of life are widely accepted in India.

In a country as diverse and complex as India, it is not surprising to find that people here reflect the rich glories of the past, the culture, traditions and values relative to geographic locations and the numerous distinctive manners, habits and food that will always remain truly Indian. According to five thousand years of recorded history, India has been invaded by armies, traders and immigrants who brought with them their own habits, faiths, practices and observances which have all contributed to the rich texture of Indian life and living.

From the eternal snows of the Himalayas to the cultivated peninsula of far South, from the deserts of the West to the humid deltas of the East, from the dry heat and cold of the Central Plateau to the cool forest foothills, Indian lifestyles clearly glorify the geography. The food, clothing and habits of an Indian differ in accordance to the place of origin. Deep-rooted family values continue to exist in Indian families. The surname of an Indian is based on his caste or place of origin or his family occupation. Men are still considered the head of a family and are consulted for all decisions though they no longer continue to be the single breadwinner. A wife will always serve her husband before she eats. Parents are looked upon with respect and regard. Children are financially supported by their parents throughout their education.

Indians believe in sharing happiness and sorrow. A festival or a celebration is never constrained to a family or a home. The whole community or neighborhood is involved in bringing liveliness to an occasion. A lot of festivals like *Diwali, Holi, Id, Christmas, Mahaveer Jayanthi* are all celebrated by sharing sweets and pleasantries with family, neighbours and friends. An Indian wedding is an occasion that calls for participation of the family and friends. Similarly, neighbours and friends always help out a family in times of need. Though ethnically Indians speak different languages, follow different religions, eat the most diverse varieties of food, there is still a richness in Indian arts and culture which is unparalleled anywhere else in the world. The beauty of the Indian people lies in the spirit of tolerance, give-and-take and a composition of cultures that can be compared to a garden of flowers of various colors and shades of which, while maintaining their own entity, lend harmony and beauty to the garden - India!

As a woman in India, I find that the society is changing a lot in terms of acceptance of women as professionals, as bread-earners in families and as independent thinking individuals. Women have proved themselves as equals in many professions as well as proved themselves even better suited than men in others. The situation for working women is improving fast.

On the other hand, in the typical Indian Society, you find that there are still expectations and assumptions about women that are not so much relevant to their current status, but a clear hangover from out suppressive past. This may be more obvious in rural societies, but it is extremely prevalent in urban ones as well.

I am speaking of "running the home" kind of stuff. Regardless of how hard the man and woman of the house work, there are certain areas of the home that are the woman's province in happy times and her nemesis in not so happy times.

"As the woman of the house, you should…." is a familiar refrain for most women in India. I think, it is high time that we as citizens of modern India took a good hard look at our automatic assumptions and investigated which among these are still applicable today, and which ones we simply need to let go.

Typical situations we see include the woman bringing a cup of hot tea for her man returning from work, or the woman returning home after her husband and heading straight to the kitchen to cook dinner, and so on.

On an average, in any home where women are working, their income is also important to the well-being of the home and the living standards. Where it is not a question of money, it is generally possible to employ someone for the work in the house. So when we speak of a traditional role of a woman being responsible for the efficient running of her home, it is something we need to be aware of as an additional expectation made from her.

The traditional role of a man has been the one of earning the money for the running of the home. This has changed to a great extent. Working women contribute to the expenses of running their homes as well. However, there has been little contribution from men in terms of shouldering some of the responsibilities of women.

One interesting insight I received into this was from a friend. He said, "See, women find the outside world challenging and attractive. They like the freedom it brings to them. So they enter the world. There is no reason for a man to find the women's traditional role appealing, so he doesn't. No one has forced the women to step into the man's role, and no one should force the men to step into a woman's role."

On the surface, this seems to strike sense. However, the flaw lies in an assumption of current roles that are the same as traditional roles and that the women are entering "a man's territory". This simply doesn't hold true in most cases today. Women are educated and often have their careers well before they get married and it is as much their right as the man's work is his. However, the other part, where the men don't find the house work appealing enough to invest effort in still holds true.

This is something that needs to be taken an honest assessment of. If we abandon the traditional perspective of division of responsibilities inside and outside the home (since it has already been broken in the outside the home area), we come to a situation where the couple are both inhabiting a home and earning and contributing toward its running. What we need to find is a sharing of responsibilities inside the home as well, that allows both some dignity. This would also help resolve many situations where a man feels threatened by a working woman. Why wouldn't he. She earns, she spends, she invests, and on top of that, she is independent in terms of being able to manage her own existence completely, including running of her own home.

There is no point pushing the women down. What needs to happen is the removal of the "un-marchioness" associated with responsibilities at home and recognize it as the actions of a responsible and independent individual, whether male or female. This would actually add some power to the increasingly "lazy" image of men among women and empower them with some self-respect, while empowering the women with acceptance and support from the one source that matters the most. Please note that I am not speaking of every man out here. There are many couples who are already on this journey and find themselves comfortable both inside and outside the home, and the mutual respect and closeness can be seen a mile off in such couples.

It is heartening to find amidst the flood of profound, philosophic, and scholarly dissertations on literature and culture and their anatomy and their varied dimensions the author, a noted thinker and a doyen and pioneer among the exponents of what is called "Bandaya Sahitya" in Kannada delving into thought-provoking pieces on contemporary issues and concerns. He is presently the head of the Kannada Development Authority, a government organ. Information technology's advent has come in for very critical treatment by the author in his piece "Mahiti tantragyanada mayabajar". He laments that this technology has turned out to be a mindless fad and that instead of being treated as either an aid or a tool, it is treated as the be-all and end-all in human existence and has enslaved governments and educational institutions leading to distortions in the scheme of civilised life, particularly in the backward nations.

It is regrettable, he says, that the western motivations for science and technology are setting the pattern for the development models in developing countries like India which are trapped by the western pursuits of commerciali-sation of science and technology geared to profiteering. Instead of promoting and fostering the springs of native and indigenous initiatives and creative pursuits relevant to the Indian context by the use of science and technology, the IT-wallahs were acquiring a stranglehold over the governments and had converted them into their slaves dancing to their tunes. It is obvious that the author, in his observations, has criticised the Congress Government of the day in the State under the chief ministership of Mr. S. M. Krishna, which is seen to be obsessed with IT to the exclusion of more important concerns that plague the bulk of the community which is faced with the problems of bread and butter and poverty and unemployment.

In the author's view, apparently widely shared by thinking sections and critics, the state government's "fixation" with it has had the effect of further glamourising the English language with its deleterious effect of emasculating the vibrancy and status of the state language, Kannada. The author's canvas is so wide that the volume runs to nearly 600 pages to accommodate his 80 and odd thought-provoking essays, written over a long period or published before and the latest ones.

They are spread over five divisions. It is a long haul from the sublime and the profound and the scholarly to the down to earth, from Kuvempu to Veerappan or Kapildev, or the magic of the Vidhana Soudha. Veerappan has been roped in for a focus on the "Inner Veerappan" meaning the inner negative and baser human instincts, which need to be fought.

The glorification of the line of Indian world beauty queens starting with Sushmita Sen symbolises the trend towards the halting of the erstwhile western monopolies characterising that pageant and a symbol of competitive abilities and of national self-confidence. There are parodies about the hijacking of the institution of democracy and egalitarianism in fake commitments and unrequited aspirations of the backward classes, etc.

The functioning of the Doordarshan is x-rayed in favour of an integrated approach to strengthen the fabric of nationhood. There is a fresh and insightful look into the life of The Buddha and Gandhiji and Talisma and Ambedkar and Marx, and Devaraj Urs and Rajkumar. The writer's philosophy is, as he himself puts it, "Bhoomi Tatva", according to which eternal struggle is the order of life and from it emerges the process of creative consciousness and refined intellectual and emotional urges. His output, tinged by this philosophy, is very satisfying to literary and discriminating palate.

PHILOSOPHY OF EDUCATION, THE ANALYTICAL MODEL

Philosophy of education in its present critical/ analytical mode owes its origin to the analytical work of British philosophers (although Plato, Kant, Dewey and several other philosophers also addressed educational problems before). Historically, C. D. Hardy's Truth and Fallacy in Educational Theory (1942) is acknowledged as the first work of this genre.

Analytical philosophy itself was the offshoot of the 'philosophical revolution' inspired by the work of Russell, Moore and Wittgenstein at the beginning of the last century. The outstanding feature of this revolution was a reinterpretation of the nature and scope of philosophy in the light of developments in the theory of knowledge and increased understanding of the relationship between language, thought and reality.

Philosophy, according to this view, is not to be looked upon as a body of knowledge (a system of true proposi-tions) but as a method or activity of analysis, clarification and criticism.

All propositional knowledge is subject to tests of public verification, reliability and coherence and these are truth criteria that are satisfied only by the deductive and empirical forms of inquiry of mathematics and science. It was realized that philosophical questions are 'second order' logical and conceptual questions and cannot be tackled by the axiomatic method of mathematics or the observational experimental method of science. The philosophical method is in essence analytical, clarificatory and critical concerned with such tasks as elucidation of concepts, logical appraisal of different kinds of statements and arguments, validation of theories and justification of grounds of belief and knowledge.

Philosophy of education is such an activity performed on education, its concepts, theories, beliefs and arguments. Since the concern of philosophy is with the purely logical and conceptual questions the philosopher of education begins his work by demarcating such areas and problems in education as legitimately belong to his domain. Discourse in education because of the practical nature of the enterprise embraces a number of different contexts cutting across the scientific, practical and ethical spheres. A fundamental task of analysis is to disentangle these different contexts in which education is discussed and consider the basic ideas and appropriate logical criteria relevant to each. The analytical function covers almost all the aspects of the language of education, its concepts, beliefs, inferences, theories. To sum up, philosophy of education, as Prof R. S. Peters the chief architect of concept analysis in education says, is to be seen not as a body of true propositions but as a method, an intellectual activity of conceptual analysis and elucidation.

It involves such formal tasks as: analysis of educational concepts, logical appraisal of different kinds of educational statements, validation of theories and justification of prescriptive conclusions of the theory. Further, as a meta activity of analysis and criticism, philosophy can be 'done' on any field of human inquiry, science, literature, art, mathematics, history, politics and education.

Philosophy of education is the analytical function carried out on educational concepts, policy, theory, programmes and practice. The concept analysis paradigm has cast enormous influence on educational theorizing; it has come to characterize most of philosophical literature produced in the English speaking West.

The lasting contributions of concept analysis (apart from the light it has shed on many of the educational concepts and theories like 'education', 'teaching', 'learning', 'knowledge'), however, are the dispositions it seeks to promote: clarity, consistency, rigour of thought, concern for semantic meaningfulness, methodological awareness and consciousness of assumptions.

These are particularly significant in the Indian context wherein philosophical thinking in education lacks clarity and rigour. The Indian scene "Philosophy of education" is used, in India, to refer either to undifferentiated discourse (sometimes empirical, sometimes historical and generally hortatory) about aims, curriculum, methodology and other aspects of education or, in its not so inarticulate form, to the application of the speculative thesis (metaphysical, epistemological, axiological) of general philosophy, to draw 'implications' for educational theory and practice.

For a long time philosophy had come to mean only the study of individual thinkers/ systems/ schools; the view that this is all there is to philosophy of education dies hard. This restrictive paradigm has spelled doom for the growth of the field. The analytical movement seems to have had little or no influence on this area of study Philosophy of education in India presents a sorry spectacle.

In all aspects - as a subject of academic study, as a foundational input in teacher education programmes, as an area of scholarly research and as a perspective for intellectual dialogue and debate – it has suffered neglect. That this should be so in a country known for its hoary philosophical traditions is indeed ironic.

The problem with philosophy of education, however, is not something unique to it. It is the general problem of low quality inputs – students, teachers, curricula – and the impact of market forces facing most liberal and humanistic studies especially in institutions of higher learning. This does not mean rationalizing the status quo. It is only a reminder to the academia to rethink ways and means of checking this downward slide and restore to philosophy of education its rightful place in educational studies. There is another problem facing philosophy of education (again this is not peculiar to India), the absence of communication between 'pure' philosophers and philosophers of education.

Whenever such communication is attempted through professional meets, the agenda of educational philosophers faces the risk of being pushed to the background in favour of 'pure' philosophical issues. I attended a national seminar on pedagogy and epistemology hoping that fresh insights would be shared on pedagogy, as we educationists understand -

something that deals with teaching, teachers, students and schools.

The domination of the academic philosophers abstracted the concept from its natural home and educational/ empirical moorings and converted the seminar into a discussion on highly abstruse philosophical theories which were way, way out of the concerns of the educational theorist not to mention the practical classroom teacher. A similar outcome resulted in another national seminar on 'value education'. Its importance lay in that general philosophers would address the issue of value education which hitherto had been debated only within and by the "educational" community.

The seminar debated conceptual and methodological issues as well as normative dimensions of the problem. But that was all; on-going, 'live' concerns having to do with educational policy, programmes and practice and the recommendations of the several committees on the theme did not engage the attention of the seminar at all. The point of mentioning these instances is to show how it is becoming difficult for philosophy of education to stand up and be counted and claim its rightful place in discussion of issues which are at heart educational.

WRITINGS WITH PHILOSOPHIC FLAVOUR

Notwithstanding these gloomy observations, it is cheering that dormant philosophical activity can be witnessed, now and then, in deliberations of national educational resource and research institutions in the form of critiques of policy, programmes and practices. There are also contributions of a philosophic kind from lay individual thinkers. These have found expression in seminar proceedings, journal articles and news paper write-ups. If one does not take too technical a view, they can be cited as philosophical contributions as they exhibit the spirit and rigour of philosophical thinking. My point is that we have to build on this tradition and strengthen it. I have enjoyed reading these contributions and appreciated the potential they carry for further philosophical work.

I quote a few to substantiate my point: NIEPA faculty's analytical articles on the NPE and critiques of different aspects of national policy relating to UEE, the planning strategy of pan-Indian reforms and centrally sponsored schemes. NCERT's in-house analysis of the concept of Minimum learning levels (which acquired a kind of policy status) attempted to lay bare hidden conceptual difficulties. Also, the institution's critique of the Planning Commission's Report on value orientation of education exposed the muddles of the value education debate. Learning without burden, the GOI report on school bag load is a philosophical commentary on learning and teaching in the nation's schools. National Curriculum Framework 2006 has interesting philosophical content interspersed with text; 'critical pedagogy', 'knowledge as construction', 'teacher as reflective practitioner' find a mention.

Most Focus Group Position Papers (Aims of Education, Education for Peace, Work and Education) have raised many philosophical questions. The Journal of the Krishnamurty Schools is a treasure house of readings (philosophical in temper) on a host of educational issues from the Krishnamurty perspective: The Three Great Arts in Education, Krishnamurty and the Scientific Temper, Observation, Leisure and Learning, A True Art of Learning: Dialogue in Education, An Experiential Approach to Language Learning and Comparison and Education, The Insight Curriculum, Knowing and Being- The Two Aspects of Education, Media and Young Minds, Creativity in Grammar Classes, And I thought I was teaching Chemistry! Effective Environmental Education Needs 'New' Science by I. Jackson, M.G., makes the point that the 'contradictions' revealed in environmental education cannot be removed without questioning the assumptions about current science and technology that school textbooks project.

The author presents an alternative coherent worldview with a more effective set of working principles in the shape of 'new' science, systems science or ecological science. The new paradigm claims that no system of knowledge is the absolute truth and that one must question all structures and evaluates them in terms of their practical consequences. A thought provoking piece of research with special significance for education ¾ History and Philosophy of Science, Cognitive Science and Science Education is a review and summing up of developments in the philosophy of science and the research responses it has triggered in curriculum and teaching methodologies of science by Homi Bhabha Centre for Science Education, Mumbai (2002). The authors point out that since the 1960s, science education research and curriculum development have been subtly or explicitly influenced by theories of learning of Piaget, work of Popper, Kuhn, Lakatos and Toulmin and developments in cognitive science.

They argue that an awareness of these trends might help avoid scientism in science education, that the philosophy of perception and representation might guide research while work in the tradition of situated cognition might hold promise for a philosophy of praxis and action. The rich terrain of philosophy of education I have already made the point how the limited, but dominant, view of philosophy of education as study of the educational ideas of individuals and institutions within the framework 'isms' has virtually made the field stagnant and aloof from on-going happenings in education. In contrast, the field remains vibrant in the English speaking West with its continuous engagement with current debates about such issues as: educational aims, policies, curriculum, pedagogy, testing and measurement, administration, access, equity, anti-racist education, indigenous knowledge and culture, democracy, citizenship and peace. Even a casual web scan will point to the dynamism of the field and the variety of activities with which it is abuzz.

By way of illustration, the British Journal of Philosophy of Education carries such titles as: Wellbeing and Education: Issues of Culture and Authority; Disability, Dependency and Indebtedness? Essentialism Regarding Human Nature in the Defense of Gender Equality in Education; How to Think about Environmental Studies; Reconstructing Pragmatism to Address Racial Injustice. Also in evidence is application of contemporary philosophical theories to education: the journal carries a review of the book: The Responsibility of Parents for the Education of their Children: A Foucauldian Analysis of the School Education Act, 1999 by Wayne S. McGowan. In Is teaching for social justice undemocratic? Eric B. Freedman examines the extent to which critical pedagogy can be considered a democratic form of education by comparing Paulo Freire's notion of dialogue to Jürgen Habermas's "ideal speech situation". It is also interesting that the JPE, Nov 2007 is a special issue devoted for The Common School.

The discussion includes sub themes like: On the Necessity of Radical State Education: Democracy and the Common School, Educational Justice and Socio-Economic Segregation in Schools, Common Schools and Multicultural Education, A Question of Universality: Inclusive Education and the Principle of Respect. The point of this elaboration is to reemphasize that as a knowledge field philosophy of education is dynamic and concerned with the understanding of 'here and now' issues of educational policies, programmes and practices as they affect children, schools and the community NUEPA concerns and philosophy of education I now turn to the main thrust of my presentation, to point out the relevance of philosophical analysis to the educational planning and administration concerns of NUEPA spanning school and non-formal education, higher education, women's empowerment and inclusive education. At the outset, it is to be appreciated that whatever be the specific nature and level of engagement in education - teaching, training, institutional management and administration, policy and programme planning, evaluation and research -one must not lose sight of the broader perspective of the real point of it all, of what education is all about.

Education can be considered as a process of transmi-ssion of knowledge, skills, attitudes and values that we consider as desirable in accordance with our concept of the good life. We value education not just for its extraneous benefits to the society but also because we consider it as something that is good in itself. The case for UEE rests as much on the intrinsic value of education as on its social and economic returns. Such education is a fundamental right of human beings. Educational aims after all emerge out of an image of the human individual and a vision of the good life and ideal society as these are conceived from time to time. In our zealous appreciation of its social and economic returns and linkage with development, we should not lose sight of the values of justice, liberty, equality and respect for the dignity of the human individual that constitute the moral foundation of the envisioned social order.

Ultimately, it is within this broader value framework that ground level activities of educational policy formulation, planning and administration are to be conceived, understood and justified. The dispositions that philosophy seeks to promote - clarity, consistency and rigour of thought, concern for semantic meaningfulness, methodolo-gical awareness, and consciousness of assumptions - are general prerequisites for the intellectual pursuit of knowledge in any field, whether it pertains to the physical or the social world. In the case education, an essentially human endeavour, they acquire an added significance for both the educational practitioner and the theoretician. Educational decisions necessarily involve value judgments and they cannot be settled by empirical methods alone; they need a good deal of hard clear thinking of a philosophic kind. Conceptual analysis increases and deepens our understanding of the various aspects of the educational enterprise and makes explicit the dimensions in which educational decisions have to be made.

Practical action relating to policies, programmes and evaluation cannot avoid dealing with logical and conceptual issues. Controversies arise many times due to lack of conceptual clarity. More than all, all practical action in education has to keep before it the aims of education as formulated by the society. It behaves on the educational policy planner and practitioner to constantly check whether action on the ground - policies, plans, programmes, strategies and practices - is in harmony with the societal vision of the good life. Philosophy of education aids us in this scrutiny. It also provides a perspective for intellectual dialogue and debate besides deepening our understanding of issues related to educational theory and practice. With this justification, I now make an attempt to delineate ideas, issues and questions that I think may be of particular interest to the NUEPA concerns.

These have been raised in journal and newspaper articles and also seminar deliberations (notably by Padma Velaskar, National Commitment to education of Dalits; Madhu Prasad, Autonomy, Privatization and Commerciali-zation; Sudesh Mukhopadhyay, Commission's vision on Inclusive Education; Anita Ghai, Gender and Inclusive Education at all levels; Seshadri, Perspectives on Society, Education and Values: The Education Commission and After; Anil Sadgopal, Learning about barriers, National Focus Group position paper on Work and Education). They deal with on going debates on educational concepts, plans, policies, strategies, programmes and practices. Some of the observations are very perceptive and critical; they have gone deep into issues laying bare assumptions, pointing out conceptual inadequacies, flaws in arguments and questioning underlying theories and generating fresh insights. Some of them may appear as speculative, some as emotive expression of fear about the future scenario.

Whatever may be their characteristic and nature, they have brought to surface issues of a more theoretical and philosophical import. The implication for NUEPA is that its institutional actions relating to teaching, training, extension, policy planning and research, programme administration and evaluation need to be perceived and understood in the light of the broader perspective provided by these observations 1. Neo-liberalization/ Globalization (a transverse theme) Ideology Globalization, neo-liberalism, neo-colonization Observations:

- Liberal ideology and developmental model endorses 'state programme of capitalistic development' laying more emphasis on modern economic development and less on social transformation. It fails to acknowledge the fundamental conflict of interest between rapid modernization and egalitarianism in a resource-poor country.

- Globalization = Neo-colonization?
- Neoliberalism is the most dangerous ideology of the current historical moment....civic discourse has given way to the language of commercialization, privatization, and deregulation and that, within the language and images of corporate culture, citizenship is portrayed as an utterly privatized affair that produces self-interested individuals...corporate culture functions largely to either ignore or cancel out social injustices in the existing social order by overriding the democratic impulses and practices of civil society through an emphasis on the unbridled workings of market relations.
- In a globalized world citizens are recast as consumers. Locus of control shifts from the public domain of politics to an individualized/privatized world of economic cost benefits analysis. The outcome would be a society of self-interested individual consumers working for personal gains.
- Globalization leads to 'state organized feminism' replacing feminist politics on the ground – government programmes aiming at empowering women only to the extent of harnessing women's contribution to growth can never be enough for empowerment.
- "Ethics of globalization has altered the sense of morality of the nation (equality, justice, democracy)."
- Globalization and free market economy lead to commoditization of knowledge and shifting of responsibility for education from State to the community.
- Globalization and neo-liberalization value privilege and exclusiveness while public education aims at fighting them ror reflection.

How shall national educational planning and administ-ration respond to forces of globalization/ neo-liberalism? How does one confront selective and uneven nature of globalization exacerbating existing inequalities, producing new divisions, reduction of the public sector expenditure, and growth of the private sector? Is economic liberalization a threat or an opportunity for educational development? Do liberal education ideals and social purposes of education face a threat under neo-liberal economic policies? "The forces of globalization are moving the global economy toward a single unified economy and, by extension, the world's education systems toward a universal model". Is such a trend in the interest of India?

The world over have agreed that the training of the teacher is of utmost importance in any educational endeavour. The Vedas call it a divine exercise and no wonder the teacher was defied. "Acharya Devo Bhava" says the Upanishads. From Vedic times, ashrams and gurukuls have insisted on the primacy of the teacher and the utmost importance of teacher training. The great Indian Universities of Taxila and Nalanda were real centres of knowledge via training. The potentialities of the child have to be nurtured, just as in Nature a mighty tree evolves from a very simple and small seed. This is not an easy task hence, the need for careful teacher training. Today, we talk of caste recruitment, appointment of teachers, reservation and salaries only. Dharnas are held for more benefits, but no one seems to talk about training teachers to make them dedicated. Teacher training perhaps gets the lowest priority in our educational scale. The Great Mother of Pondicherry said, "One must be a saint and a hero to be a good teacher." A great teacher is born not made.

Dedication and devotion are among the noble qualities a teacher should have. Mahatma Gandhi, started a free school in South Africa, and was the sole teacher with no salary. Kasturba was his assistant. They swept the classroom and cleaned the toilets. They bathed children who lived in abject poverty. Gandhiji felt that "we cannot ask anyone to do a task which we don't do ourselves". This is the "Nish-kamya Karma," an ideal where you do your duty without fear or favour, and without expecting any reward. But you should seek returns in the form of the student's upliftment. This is the true Gandhian philosophy, which has been forgotten completely. Great educational thinkers such as Pestolozzi and Herbert believed that the teacher should have total self-control. He should never get angry or lose his temper. Calmness at all times should be his motto. Another attribute of the teacher as per Makernko, the Russian thinker is "self-confidence". Aristotle said that the teacher should be "thoroughly knowledgeable" and should seek knowledge incessantly.

All thinkers today want India to be shaped as a knowledge super power. Whose work is this? Work of the politician? Certainly not. Work of the multi-millionaires? No. Then, who should shape our country as a super knowledge power? Only the teacher can do this. Nani Palkhivala pointed out that the teacher was the architect of the nation. Swami Vivekananda entrusted man-making assignment to education, i.e., to the teacher. Having established the primacy of the teacher in nation building, we should now look at the tools he should employ. The teacher should use his example as a teaching tool to create an influence on the taught, as per Sri Aurobindo, the Great Master. Teaching, example and influence are the three tools he should employ to have the desired effect. A teacher has to be a yogi. This concept of Sri Aurobindo does not mean that the teacher should be a sanyasin. A teacher should never tell a lie, not lose his temper, and be patient, impartial, honest and unselfish. These are the traits we expect from a true teacher. But above all, he should possess the soul force. Once he has this, he can use the Troika "Teaching, Example and Influence." Then he will be able to shape his disciple. A teacher's work, as per the Mother, is a sadhana.

Education in India has a history stretching back to the ancient urban centres of learning at Taxila and Nalanda. Western education became ingrained into Indian society with the establishment of the British Raj.

Education in the Republic of India falls under the control of both the central government and the states, with some responsibilities lying with the centre and the state having autonomy for others. The various articles of the Indian constitution provide for education as a fundamental right. India has made huge progress in terms of increasing primary education attendance rate and expanding literacy to approximately two thirds of the population. However, education is still far behind developing countries such as China or Thailand. Most children never attend secondary schools.

An optimistic estimate is that only one in five job-seekers in India has ever had any sort of vocational training. Not a single Indian university was in the top 300 of Academic Ranking of World Universities in 2006. However, five Indian Institutes of Technology were listed among the top 10 science and technology schools in Asia by *Asia Week*. The Indian School of Business was ranked number 15 in global MBA rankings by the *Financial Times* of London in 2009 while the All India Institute of Medical Sciences has been recognized as a global leader in medical research and treatment.

A monastic order of education under the supervision of a guru was a favoured form of education for India's noble castes. The knowledge in these orders was often related to the tasks a section of the society had to perform. The priest class, the *Brahmans*, was imparted knowledge of religion, philosophy, and other ancillary branches while the warrior class, the *Kshatriya*, was trained in the various aspects of warfare. The business classes, the Vaiṣhya, were taught their trade and the lowest class of the *Shudras* was generally deprived of educational advantages. The book of laws, the *Manusmriti*, and the treatise on statecraft the *Arthashastra* were among the influential works of this era which reflect the outlook and understanding of the world at the time.

Apart from the monastic orders, institutions of higher learning and universities flourished in India well before the Common Era, and continued to deliver education into the Common Era. Secular Buddhist institutions cropped up along with monasteries. These institutions imparted practical education, e.g. medicine. A number of urban learning centres became increasingly visible from the period between 200 BCE to 400 CE. The important urban centres of learning were Taxila and Nalanda, among others. These institutions systematically imparted knowledge and attracted a number of foreign students to study topics such as logic, grammar, medicine, metaphysics, and arts and crafts. By the time of the visit of the Islamic scholar Alberuni (973-1048 CE), India already had a sophisticated system of mathematics and science in place, and had made a number of inventions and discoveries.

With the arrival of the British Raj in India a class of Westernized elite was versed in the Western system of education which the British had introduced. This system soon became solidified in India as a number of primary, secondary, and tertiary centres for education cropped up during the colonial era. Following independence in 1947, Maulana Azad, India's first education minister envisaged strong central government control over education throughout the country, with a uniform educational system. However, given the cultural and linguistic diversity of India, it was only the higher education dealing with science and technology that came under the jurisdiction of the central government. The government also held powers to make national policies for educational development and could regulate selected aspects of education throughout India.

The central government of India formulated the National Policy in Education (NPE) in 1986 and also re-enforced the Programme of Action (POA) in 1986. The government initiated several measures including the setting up of *Navodaya Vidyalaya* selective schools in every district, advances in female education, inter-disciplinary research and establishment of open universities. India's NPE also contains the National System of Education, which ensures some uniformity while taking into account regional education needs. The NPE also stresses on higher spending on education, envisaging a budget of more than 6% of the overall national budget. While the need for wider reform in the primary and secondary sectors is recognized as an issue, the emphasis is also on the development of science and technology education infrastructure.

The National Council of Educational Research and Training (NCERT) is the apex body for school education in India. The NCERT provides support and technical assistance to a number of schools in India and oversees many aspects of enforcement of education policies. In India, the various bodies governing school education system are:

- The state government boards, in which the majority of Indian children are enrolled.
- The Central Board of Secondary Education (CBSE) board.
- The Council for the Indian School Certificate Examinations (CISCE) board.
- The National Institute of Open Schooling.
- International schools affiliated to the International Baccalaureate Programme and/or the Cambridge International Examinations.
- Islamic Madrasah schools, whose boards are controlled by local state governments, or autonomous, or affiliated with Darul Uloom Deoband.
- Autonomous schools like Woodstock School, Auroville, Patha Bhavan and Ananda Marga Gurukula.

PRIMARY EDUCATION

The Indian government lays emphasis to primary education up to the age of fourteen years. The Indian government has also banned child labor in order to ensure that the children do not enter unsafe working conditions. However, both free education and the ban on child labor are difficult to enforce due to economic disparity and social conditions.

The District Primary Education Programme (DPEP) was launched in 1994 with an aim to universalize primary education in India by reforming and vitalizing the existing primary education system. 85% of the DPEP is funded by the central government and the remaining 15 percent is funded by the state. The DPEP, which has opened 160000 new schools including 84000 alternative education schools delivering alternative education to approximately 3.5 million children, is also supported by UNICEF and other international programmes.

This primary education scheme has also shown a high Gross Enrollment Ratio of 93–95% for the last three years in some states. Significant improvement in staffing and enrollment of girls has also been made as a part of this scheme. The overall primary school conditions in India as a whole continued to remain lag behind internationally due to understaffing coupled with lack of developed infrastructure and sufficient financing.

SECONDARY EDUCATION

The National Policy on Education (NPE), 1986, has provided for environment awareness, science and technology education, and introduction of traditional elements such as Yoga into the Indian secondary school system. A significant feature of India's secondary school system is the emphasis on inclusion of the disadvantaged sections of the society Professionals from established institutes are often called to support in vocational training. Another feature of India's secondary school system is its emphasis on profession based vocational training to help students attain skills for finding a vocation of his/her choosing.

A special Integrated Education for Disabled Children (IEDC) programme was started in 1974. Another notable special programme, the *Kendriya Vidyalaya* project, was started for the employees of the central government of India, who are distributed throughout the country. The government started the *Kendriya Vidyalaya* project in 1965 to provide uniform education in institutions following the same syllabus at the same pace regardless of the location to which the employee's family has been transferred.

TERTIARY EDUCATIONT

Our university system is, in many parts, in a state of disrepair...In almost half the districts in the country, higher education enrollments are abysmally low, almost two-third of our universities and 90 per cent of our colleges are rated as below average on quality parameters... I am concerned that in many states university appointments, including that of vice-chancellors, have been politicised and have become subject to caste and communal considerations, there are complaints of favouritism and corruption. – *Prime Minister Manmohan Singh in 2007*

India's higher education system is the third largest in the world, after China and the United States. The main governing body at the tertiary level is the University Grants Commission (India), which enforces its standards, advises the government, and helps coordinate between the centre and the state. Accreditation for higher learning is overseen by 12 autonomous institutions established by the University Grants Commission.

As of 2009, India has 20 central universities, 215 state universities, 100 deemed universities, 5 institutions established and functioning under the State Act, and 13 institutes which are of national importance. Other institutions include 16000 colleges, including 1800 exclusive women's colleges, functioning under these universities and institutions. The emphasis in the tertiary level of education lies on science and technology. Indian educational institutions by 2004 consisted of a large number of technology institutes. As of 2006 some 1200 engineering colleges awarded degrees in India and approximately 380000 students were admitted in them. Distance learning is also a feature of the Indian higher education system.

Some institutions of India, such as the Indian Institutes of Technology (IITs), have been globally acclaimed for their standard of education. The IITs enroll about 4000 students annually and the alumni have contributed to both the growth of the private sector and the public sectors of India. IIT graduates of India have also contributed significantly to the global software industry, with an estimated 30000 graduates employed in the United States as of 2006.

TECHNICAL EDUCATION

From the first Five Year Plan onwards India's emphasis was to develop a pool of scientifically inclined manpower. India's National Policy on Education (NPE) provisioned for an apex body for regulation and development of higher technical education, which came into being as the All India Council for Technical Education (AICTE) in 1987 through an act of the Indian parliament. At the level of the centre the Indian Institutes of Technology are deemed of national importance. The Indian Institutes of Management are also among the nation's premier education facilities. Several Regional Engineering Colleges (REC) have been converted into National Institutes of Technology. The UGC has inter-university centres at a number of locations throughout India to promote common research, e.g. the Nuclear Science Centre at the Jawaharlal Nehru University, New Delhi. Tertiary education in India is accessible to 1 in 10 young Indians. Nevertheless, India's higher education system is the third largest in the world, after China and the United States. Out of those who reach higher level education, Mercer Consulting estimates that only a quarter of graduates are employable.

Higher education in India has evolved in divergent streams with each stream monitored by an apex body, indirectly controlled by the Ministry of Human Resource Development and funded jointly by the state governments. Most universities are administered by the States, however, there are 18 important universities called Central Universities, which are maintained by the Union Government. The increased funding of the central universities give them an advantage over their state competitors. Apart from the several hundred state universities, there is a network of research institutions that provide opportunities for advanced learning and research leading up to a PhD in branches of science, technology and agriculture. Several have won international recognition. 25 of these institutions come under the umbrella of the CSIR - Council of Scientific and Industrial Research and over 60 falls under the ICAR - Indian Council of Agricultural Research. In addition, the DAE - Department of Atomic Energy, and other ministries support various research laboratories.

The Indian Institutes of Technology were placed 50th in the world and 2nd in the field of Engineering (next only to MIT) by Times Higher World University Rankings Earlier; an Asia Week study had ranked them as the best technical universities in Asia. Indian Institute of Science is the premier research institute in the field of science and engineering.

There are several thousand colleges (affiliated to different universities) that provide undergraduate science, agriculture, commerce and humanities courses in India. Amongst these, the best also offer post graduate courses while some also offer facilities for research and PhD studies.

Technical education has grown rapidly in recent years. With recent capacity additions, it now appears that the nation has the capability to graduate over 500,000 engineers (with 4-yr undergraduate degrees) annually, and there is also a corresponding increase in the graduation of computer scientists (roughly 50,000 with post-graduate degree). In addition, the nation graduates over 1.2 million scientists. Furthermore, each year, the nation is enrolling at least 350,000 in its engineering diploma programs (with plans to increase this by about 50,000). Thus, India's annual enrollment of scientists, engineers and technicians now exceeds 2 million.

2008 data from Maharashtra's Higher Secondary Board reveals that 87 million passed the school leaving exam and enrolled in college for undergraduate studies. Adding enrolment in polytechnic programs and graduates from other boards puts Maharashtra's total at close to a million and its college enrolment ratio at roughly 39%. States like Tamil Nadu, Haryana and Kerala also have comparably high tertiary enrollment ratios. In Andhra Pradesh, the tertiary enrolment rate is now approaching 25%. Across the country, tertiary enrollment rates have been increasing at a rate between 5-10% in the last decade, which has led to a doubling of the tertiary enrolment rate to near 20%. (However, outdated government data does not yet capture this trend, which can be seen from analyzing individual state data.)

International league tables produced in 2006 by the London-based Times Higher Education Supplement (THES) confirmed Jawaharlal Nehru University (JNU)'s place among the world's top 200 universities. Likewise, THES 2006 ranked JNU's School of Social Sciences at the 57th position among the world's top 100 institutes for social sciences. The University of Calcutta was the first multi-disciplinary university of modern India. According to The Times Higher

Education Supplement's survey of the world's top arts and humanities universities, dated November 10, 2005, this university, ranked 39, was the only Indian university to make it to the top 50 list in that year. Other research institutes are the Saha Institute of Nuclear Physics, the Asiatic Society, and the Indian Statistical Institute.

The National Law School of India University is highly regarded, with some of its students being awarded Rhodes Scholarships to Oxford University, and the All India Institute of Medical Sciences is consistently rated the top medical school in the country. Indian Institutes of Management (IIMs) are the top management institutes in India. The private sector is strong in Indian higher education. This has been partly as a result of the decision by the Government to divert spending to the goal of universalisation of elementary education. Within a decade different state assemblies has passed bills for private universities, including Birla Institute of Technology and Science, Amity University and Xavier Labour Relations Institute.

Accreditation for universities in India is required by law unless it was created through an act of Parliament. Without accreditation, the government notes "these fake institutions have no legal entity to call themselves as University/ Vishwvidyalaya and to award 'degree' which are not treated as valid for academic/employment purposes". University Grants Commission Act 1956 explains, "the right of conferring or granting degrees shall be exercised only by a University established or incorporated by or under a Central Act carlo bon tempo, or a State Act, or an Institution deemed to be University or an institution specially empowered by an Act of the Parliament to confer or grant degrees. Thus, any institution which has not been created by an enactment of Parliament or a State Legislature or has not been granted the status of a Deemed to be University is not entitled to award a degree."

LITERACY

2001 government statistics hold the national literacy to be around 64.84%. Government statistics of 2001 also hold that the rate of increase of literacy is more in rural areas than in urban areas. Female literacy is was at a national average of 53.63% whereas the male literacy was 75.26%. Within the Indian states, Kerala has shown the highest literacy rates of 90.02% whereas Bihar averaged lower than 50% literacy, the lowest in India. The 2001 statistics also indicated that the total number of 'absolute non literates' in the country was 304 million.

Attainment

World Bank statistics found that fewer than 40 percent of adolescents in India attend secondary schools. *The Economist* reports that half of 10-year-old rural children could not read at a basic level, over 60% were unable to do division, and half dropped out by the age 14. Only one in ten young people have access to tertiary education. Out of those who receive higher education, *Mercer Consulting* estimates that only a quarter of graduates are "employable".An optimistic estimate is that only one in five job-seekers in India has ever had any sort of vocational training.

PRIVATE EDUCATION

Because of poor quality of public education, 27% of Indian children are privately educated. Private schools provide often superior results at a fraction of the unit cost of government schools. Private schools cover the entire curriculum and offer extra-curricular activities such as science fairs, general knowledge, sports, music and drama. Most teachers in private schools are female, graduates and reasonably experienced. The competition in the school market is intense, yet most schools make profit.

Even the poorest often go to private schools despite the fact that government schools are free. A study found that 65% of schoolchildren in Hyderabad's slums attend private schools. Private schools are often operating illegally. A 2001 study found that it takes 14 different licenses from four different authorities to open a private school in New Delhi and could take years if done legally.

Women have much lower literacy rate. Compared to boys, far fewer girls are enrolled in the schools, and many of them drop out. According to a 1998 report by U.S. Department of Commerce, the chief barrier to female education in India are inadequate school facilities (such as sanitary facilities), shortage of female teachers and gender bias in curriculum (majority of the female characters being depicted as weak and helpless). The number of literate women among the female population of India was between 2-6% from the British Raj onwards to the formation of the Republic of India in 1947. Concerted efforts led to improvement from 15.3% in 1961 to 28.5% in 1981. By 2001 the literacy for women had exceeded 50% of the overall female population, though these statistics were still very low compared to world standards and even male literacy within India.

Sita Anantha Raman outlines the progress of women's education in India:

Since 1947 the Indian government has tried to provide incentives for girls' school attendance through programs for midday meals, free books, and uniforms. This welfare thrust raised primary enrollment between 1951 and 1981. In 1986 the National Policy on Education decided to restructure education in tune with the social framework of each state, and with larger national goals. It emphasized that education was necessary for democracy, and central to the improvement of women's condition.

The new policy aimed at social change through revised texts, curricula, increased funding for schools, expansion in the numbers of schools, and policy improvements. Emphasis was placed on expanding girls' occupational centers and primary education; secondary and higher education; and rural and urban institutions. The report tried to connect problems like low school attendance with poverty, and the dependence on girls for housework and sibling day care. The National Literacy Mission also worked through female tutors in villages. Although the minimum marriage age is now eighteen for girls, many continue to be married much earlier. Therefore, at the secondary level, female dropout rates are high.

Sita Anantha Raman also maintains that while educated Indian women workforce maintains professionalism, the men outnumber them in most fields and, in some cases, receive higher income for the same positions.

RURAL EDUCATION

Following independence, the Republic of India viewed education as an effective tool for bringing social change through community development. The administrative control was effectively initiated in the 1950s, when, in 1952, the government grouped villages under a Community Development Block—an authority under national programme which could control education in up to 100 villages. A Block Development Officer oversaw a geographical area of 150 square miles which could contain a population of as many as 70000 people.

Setty and Ross elaborate on the role of such programmes, themselves divided further into *individual-based, community based*, or the *Individual-cum-community-based*, in which microscopic levels of development are overseen at village level by an appointed worker.

The community development programmes comprise agriculture, animal husbandry, cooperation, rural industries, rural engineering (consisting of minor irrigation, roads, buildings), health and sanitation including family welfare, family planning, women welfare, child care and nutrition, education including adult education, social education and literacy, youth welfare and community organisation. In each of these areas of development there are several programmes, schemes and activities which are additive, expanding and tapering off covering the total community, some segments, or specific target populations such as small and marginal farmers, artisans, women and in general people below the poverty line.

Despite some setbacks the rural education programmes continued throughout the 1950s, with support from private institutions. A sizable network of rural education had been established by the time the *Gandhigram Rural Institute* was established and 5, 200 Community Development Blocks were established in India. Nursery schools, elementary schools, secondary school, and schools for adult education for women were set up. The government continued to view rural education as an agenda that could be relatively free from bureaucratic backlog and general stagnation. However, in some cases lack of financing balanced the gains made by rural education institutes of India. Some ideas failed to find acceptability among India's poor and investments made by the government sometimes yielded little results.

Issues

One study found out that 25% of public sector teachers and 40% of public sector medical workers were absent during the survey. Among teachers who were paid to teach, absence rates ranged from 15% in Maharashtra to 71% in Bihar. Only 1 in nearly 3000 public school head teachers had ever dismissed a teacher for repeated absence. A study on teachers by Kremer etc. found that 'only about half were teaching, during unannounced visits to a nationally representative sample of government primary schools in India'.

Modern education in India is often criticized for being based on rote learning rather than problem solving. *Business Week* denigrates the Indian curriculum saying it revolves around rote learning. And Express India suggests that students are focused on cramming. A study of 188 government-run primary schools found that 59% of the schools had no drinking water and 89% had no toilets. 2003-04 data by National Institute of Educational Planning and Administration revealed that only 3.5% of primary schools in Bihar and Chhattisgarh had toilets for girls. In Madhya Pradesh, Maharashtra, Andhra Pradesh, Gujarat, Rajasthan and Himachal Pradesh, rates were 12-16%.

Fake degrees are a problem. One raid in Bihar found 0.1 million fake certificates. In February 2009, the University Grant Commission found 19 fake institutions operating in India. Only 16% of manufacturers in India offer in-service training to their employees, compared with over 90% in China.

Following India's independence a number of rules were formulated for the backward Scheduled Castes and the Scheduled Tribes of India, and in 1960 a list identifying 405 Scheduled Castes and 225 Scheduled Tribes was published by the central government. An amendment was made to the list in 1975, which identified 841 Scheduled Castes and 510 Scheduled Tribes. The total percentage of Scheduled Castes and Scheduled Tribes combined was found to be 22.5 percent with the Scheduled Castes accounting for 17 percent and the Scheduled Tribes accounting for the remaining 7.5 percent. Following the report many Scheduled Castes and Scheduled Tribes increasingly referred to themselves as *Dalit*, a Marathi language terminology used by B. R. Ambedkar which literally means "oppressed".

The Scheduled Castes and Scheduled Tribes are provided for in many of India's educational programmes. Special reservations are also provided for the Scheduled Castes and Scheduled Tribes in India, e.g. a reservation of 15% in *Kendriya Vidhyala* for Scheduled Castes and another reservation of 7.5% in *Kendriya Vidhyala* for Scheduled Tribes. Similar reservations are held by the Scheduled Castes and Scheduled Tribes in many schemes and educational facilities in India. The remote and far-flung regions of North East India are provided for under the Non Lapsable Central pool of Resources (NLCPR) since 1998-1999. The NLCPR aims to provide funds for infrastructure development in these remote areas.

The government objective for the *Sarva Shiksha Abhiyan* (SSA), started in 2001, is to provide education to children between 6–14 years by 2010. The programme focuses specially on girls and children with challenged social or financial backgrounds. The SSA also aims to provide practical infrastructure and relevant source material in form of free textbooks to children in remote areas. The SSA also aims at widening computer education in rural areas. However, some objectives of the SSA, e.g. enrollment of all children under the scheme in schools by 2005 remain unfulfilled. Education Guarantee Scheme and Alternative and Innovative Education are components of the SSA.

Women from remote, underdeveloped areas or from weaker social groups in Andra Pradesh, Assam, Bihar, Jharkhand, Karnataka, Kerala, Gujarat, Uttar Pradesh, and Uttarakhand, fall under the *Mahila Samakhya Scheme,* initiated in 1989. Apart from provisions for education this programme also aims to raise awareness by holding meetings and seminars at rural levels. The government allowed 340 million rupees during 2007–08 to carry out this scheme over 83 districts including more than 21, 000 villages. Currently there are 68 *Bal Bhavans* and 10 *Bal Kendra* affiliated to the *National Bal Bhavan.*

The scheme involves educational and social activities and recognising children with a marked talent for a particular educational stream. A number of programmes and activities are held under this scheme, which also involves cultural exchanges and participation in several international forums.

India's minorities, especially the ones considered 'educationally backward' by the government, are provided for in the 1992 amendment of the Indian National Policy on Education (NPE).

The government initiated the Scheme of Area Intensive Programme for Educationally Backward Minorities and Scheme of Financial Assistance or Modernisation of Madarsa Education as part of its revised Programme of Action (1992). Both these schemes were started nationwide by 1994. In 2004 the Indian parliament allowed an act which enabled minority education establishments to seek university affiliations if they passed the required norms.

CENTRAL GOVERNMENT INVOLVEMENT

As a part of the tenth Five year Plan (2002–2007), the central government of India outlined an expenditure of 65.6% of its total education budget of Rs. 438250 million, or (Rs. 287500 million) on elementary education; 9.9% (Rs. 43250 million) on secondary education; 2.9% (Rs. 12500 million) on adult education; 9.5% (Rs. 41765 million) on higher education; 10.7% (Rs. 47000 million) on technical education; and the remaining

1.4% (Rs. 6235 million) on miscellaneous education schemes.

According to the United Nations Educational, Scientific and Cultural Organization (UNESCO), India has the lowest public expenditure on higher education per student in the world.

Public Expenditure on Education in India

In recent times, several major announcements were made for developing the poor state of affairs in education sector in India, the most notable ones being the National Common Minimum Programme (NCMP) of the United Progressive Alliance (UPA) government. The announcements are;

a. To progressively increase expenditure on education to around 6 percent of GDP.

b. To support this increase in expenditure on education, and to increase the quality of education, there would be an imposition of an education cess over all central government taxes.

c. To ensure that no one is denied of education due to economic backwardness and poverty.

d. To make right to education a fundamental right for all children in the age group 6-14 years.

e. To universalize education through its flagship programmes such as Sarva Siksha Abhiyan and Mid Day Meal.

However, even after five years of implementation of NCMP, not much progress has been done on these promises or announcements. The public expenditure on education has actually declined from around 3.23 percent of GDP in 2000-2001 to 2.88 percent in the recent times. As a proportion of total government expenditure, it has declined from around 11.1 percent in 2000-2001 to around 9.98 percent during UPA rule. A policy brief issued by [Network for Social Accountability (NSA)] titled "[NSA Response to Education Sector Interventions in Union Budget: UPA Rule and the Education Sector]" provides significant revelation to this fact. Due to a declining priority of education in the public policy paradigm in India, there has been an exponential growth in the private expenditure on education also. [As per the available information, the private out of pocket expenditure by the working class population for the education of their children in India has increased by around 1150 percent or around 12.5 times over the last decade].

Legislative Framework

Article 54, of the Constitution of India originally stated:

"The State shall endeavour to provide, within a period of ten years from the commencement of this Constitution, for free and compulsory education for all children until they complete the age of fourteen years."

This chapter was a directive principle of state policy within India, effectively meaning that it was within a set of rules that were meant to be followed in spirit and the government could not be held to court if the actual letter was not followed. However, the enforcement of this directive principle became a matter of debate since this principle held obvious emotive and practical value, and was legally the only directive principle within the Indian constitution to have a time limit.

Following initiatives by the Supreme Court of India during the 1990s the Ninety-third amendment bill suggested three separate amendments to the Indian constitution:

- The constitution of India was amended to include a new article, 21A, which read:

"The State shall provide free and compulsory education to all children of the age of six to fourteen years in such a manner as the State may, by law, determine."

Article 45 was proposed to be substituted by the article which read:

"Provision for early childhood care and education to children below the age of six years: The State shall endeavour to provide early childhood care and education for all children until they complete the age of sixteen years."

Another article, 51A, was to additionally have the clause:

"..a parent or guardian [shall] provide opportunities for education to his child or, as the case may be, [a] ward between the ages of six to fourteen years."

The bill was passed unanimously in the *Lok Sabha*, the lower house of the Indian parliament, on November 28, 2001. It was later passed by the upper house—the *Rajya Sabha*—on May 14, 2002. After being signed by the President of India the Indian constitution was amended formally for the eighty sixth time and the bill came into effect. Since then those between the age of 6–14 have a *fundamental right* to education.

Article 46 of the Constitution of India holds that:

"The State shall promote, with special care, the education and economic interests of the weaker sections of the people, and in particular of the Scheduled Castes and Scheduled Tribes, and shall protect them from social injustice and all forms of social exploitation."

Other provisions for the Scheduled Castes and Scheduled Tribes can be found in Articles 330, 332, 335, 338–342. Both the 5th and the 6th Schedules of the Constitution also make special provisions for the Scheduled Castes and Scheduled Tribes.

Literacy in India is an indispensable means for effective social and economic participation, contributing to human development and poverty reduction, says UNESCO. The right to education is also a fundamental human right. UNESCO aims at education for all by 2015. India is one of the countries (along with the Arab states and sub-Saharan Africa) where the literacy levels are still below the threshold level of 75% but gigantic efforts are on to achieve that level. More than three fourths of the country's male population and above half of the female population is literate. The thrust forward for achieving at least the threshold level of literacy represents the largest ever civil and military mobilization in the country.

Adult literacy rate is for the age group 15 years and above. Youth literacy rate is for the age group 15–24 years (i.e., youth represents a subset of adults). The youth literacy rate for India relates to 2001.

Literacy as defined by UNESCO is given below:

1. A literate person is one who can with understanding both read and write a short simple statement relevant to his everyday life.
2. Literacy is not the simple reading of a word or a set of associated symbols and sounds, but an act of critical understanding of men's situation in the world.
3. Literacy is not an end in itself but a means of personal liberation and development and extending individuals educational efforts involving overall inter-disciplinary responses to concrete problems.
4. A literate person is one who has acquired all the essential knowledge and skills which enable him to engage in all those activities in which literacy is required for effective functioning in his group and community and whose attaining in reading, writing and numeracy make it possible to use these skills towards his own and his community's development.

The National Literacy Mission defines literacy as acquiring the skills of reading, writing and arithmetic and the ability to apply them to one's day-to-day life. The achievement of functional literacy implies:

- Self-reliance in 3 R's.
- Becoming aware of the causes of deprivation and moving towards amelioration of their condition by participating in the process of development.
- Acquiring skills to improve their economic status and general well being.
- Imbibing values of national integration, conservation of environment, women's equality, observance of small family norms, etc.

The working definition of literacy in the Indian census since 1991 is as follows:

- "Literacy rate":

The total percentage of the population of an area at a particular time aged seven years or above who can read and write with understanding. Here the denominator is the population aged seven years or more.

- "Crude literacy rate":

The total percentage of the people of an area at a particular time aged seven years or above who can read and write with understanding, taking the total population of the area (including below seven years of age) as the denominator.

GROWTH OF LITERACY

During the British period, progress of education was rather tardy. Between 1881-82 and 1946-47, the number of primary schools grew from 82,916 to 134,866 and the number of students grew from 2,061,541 to 10,525,943. Literacy rates in British India rose from 3.2 per cent in 1881 to 7.2 per cent in 1931 and 12.2 per cent in 1947. In 2000-01, there were 60,840 pre-primary and pre-basic schools, and 664,041 primary and junior basic schools. Total enrolment at the primary level has increased from 19,200,000 in 1950-51 to 109,800,000 in 2001-02. The number of high schools in 2000-01 was higher than the number of primary schools at the time of independence.

The provision of universal and compulsory education for all children in the age group of 6-14 was a cherished national ideal and had been given overriding priority by incorporation as a Directive Policy in Article 45 of the Constitution, but it is still to be achieved more than half a century since the Constitution was adopted. Parliament has passed the Constitution 86th Amendment Act, 2002, to make elementary education a Fundamental Right for children in the age group of 6–14 years. In order to provide more funds for education, an education cess of 2 per cent has been imposed on all direct and indirect central taxes through the Finance (No. 2) Act, 2004. Since independence, the literacy rate grew from 18.33 per cent in 1951, to 28.30 per cent in 1961, 34.45 per cent in 1971, 43.57 per cent in 1981, 52.21 per cent in 1991, and 64.84 per cent in 2001. During the same period, the population grew from 361 million to 1,028 million.

LITERACY RATES

The bar chart below shows the position of different states concerning literacy in 2001. Kerala is at one end of the table and Bihar at the other. An analysis of important social indicators highlights the social differences in the two states. Literacy rate (2001) in Kerala was 90.86 per cent against 47.00 per cent in Bihar. Life expectancy at birth (2001-2006) is 71.61 for males and 75 for females in Kerala. In Bihar, it is 65.66 for males and 64.79 for females. Infant mortality (per 1,000 live births, 2002 provisional data) was only 10 in Kerala against 61 in Bihar. Birth rate (per 1,000, provisional) is 16.9 in Kerala against 30.9 in Bihar. Death rate (per 1,000, provisional) is 6.4 in Kerala against 7.9 in Bihar. The differences clearly indicate that literacy is the key to improvement in quality of life. Kerala's achievement is remarkable because the proportion of literate people in the area that now constitutes that state at the time of independence was, although higher than rest of India, still low. According to the 1991 census, Kottayam District of Kerala is the first district in India to achieve highest literacy rate i.e. 90.52 per cent.

In the graph showing literacy rates in different states for 1981 and 2001, there is considerable variance throughout the country. Large variations can be observed even amongst contiguous states. Union Territories are not included in the graph. It can be seen that while there are a few states at the top and bottom, most of the states are just above or below the national average. In his essay on *Social Infrastructure As Important As Physical Infrastructure* published in *India Development Report 2002*, Kirit S. Parikh had pointed out, "With a literacy rate of 65, we have 296 million illiterates, age seven years and above, as per the 2001 census. The number of illiterates today exceeds the population of the country of around 270 million at Independence, age seven and above." The largest segment of the world's illiterates is in India.

In his book *The Argumentative Indian*, Amartya Sen notes, on the basis of investigations by Pratichi Trust, set up with the proceeds of his Nobel award, carried out in West Bengal and Jharkhand, that absenteeism of comparatively well-paid teachers, particularly where bulk of the students come from scheduled castes and tribes, poses a major problem. Students are circumstantially forced to go in for private tuitions. He concludes, "Sometimes the very institutions that were created to overcome disparities and barriers have tended to act as reactionary influences in reinforcing inequality... The teachers' unions, which have a very positive role to play in protecting the interests of teachers and have played that part well in the past, are often are turning into an influence that reinforces the neglect of the interests of children from desperately underprivileged families. There is evidence of hardening of class barriers that separate the newly affluent teachers from the impoverished rural poor."

The Sarva Siksha Abhiyan was launched in 2001 to ensure that all children in the age group 6–14 years attend school and complete eight years of schooling by 2010. Important components of the scheme are the Education Guarantee Scheme and Alternative and Innovative Education meant primarily for children where there is no formal school within a radius of one kilometer. The centrally sponsored District Primary Education Programme launched in 1994, has so far opened more than 160,000 new schools, including almost 84,000 alternative schools. Of the estimated population of 205 million in the age group 6–14 years on March 1, 2002, nearly 82.5 per cent was enrolled in schools. However, drop out in 2002-03 at the primary level was 34.9 per cent and at the upper primary level, it was 52.8 per cent.

The high drop out rate has been a matter of major concern. One of the most popular schemes adopted to attract children to schools is the mid-day meals programme launched in 1995. Several other special programmes have been launched with varying degrees of success. The National Literacy Mission launched in 1988 aims at attaining a literacy rate of 75 per cent by 2007. It imparts functional literacy to non-literates in the age group of 15–35 years. The Total Literacy Campaign is the principal strategy of the NLM for eradication of illiteracy. The Continuing Education Scheme provides a learning continuum to the efforts of the Total Literacy and Post literacy programmes. International Literacy Day is celebrated each year on 8 September with the aim to highlight the importance of literacy to individuals, communities and societies.

SOCIAL REFORMATION EFFORTS

Bulk of the illiterates is in the rural areas, where social and economic barriers play an important role in keeping the lowest strata of society illiterate. Government programmes alone, however well intentioned, may not be able break barriers built over the centuries. Major social reformation efforts are required to bring about a change in the rural scenario. Examples of two such efforts are given below. There are many but more are required. In 2002, Sandeep Pandey won the prestigious Magsaysay Award. While pursuing a Ph.D. in control theory at the University of California-Berkeley, he joined his friends to form Asha (Hope), to support education for poor children in India by tapping the resources of Indians abroad. The enterprising founders raised ten thousand dollars in one year, an auspicious beginning for an organization that now claims thirty-six North-American chapters and has disbursed nearly one million dollars for programs in India.

After launching Asha, he himself returned to India, doctorate in hand. He taught briefly at the prestigious Indian Institute of Technology and, in 1992, left the institute to devote himself full-time to Asha's larger purpose: to bring about socio-economic change in India through education. The flow of money apart, it was not an easy task. In Ballia district of Uttar Pradesh, he confronted the impoverished world of low-caste families and dalits, or untouchables. Few children went to school at all; even those who did grew up to swell India's vast unemployment rolls. With local volunteers in the villages of Reoti and Bhainsaha, Pandey has created schools that instill self-reliance and values for a just society. Asha's teachers take no pay. Instead, they support themselves with sidelines such as making candles and greeting cards from handmade paper. A fuller expression of his vision is the Asha ashram in the dalit village of Lalpur, outside Lucknow. There, students live and study among traditional artisans and engage in bee-keeping, vegetable gardening and cottage industries. His award was in recognition of "the empowering example of his commitment to the transformation of India's marginalized poor."

The Magsaysay Award for Shantha Sinha in 2003 was in recognition of "her guiding the people of Andhra Pradesh to end the scourge of child labour and send all of their children to school." As head of an extension program at the University of Hyderabad in 1987, she organized a three-month-long "camp" to prepare children rescued from bonded labour to attend school. Later, in 1991, she guided her family's Mamidipudi Venkatarangaiya Foundation to take up this idea as part of its overriding mission in Andhra Pradesh. Her original transition camps grew into full-fledged residential "bridge schools." The foundation is creating a social climate hostile not only to child labour but also to child marriage and other practices that deny children the right to a normal childhood. Today the MV Foundation's bridge schools and programs extend to 4,300 villages.

2

Education in a Contemporary Scene

The history of education in India began with teaching of traditional elements such as Indian religions, Indian mathematics, Indian logic at early Hindu and Buddhist centres of learning such as Taxila and Nalanda before the Common Era. Islamic education became ingrained with the establishment of the Islamic empires in India in the middle ages while the coming of the Europeans later bought western education to colonial India. A series of measures continuing throughout the early half of the 20th century ultimately laid the foundation of education in the Republic of India. Early education in India commenced under the supervision of a *guru*. The education was imparted on the basis of caste and the related duties that one had to perform as a member of a specific caste. The *Brahmans* learned about scriptures and religion while the *Kshatriya* was educated in the various aspects of warfare.

The *Vaishya* caste learned commerce and other specific vocational courses while education was largely denied to the *Shudras,* the lowest caste. The earliest venues of education in India were often secluded from the main population. Students were expected to follow strict monastic guidelines prescribed by the *guru* and stay away from cities in *ashrams*. However, as population increased under the Gupta empire centres of urban learning became increasingly common and cities such as Varanasi and the Buddhist centre at Nalanda became increasingly visible. Education in India in its traditional form was closely related to religion. Among the Heterodox schools of belief were the Jain and Buddhist schools. Heterodox Buddhist education was more inclusive and aside of the monastic orders the Buddhist education centres were urban institutes of learning such as Taxila and Nalanda where grammar, medicine, philosophy, logic, metaphysics, arts and crafts etc. were also taught.

Early secular Buddhist institutions of higher learning like Taxila and Nalanda continued to function well into the Common Era and were attended by students from China and Central Asia. On the subject of education for the nobility Joseph Prabhu writes: "Outside the religious framework, kings and princes were educated in the arts and sciences related to government: politics (*danda-nýti*), economics (*vartta*), philosophy (*anvýksiki*), and historical traditions (*itihasa*). Here the authoritative source was Kautilya's *Arthashastra*, often compared to Niccolò Machiavelli's *The Prince* for its worldly outlook and political scheming." The *Rigveda* dating from 1500 BCE mentions female poets called *brahmavadinis*, specifically Lopamudra and Ghosha. By 800 BCE women such as Gargi and Maitreyi were mentioned as scholars in the religious *Upnishads*. Maya, mother of the historic Buddha, was an educated queen while other women in India contributed to writing of the *Pali canon*. Out of the composers of the Sangam literature 154 were women. However, the education and society of the era continued to be dominated by educated male population.

Chinese scholars such as Xuanzang and Yi Jing arrived in Indian institutions of learning to survey Buddhist texts. Yi Jing additionally noted the arrival of 56 scholars from China, Japan, and Korea. However, the Buddhist institutions of learning were slowly giving way to a resurgent tradition of Brahmanism during that era. Scholars from India also journeyed to China to translate Buddhist texts. During the 10th century a monk named Dharmadeva from Nalanda journeyed to China and translated a number of texts. Another centre at Vikramshila maintained close relations with Tibet.

The Buddhist teacher Atisa was the head monk in Vikramshila before his journey to Tibet.

Examples of royal patronage include construction of buildings under the Rastrakuta dynasty in 945 CE. The institutions arranged for multiple residences for educators as well as state sponsored education and arrangements for students and scholars. Similar arrangements were made by the Chola dynasty in 1024 CE, which provided state support to selected students in educational establishments. Temple schools from 12–13th centuries included the school at the Nataraja temple situated at Chidambaram which employed 20 librarians, out of whom 8 were copiers of manuscripts and 2 were employed for verification of the copied manuscripts. The remaining staff conducted other duties, including preservation and maintained of reference material.

Another establishment during this period is the Uddandapura institute established during the 8th century under the patronage of the Pala dynasty. The institution developed ties with Tibet and became a centre of Tantric Buddhism. During the 10–11th centuries the number of monks reached a thousand, equaling the strength of monks at the sacred Mahabodhi complex.

By the time of the arrival of the Islamic scholar Al Biruni India already had an established system of science and technology in place. Also by the 12th century, invasions from India's northern borders disrupted traditional education systems as foreign armies' raided educational institutes, among other establishments.

With the advent of Islam in India the traditional methods of education increasingly came under Islamic influence. Pre-Mughal rulers such as Qutb-ud-din Aybak and other Muslim rulers initiated institutions which imparted religious knowledge. Scholars such as Nizamuddin Auliya and Moinuddin Chishti became prominent educators and established Islamic monasteries. Students from Bukhara and Afghanistan visited India to study humanities and science.

Islamic institution of education in India included traditional *madrassas* and *maktabs* which taught grammar, philosophy, mathematics, and law influenced by the Greek traditions inherited by Persia and the Middle East before Islam spread from these regions into India. A feature of this traditional Islamic education was its emphasis on the connection between science and humanities.

Among the centres of education in India was 18th century Delhi was the *Madrasa Rahimiya* under the supervision of Shah Waliullah, an educator who favored an approach balancing the Islamic scriptures and science. The course at the *Madrasa Rahimiya* prescribed 2 books on grammar, 1 book on philosophy, 2 books on logic, 2 books on astronomy and mathematics, and 5 books on mysticism. Another centre of prominence arose in Lucknow under Mulla Nizamuddin Sahlawi, who educated at the *Firangi Mahal* and prescribed a course called the *Dars-i-Nizami* which combined traditional studies with modern and laid emphasis on logic.

The education system under the rule of Akbar adopted an inclusive approach with the monarch favoring additional courses comprising of medicine, agriculture, geography, and even from texts from other languages and religions, such as Patanjali's work in Sanskrit. The traditional science in this period was influenced by the ideas of Aristotle, Bhaskara, Charaka and Ibn Sina. This inclusive approach was not uncommon in Mughal India. The more conservative monarch Aurangzeb also favored teaching of subjects which could be applied to administration. The Mughals, in fact, adopted a liberal approach to sciences and as contact with Persia increased the more intolerant Ottoman school of *manqul* education came to be gradually substituted by the more relaxed *maqul* school.

The middle ages also saw the rise of private tuition in India. A tutor, or *Riyazi*, was an educated professional who could earn a suitable living by performing tasks such as creating calenders or generating revenue estimates for nobility. Another trend in this era is the mobility among professions, exemplified by Qaim Khan, a prince famous for his mastery in crafting leather shoes and forging cannons.

During the 19th and 20th centuries most of the Indian princely states fell under the British Raj. The British rule during the 19th century did not take adequate measures to help develop science and technology in India and instead focused more on arts and humanities.

Till 1899 only the University of Bombay offered a separate degree in sciences. In 1899 B.Sc and M.Sc. courses were also supported by the University of Calcutta. By the late 1800s India had lagged behind in science and technology and related education. However, the nobility and aristocracy in India largely continued to encourage the development of sciences and technical education, both traditional and western.

While some science related subjects were not allowed in the government curriculum in the 1850s the private institutions could also not follow science courses due to lack of funds required to establish laboratories etc. The fees for scientific education under the British rule were also high. The salary that one would get in the colonial administration was meager and made the prospect of attaining higher education bleak since the native population was not employed for high positions in the colonial setup. Even the natives who did manage to attain higher education faced issues of discrimination in terms of wages and privileges.

One argument for the British detachment towards the study of science in India is that England itself was gradually outpaced in science and technology by European rival Germany and a resurgent United States of America so the prospects of the British Raj adopting a world class science policy towards its colonies increasingly decreased.

However, Deepak Kumar notes the British turn to professional education during the 1860s and the French initiatives at raising awareness on science and technology in French colonies. The British themselves undertook science initiatives in Canada and South Africa. Growing awareness for the need of technical education in India gave rise to establishment of institutions such as the Indian Institute of

Science, established by philanthropist Jamshetji Tata in 1909. By the 1930s India had a total of only 10 institutions offering engineering courses. However, with the advent of the Second World War in 1939 the "War Technicians Training Scheme" under Ernest Bevin was initiated, thereby laying the foundation of modern technical education in India. Later, planned development of scientific education under Ardeshir Dalal was initiated in 1944.

The Madras Medical College opened in 1875, and imparted medical education to women so that they could treat the female population who traditionally shied away from medical treatments under qualified male professionals. The concept of educated women among medical professionals gained popularity during the late 1800s and by 1894, the Women's Christian Medical College, an exclusive medical school for women, was established in Ludhiana of Punjab. British education became solidified into India as missionary schools were established during the 1920s. New policies in 1835 gave rise to the use of English as a medium of education of western science. Fritz Blackwell writes: 'With the establishment of five universities in major cities in the middle of the century and the increase in primary and secondary schools, political consciousness also increased. The curriculum was Western, and the response was impressive; for example, the University of Calcutta in 1900 was reportedly the largest university in the world, with more than eight thousand students. Further, a number of Indians, including Gandhi and Nehru attended university in England.

UNIVERSALISATION OF PRIMARY EDUCATION

Universalisation of Elementary Education (UEE) is a constitutional provision and a national commitment in India. Universalisation implies educating all children up to the age of 14 which is equivalent to completion of upper primary level of education. Over the years, efforts by the government towards achieving the goal of UEE were focussed more on the primary stage than on the upper primary level of education. With the expansion of enrollment at the primary level of education, the pressure for expansion of the upper primary level of education has increased. The present study was an effort to analyze implications for provision of upper primary education facilities to ensure that this level of education is provided to all eligible children.

This implies creation of easy geographical access conditions to enroll all the eligible children in upper primary schools, provision reasonable levels of physical and infrastructural facilities in upper primary schools and teaching learning materials in the classrooms to facilitate meaningful curriculum transaction. Universalisation of upper primary education in India is normally discussed in terms of enrolling and retaining all children belonging to the age group 11 to 14. This seems more to be a desirable goal to be achieved in the long run than a realisable target at the present levels of development of primary education. Enrollment is a function of the relevant age group at the primary level of education. However, enrolment in upper primary schools is more a function of primary education completion rates than a function of the relevant age group.

It is logical to argue that all children in the relevant age group (11 to 14) cannot be enrolled in upper primary classes unless they complete primary level of education. In other words, all relevant age group children can be provided upper primary education only when all children of the primary school going age group are enrolled, retained and successfully complete the primary stage of education.

Since primary education is not yet universalised, this implies that universalisation of upper primary education means providing upper primary education for all children who have successfully completed primary level of education. The present study has adopted this as the operational definition of universalisation of upper primary education in India. However, once universalisation of primary education is attained, then there cannot be any difference between providing upper primary level of education to all age group children and those who complete primary stage of education. The effort at present needs to be to improve the inter-stage transition ratios from primary to upper primary levels of education.

STUDY DESIGN

The stage transition ratios from primary to upper primary levels of education indicate that they are very high in most of the states. Further expansion of primary education will have a demand for expansion of upper primary education even when transition ratios remain the same. In certain cases expansion of primary education may be accompanied by an increase in the inter-stage transition ratios. Under such circumstances, the demand for expansion of upper primary education system may be rather high. In states which are educationally more advanced, the primary stage completion rates and inter-stage transition rates are nearing 100%. In states which are educationally less advanced, the primary stage completion rates are not yet nearing 100% but inter-stage transition rates are very close to 100%. Educationally backward states have lower primary stage completion rates and lower inter-stage transition rates than states which are educationally advanced.

Hence implications for expansion of upper primary education facilities may be different in these varying situations. The future demand for expansion of upper primary education may be more in educationally backward states than in educationally the most advanced states. States and districts in India belong to different levels of development of primary education. States like Kerala have almost achieved universal enrollment and retention at the primary levels of education. But there are states which are educationally backward where universal enrollment at the primary level of education is still a distant dream. Therefore, it is not perhaps desirable to have a uniform strategy and the same level of investments to achieve the target of universalisation of upper primary education. Needless to add, the institutional arrangements for universalisation of upper primary level of education will vary depending upon the level of development of primary education.

Keeping these factors in view, this study attempts to make a realistic assessment of the extent of provisions required to universalise upper primary education in India. The study was visualised in two phases. The first phase of the study focussed on the existing institutional arrangements to provide upper primary education, patterns of expansion of upper primary education in different states, estimation of future enrollments, trends in teacher-pupil ratios, transition rates from primary to upper primary levels of education and cost estimations to arrive at the magnitude of investment required to universalise upper primary education in India. This part of the study report was based on secondary sources of information and the analysis covered major states of India and was completed in May 1998. The phase II of the study (the present report) focuses more on a direct assessment of level of provisions available in upper primary schools including infrastructural and academic facilities and on the functioning of upper primary schools.

More specifically the objectives of the present study are:

i. To study provision of upper primary schooling facilities in relation to provision of primary schooling facilities in a given locality;
ii. To analyse provision of infrastructural and other academic facilities available in upper primary schools;
iii. To analyse functioning of upper primary schools in the selected localities; and
iv. To estimate cost of providing upper primary schooling facilities under different organisational arrangements.

This phase of the study was based on primary data collected from four districts selected from four states of India. While selecting the locations for the study, special care was taken to ensure that the expansion requirements of upper primary education under varying levels of development of primary education are taken care of. The effort was to evolve an educational developmental continuum and hence the study locations are selected from the least developed to the most developed educational localities. The block forms the unit for the study. There are 8 blocks in the study and these blocks are selected from Malappuram district of Kerala, Bilaspur district of Madhya Pradesh, Aurangabad district of Maharashtra and Muradabad district of Uttar Pradesh. These districts vary in terms of literacy levels, population composition and levels of attainment of primary education. For example, the female literacy rates in the district of Muradabad are only 18.3%; it is 27.3% in Bilaspur; 39.6% in Aurangabad and 84.1% in Malappuram.

In other words these districts represent varying levels of educational development with Malappuram at the one end and Muradabad at the other end of the spectrum. The other socio-economic indicators also support the developmental continuum reflected in the selection of these districts. Another consideration to select the districts was the size of the districts. All the selected districts are the largest districts in the respective stages covered under externally funded projects.

The sample consisted of 71 upper primary schools from the blocks of Nilambur and Parappanangadi in Malappuram, 80 schools from the blocks of Mungeli and Kota in Bilaspur, 90 schools from the blocks of Khultabad and Soyagaon in Aurangabad and 43 schools from the blocks of Baniyakheda and Mundepandey in Moradabad and 1391 teachers from these schools.

ACCESS TO UPPER PRIMARY EDUCATION

It is generally believed that access conditions at the elementary level of education are poorly provided in many regions of the country. Our analysis in the study shows that the pattern of provisions for expansion of upper primary education indicates certain features. The districts which are now educationally advanced were historically well endowed with institutions providing upper primary education. For example, majority of the upper primary schools in Malappuram (69%) were established before the formation of the state in 1956. Similarly, half of the upper primary schools in Aurangabad were also established before 1956. However, majority of the schools in Bilaspur and Moradabad were established in the recent decades and the expansion still continues.

The expansion was higher during the 1980s in Bilaspur and during the 1990s in Moradabad. Upper primary schools are mostly controlled by the Government in Bilaspur and by local bodies in Aurangabad. However, in Kerala it is a shared responsibility between Government and private aided sector; in Moradabad the private un-aided sector is a significant partner with nearly 1/3 of the upper primary schools in the sample managed by the un-aided private sector.

An analysis of geographical access to upper primary schools indicates that there is at least one upper primary school within a distance of less than 1 km. for most of the primary schools. More than 90% of the upper primary schools have primary school within less than 1 km in all districts except Aurangabad. Even in Aurangabad 90% of the upper primary schools are having a primary school within 3 kms. of distance. Further, nearly 80% of the upper primary schools in Malappuram and 75% in Bilaspur and Aurangabad have another upper primary school within 3 kms distance.

This shows that upper primary schools are reasonably well provided in most of the locations. The arrangements to provide upper primary education vary from state to state. The single most dominant arrangement for provision of upper primary schools in Bilaspur is in the form of independent upper primary schools. The dominant pattern of provision of upper primary education in Malappuram and Aurangabad are in the form of upper primary schools as part of primary schools.

The other pattern which is found in around 20 to 25% of the upper primary schools is that of upper primary sections attached to secondary schools. In other words elementary schools are more common in educationally developed localities and independent primary schools are more common in educationally less developed areas. The logistics may demand such varying arrangements since a school also need to be seen from the point of view of economic and educational viability. One upper primary school may be sufficient to enroll all the primary stage graduates of 2-3 primary schools in locations where primary schools are small in size. In general, primary schools are small in age in remote rural areas of the educationally backward states. Hence, independent upper primary schools may be a better institutional arrangement to provide upper primary education in the short run.

Discussions on the desirability of independent or integrated upper primary schools elicit varying responses. Many teachers and educational administrators feel that it is better to have primary and upper primary schools together i.e. elementary schools are considered to be the best arrangement. The reasons are many. It is easier from the point of view of administration of elementary education especially on matters pertaining to recruitment, posting and transfer and training of teachers. Another reason for favouring the arrangement of elementary schools is the possibility of having a Headmaster to look after the affairs of upper primary section under such arrangement. However, teachers in some of the upper primary schools feel that the subjects like science and mathematics are difficult to handle and therefore attaching upper primary schools with secondary schools has an advantage.

They expect that under such arrangements teachers from the secondary schools, who are more qualified, can be drawn to teach these subjects at the upper primary level. However, this argument is not empirically valid since such arrangement rarely operates at the school level. It seems that even teachers in the independent upper primary schools do not prefer independent upper primary schools. Most of them prefer alternative arrangements like upper primary schools attached to high schools or primary schools attached to upper primary schools. These two arrangements alone to provide upper primary education do create some logistic problems. The logistics of provision may indicate that all upper primary schools can not be attached to high schools, since the number of high schools required will be less than the number of upper primary schools required.

Similarly all primary schools can not be upgraded to upper primary schools since they may not be getting enough children to make it a viable unit. Therefore, one can reasonably argue that independent upper primary schools may be needed in educationally backward localities. However, such schools may not be sustained in the long run when a locality approaches universalisation of primary education. Therefore, independent upper primary schools may be seen as short term solution in educationally less developed regions. This independent upper primary school may be seen as potential secondary schools or elementary schools in the long run.

UPPER PRIMARY FACILITIES

Many primary schools in India are not well equipped which formed the premise for introduction of Operation Blackboard Scheme. The empirical analysis in the study shows that upper primary schools are better placed in terms of provision of facilities. Most of the upper primary schools are not operating under deplorable conditions as in case of primary schools. More than 90% of the schools in our sample had buildings and similarly nearly 95% of the schools in all districts, except Bilaspur, had *pucca* buildings. However, the condition of upper primary school buildings is far from satisfactory.

Therefore, the study argues that investment requirements of providing upper primary education is more in terms of making additional provisions in the existing schools than in terms of opening of new upper primary schools in new locations. Multigrade teaching is almost absent in most of upper primary schools. Most of the schools have at least three rooms and three teachers even when teacher pupil ratios may not warrant it. This is a situation most common in educationally backward districts. For example, a number of schools in Bilaspur and Muradabad have enrollment levels less than 100 or 150 (at times less than 50 students in a school). However, classrooms in schools located in developed localities are over-crowded in districts like Malappuram. These schools may require additional space and other related facilities. Enrolments in some of the schools are rather low.

Most of the schools are provided with well qualified teachers. In fact, the share of university level educated teachers is quite substantial in all the districts, although the educational qualification requirements for recruitment of teachers to upper primary school are higher secondary level of education. Interestingly, larger share of university graduate and post-graduate teachers are found in educationally backward districts like Bilaspur and Muradabad. This is partly due to the fact that many of the teachers in these districts are not regular and many of them continue as temporary or adhoc teachers. Many teachers are working at low levels of salaries in Muradabad. Many of these teachers are working in the un-aided sector. In fact more than 45% of the teachers in Muradabad receive a salary of less than Rs.2000/- p.m.

Female teachers are very rare at the upper primary levels of education. In fact, the share of female teachers is very low in all districts except in Malappuram, where they form the majority. The share of female teachers in educationally backward districts varies from 12.5% in Muradabad to 17.6% in Bilaspur. Many schools in Malappuram are not only having large size enrollment but also have large number of rooms in the schools. More than 85% of the schools in Malappuram have more than 11 rooms and there are also schools in the sample which have 20 to 25 rooms. However, in other districts the most common pattern is that of 3 to 6 rooms.

Even in terms of provision of other facilities like teaching-learning materials and other physical facilities, most of the schools in Malappuram and Aurangabad are well placed. However, very few schools have separate toilets for girls in all districts. However, the high inter-stage transition rates indicate that non-availability of separate toilet for girls is not a constraining factor for parents to send their girl children to upper primary schools. Girls who come to upper primary level of education belong to the age group of 11 and above. Therefore, separate toilets for them may become a necessity. However, our discussions indicated that lack of separate toilets for girls is not a constraining factor for sending them to school by their parents. Perhaps in most of the rural areas households are not used to such facilities and hence they do not expect such facilities to be provided in schools too.

STUDENT TRANSITIONS IN UPPER PRIMARY SCHOOLS

Upper primary schools operate under different managements in India. A pattern that can be generalised in case of enrolment is that the share of enrollment in aided schools is consistently higher than their share in the total number of schools. This is not true in schools under other types of management, especially so in case of un-aided schools. During our discussions in the schools, it was found that many parents prefer aided private schools over other schools for many reasons. Many parents feel that teaching-learning process is better in aided private schools than in government managed schools. Aided private school does not charge high fees as in un-aided schools and hence aided schools are affordable from the financing point of view. More importantly, many parents consider that English as a subject is taught better in aided schools. This is more so in Aurangabad and Malappuram. For these reasons, parents prefer to send their children to aided private schools wherever they are available. Transition ratios are very high at the upper primary level of education. This is in contrast to the situation at the primary level where dropout rates are very high.

Drop out rates are very low; and repetition rates are higher than dropout rates at the upper primary level. Interestingly, repetition rates are higher at the terminal grades than in other grades of upper primary education. In many localities repetition rates of boys are more than that of girls. Repetition rates in general are low in Aurangabad and Moradabad when compared to other districts. The input-output ratio, which is an indicator of efficiency of the system, indicates that wastages are relatively less at the upper primary level of education than at the primary levels of education. The input output ratios are 1:1.24 in case of Malappuram; 1:1.41 in case of Bilaspur; 1:1.11 in case of Aurangabad and 1:1.20 in case of Moradabad. These input-output ratios show that wastage is less in upper primary schools except in Bilaspur. More importantly wastage on account of repetition is atleast three times higher than that on account of drop-outs.

TEACHING-LEARNING CONDITIONS

Most of the upper primary school teachers come from agricultural families with illiterate mothers. The only exception to this pattern is Malappuram in case of educational levels of parents and Aurangabad in case of sector of employment. In Malappuram the parents are literate and school level educated and in Aurangabad many parents are engaged in non-agricultural activities. The teacher spouses are well educated and definitely better educated than teacher parents in all districts. In Malappuram the spouses are better educated and well employed than the teachers themselves.

This is partly due to the fact that this district has a very high share of female teachers. It is an accepted social norm in India that educated and employed females look for husbands who are equally qualified or more educated and better placed than them. Interestingly, many teachers prefer to send their children to private schools, even though many of them are still teaching in the government schools. As noted earlier most of the teachers in upper primary schools are qualified and a good percentage of them are trained in Malappuram and Aurangabad. However, the share of trained teachers is less in Moradabad or Bilaspur. At the same time a larger share of teachers employed in Bilaspur and Muradabad are university graduates or post-graduates. As explained earlier, this may be due to the nature of appointment (in the category of temporary teachers) and sector of employment (unaided school).

In-service training is more common in Malappuram followed by Aurangabad. Only 50% of the teachers in Bilaspur and 36% of the teachers in Moradabad are in-service trained at least once. However, in terms of frequency of in-service training programmes, the teachers in Aurangabad are better placed. In Aurangabad, nearly 43% of the teachers are trained atleast three times as against 8% in Malappuram and none at all in Muradabad. However, DIETs are not the organizations which provide in-service training to these teachers.

For example, most of the teachers who receive in-service training in Muradabad got it from BRCs which implies that they are essentially trained for primary school teaching. Most of the teachers in Aurangabad and Bilaspur received in-service training from institutions other than DIETs.

The state government of Maharashtra had introduced SMART which was conducted mostly in Zilla Parishad buildings. Language teaching takes larger share of teaching time at the upper primary level of education. Infact, on an average one finds that language teaching is at least three times more than teaching of any other single subject area. This is understandable because three languages are taught in most of the upper primary schools. However, schools located in different localities vary in terms of number of hours of instruction. Malappuram has lowest hours of instruction at the upper primary level of education and Aurangabad has the highest number of hours of instruction in the upper primary level of education.

This may be partly due to the fact that Malappuram is a Muslim majority area and Friday is a holiday in those schools which have majority of students belonging to Muslim community. Any school holiday cannot be compensating by working on a Saturday, since, Saturday is a regular working day in Malappuram. Malappuram is poorly placed in terms of instructional hours per week and total number of working days of a school in a year. Therefore, students in Malappuram have the lowest in-school learning time. Teachers have access to most of the teaching-learning materials only in Malappuram and Aurangabad; they are deprived of these facilities in Moradabad and Bilaspur. Most of the teachers say that they are regular in giving class-work and homework to children. Analyses of the distribution of teaching time of teachers indicate that the pattern varies across districts.

For example, in Aurangabad 70% of the teaching time is spending on classroom lectures with very little time available for other activities. In other districts lecture time is only 27% to 35% of the total instructional time. In schools of these districts an equal emphasis is given to class-work, correction, feedback and students copying from the black-board. Most of the teachers indicate that the most commonly used teaching aid is teachers guide in Aurangabad, Maps in all districts and dictionary in Malappuram. Many teachers feel that they do not get much support from the inspecting officers except in Aurangabad. Most of them feel that support and help from the head of the school and from other teachers of the school are more easily available. However, all the teachers in Aurangabad feel that the support that they receive from the head of the school complex teacher is very substantial and satisfactory.

The teachers feel that when the head of the school complex visits the school academic matters are discussed and moreover, teachers respect them but are not scared of them since they can be better equate with them than with a typical school inspector. PTA meetings are not very regular in any district except in Malappuram. Many teachers feel that they need to improve their academic competency and therefore they need more in-service training in the subject areas to improve their subject knowledge while teachers in Malappuram feel that the training should be in-school based, teachers in other district feel that training may be organised in separate institutions far away from the schools. Most of the teachers express difficulty in teaching subjects like Science, Mathematics and English. In fact, many of them suggested that they are unable to teach these subjects.

In the absence of teacher guide books and adequate training programmes they feel helpless. It seems that the teacher competency development programmes have not kept pace with the changes in the curriculum and text-books. Perhaps one may have to seriously look into the qualification requirements while recruiting upper primary school teachers. Although many teachers are university graduates, most of them had specialization in arts and humanity and hence they are equally ill-equipped as their less educated counterparts to teach Mathematics and Science. Many of them have taken these degrees through correspondence courses while on job and that too at times in regional language medium. Therefore, they are not better equipped to teach English language.

SCHOOL MANAGEMENT

School management has two dimensions:

i. Efforts made by Headmasters of the schools and by other administrative authorities; and

ii. The support received by the schools from the community. The support from PTAs is rather limited except in Malappuram. The VECs focus more on issues related to primary education and therefore, VECs have not yet become effective mechanisms of community support at the upper primary level of education. The Head-masters do not have much control in the selection of teachers. This is true in schools under any management. Teacher selection in government schools is a responsibility of the Public Service Commissions; it is the responsibility of the school management in aided and unaided primary schools. This shows that headmasters in upper primary schools can only re-organise the human resources already provided to them. Our study shows that a considerable amount of time of the head master is spent on non-teaching activities. In fact, we made a detailed analysis of the time spend by head-teacher on various activities and it is estimated that nearly 5 to 10 days of a headmaster is spend every month on school related activities taking place outside the schools.

Similarly, the headmaster also devotes time for administration of schools activities in the schools. Our estimation indicates that a total nearly 40% of the working time of the headmaster in Malappuram is spending on administrative activities. The corresponding percentages are 21% in Bilaspur and 29% each in Aurangabad and Muradabad. It seems that if we expect the head-teacher to closely monitor the school activities one may have to devote at least half of the total working time of the Headmasters on non-teaching activities. In Kerala such responsibilities may account for 2/3 to 3/4 of the total working time of the Headmaster because the schools are large. This implies that treating headmaster as just another teacher is not realistic. The teaching time of the head-teacher needs is to be reduced and his/her managerial role needs to be increased.

However, from the academic point of view it is important that the headmaster also teaches. But teaching responsibility of the headmaster may by keep at a minimum level. What is more important to improve school functioning is to raise the status of headmaster as educational managers than as teachers. Unfortunately, many upper primary schools do not have separate headmasters unless it is an independent upper primary school. Therefore, the argument is to devise mechanisms to have separate head-masters for the upper primary sections/schools. At present the headmasters are not in a position to do any evaluation of teachers either through observation of classes through or checking of notes prepared by the teachers. He/she plays limited role in planning of school activities. Therefore, one may have to develop a system by which the headmaster will be actively taking up these managerial responsibilities. This further confirms our argument for separate headmasters with limited teaching responsibilities for upper primary schools in India.

COST OF EDUCATION

The study also made an analysis of cost of upper primary education provided under alternative arrangements. The cost composition of upper primary education varies between schools under other managements. For example, salaries account for nearly 95% of the total educational expenditure in all schools under the government, aided private and local body schools. Teacher salary accounts for the major share in government and local body schools. The share of non-teaching salary is higher in private schools than their counter parts in the government sector.

This implies that the support system that the school

receives in terms of non-teaching staff is very poor in the government schools.

The per school expenditure varies from locality to locality. It is found that schools managed by Zila Parishad have less per school expenditure than the schools managed by the state governments. But per school expenditure in government schools, on an average, are less than that in private aided schools in all districts except Moradabad and unaided schools has the lowest per school expenditure in all the districts. However, expenditure per school in un-aided school is very low in Malappuram and very high in Moradabad and Bilaspur. Per school expenditure is influenced by the number of teachers. Small schools, in general may have low per school expenditure.

Therefore, unit cost, unless adjusted for the size of the school may be misleading. Per student expenditure may be a more reliable indicator from this point of view. Per student expenditure in Malappuram and Aurangabad are very similar in schools managed by the government and local bodies. Per student expenditure in government schools is high in Bilaspur and it is the highest in Moradabad. Per student expenditure variations are not substantial in aided private schools. However, per student expenditure in private unaided schools seems to be lower than that in other types of managements.

Per student expenditure in government schools is the lowest in Malappuram and the highest in Moradabad; per student expenditure in aided private schools is the lowest in Malappuram and the highest in Aurangabad; and per student expenditure in unaided schools is the highest in Aurangabad and the lowest in Bilaspur.

Within a given locality private unaided schools have the lowest per student expenditure in all districts except Aurangabad where local body schools have the lowest per student expenditure. The low per student expenditure in unaided schools is primarily due to the low level of salaries paid to the teachers in these schools. However, one crucial distinction between unaided and schools under other managements needs to be noted.

The burden of cost of education in unaided schools is entirely borne by the parents. Hence, even when per student expenditure is lower in unaided schools, it is the most expensive form of education from the parental point of view. Total cost of providing upper primary education in a block varies widely. It varies from Rs.3.8 millions in Mundapandey to Rs. 31.7 millions in Nilambur. Needless to add, the total expenditure of a block is a function of total number of schools in a block and the number of teachers in a school which is determined by the size of student enrolment. Schools in Malappuram have large student enrolment and hence the total number of teachers and the total expenditure are also substantially higher than that in other localities. In general one can argue that provision of upper primary schools in developed districts may cost around Rs. 22 to Rs. 32 millions; While it may cost between Rs. 12 millions to 22 millions in blocks located in moderately developed areas; it may cost between Rs. 4 millions to Rs. 17 millions per block in the least developed areas like Muradabad; and it may cost between Rs. 14 to 20 millions in blocks in Bilaspur.

Although, the number of schools in Bilaspur is less than that in Aurangabad, the level of teacher salaries are higher in Bilaspur and hence total expenditure is also high in this district. In other words, the cost of providing upper primary education to all children in a block will increase from a minimum of Rs. 4 millions when most of the age-group children remain outside the school to around Rs. 32 millions when all age-group children will be enrolled and retained in the upper primary schools. Which is the least expensive institutional arrangement to provide upper primary education in India? The cost of independent upper primary schools varies from block to block. Independent upper primary schools are the most expensive in Baniyakheda with per school expenditure of Rs. 1 million and it is the least expensive in Kota with a per school expenditure of around Rs. 0.3 million. Upper primary schools with primary schools are the least expensive in Mungeli with a per school expenditure of Rs. 0.2 millions and the most expensive in Nilambur with a per school expenditure of Rs. 0.8 millions.

The per school expenditure in integrated schools (upper primary schools with Higher Secondary) is the lowest in Mundapandey with Rs. 0.4 million and the most expensive in Nilambur with Rs. 1.1 millions. Integrated schools from primary to secondary levels are the least expensive in Kota with Rs. 55.4 thousand and most expensive in Nilambur with Rs. 0.7 millions. The integrated upper primary schools primary to secondary is the least expensive arrangement in Malappuram, Bilaspur and Moradabad. Independent upper primary schools are the most expensive arrangement in Malappuram and Moradabad.

Upper primary schools attached to secondary schools are the most expensive arrangement in Bilaspur and Aurangabad. Incidentally, Aurangabad does not have any independent upper primary schools. As argued earlier, cost cannot be the only criterion to provide compulsory levels of education. And hence independent upper primary schools may become an unavoidable institutional arrangement in the educationally backward districts. However, it is important to visualise any independent upper primary school as an interim arrangement which in the long run may be converted into integrated schools either as elementary schools or as secondary schools.

3

Philosophical Idealism of Indian Society

PHILOSOPHY OF EDUCATION

The theme of my talk (philosophy of education as a knowledge field) is mainly inspired by the consideration that my academic training and professional engagement has been, for the most part, in the area of philosophy of education although during the past few years I have been doing mostly project work of the kind that field educa-tionists do in the areas of basic education, literacy training and teacher training, an engagement qualitatively different from serious academics. A further justification arises from NIEPA becoming NUEPA; the change entails a drastic qualitative change in the institution's lifestyle and culture; it also raises new hopes and expectations. A university is a university; it cannot be conceived without values integrally linked with it: academic freedom, autonomy, liberalism and pursuit of excellence.

The change implies that NUEPA would now address its mandated functions in educational planning and administration with greater freedom and its contributions will be characterized by intellectual scholarship of a high order and deep understanding of educational theory and practice. I hold that philosophy of education contributes to the development of such understanding and also provides the needed perspective for intellectual dialogue and debate. Like in other disciplines, there are different traditions in philosophy as well.

The dominating one is conceptual analysis (I also use the terms 'analytical', 'critical' to denote this trend) which characterizes most of current writings in the field. I hold this as the paradigm tradition and begin by giving a summary account of analytical philosophy of education. I follow this up with a critique of philosophy of education as it is understood in India and its status, alongside citing work that I consider as contributions of a philosophical kind to the field. As the meager output and general lack of quality in this area appear to stem from a lack of appreciation of the wide scope and richness of the field, I provide illustrations of the nature and variety of philosophical work carried out drawing from national and international sources. I then turn to the NUEPA function areas of school and higher education, NFE, inclusive education and women's empowerment and provide illustrations of issues and problems of a philosophical/ theoretical kind that, in my view, provide a broader perspective for addressing practical tasks related to educational planning and administration.

In relation to Western philosophical thought, Indian philosophy offers both surprising points of affinity and illuminating differences. The differences highlight certain fundamentally new questions that the Indian philosophers asked. The similarities reveal that, even when philosophers in India and the West were grappling with the same problems and sometimes even suggesting similar theories, Indian thinkers were advancing novel formulations and argumentations. Problems that the Indian philosophers raised for consideration, but that their Western counterparts never did, include such matters as the origin (*utpatti*) and apprehension (*jnapti*) of truth (*pramanya*). Problems that the Indian philosophers for the most part ignored but that helped shape Western philosophy include the question of whether knowledge arises from experience or from reason and distinctions such as that between analytic and synthetic judgments or between contingent and necessary truths.

Indian thought, therefore, provides the historian of Western philosophy with a point of view that may supplement that gained from Western thought. A study of Indian thought, then, reveals certain inadequacies of Western philosophical thought and makes clear that some concepts and distinctions may not be as inevitable as they may otherwise seem. In a similar manner, knowledge of Western thought gained by Indian philosophers has also been advantageous to them. Vedic hymns, Hindu scriptures dating from the 2nd millennium B.C., are the oldest extant record from India of the process by which the human mind makes its gods and of the deep psychological processes of mythmaking leading to profound cosmological concepts. The *Upanisads* (Hindu philosophical treatises) contains one of the first conceptions of a universal, all-pervading, spiritual reality leading to a radical monism (absolute non dualism, or the essential unity of matter and spirit). The *Upanisads* also contain early speculations by Indian philosophers about nature, life, mind, and the human body, not to speak of ethics and social philosophy.

The classical, or orthodox, systems (*darsanas*) debate, sometimes with penetrating insight and often with a degree of repetition that can become tiresome to some, such matters as the status of the finite individual; the distinction as well as the relation between the body, mind, and the self; the nature of knowledge and the types of valid knowledge; the nature and origin of truth; the types of entities that may be said to exist; the relation of realism to idealism; the problem of whether universals or relations are basic; and the very important problem of *moksa*, or salvation—its nature and the paths leading up to it. The various Indian philosophies contain such a diversity of views, theories, and systems that it is almost impossible to single out characteristics that are common to all of them. Acceptance of the authority of the Vedas characterizes all the orthodox (*astika*) systems, but not the unorthodox (*nastika*) systems, such as Carvaka (radical materialism), Buddhism, and Jainism.

Moreover, even when philosophers professed allegiance to the Vedas, their allegiance did little to fetter the freedom of their speculative ventures. On the contrary, the acceptance of the authority of the Vedas was a convenient way for a philosopher's views to become acceptable to the orthodox, even if a thinker introduced a wholly new idea. Thus, the Vedas could be cited to corroborate a wide diversity of views; they were used by the Vaisesika thinkers (*i.e.*, those who believe in ultimate particulars, both individual souls and atoms) as much as by the Advaita (monist) philosophers. In most Indian philosophical systems, the acceptance of the ideal of *moksa*, like allegiance to the authority of the scriptures, was only remotely connected with the systematic doctrines that were being propounded.

Many epistemological, logical, and even metaphysical doctrines were debated and decided on purely rational grounds that did not directly bear upon the ideal of *moksa*. Only the Vedanta ("end of the Vedas") philosophy and the Samkhya (a system that accepts a real matter and a plurality of the individual souls) philosophy may be said to have a close relationship to the ideal of *moksa*. The logical systems—Nyaya, Vaisesika, and Purva-mimamsa—are only very remotely related. Also, both the philosophies and other scientific treatises, including even the *Kama-sutra* ("Aphorisms on Love") and the *Arthasastra* ("Treatise on Material Gain"), recognized the same ideal and professed their efficacy for achieving it. When Indian philosophers speak of intuitive knowledge, they are concerned with making room for it and demonstrating its possibility, with the help of logic—and there, as far as they are concerned, the task of philosophy ends. Indian philosophers do not seek to justify religious faith; philosophic wisdom itself is accorded the dignity of religious truth.

Theory is not subordinated to practice, but theory itself, as theory, is regarded as being supremely worthy and efficacious. Three basic concepts form the cornerstone of Indian philosophical thought: the self, or soul (*atman*), works (*karma*, or *karman*), and salvation (*moksa*). Leaving the Carvakas aside, all Indian philosophies concern themselves with these three concepts and their interrelations, though this is not to say that they accept the objective validity of these concepts in precisely the same manner. Of these, the concept of *karma,* signifying moral efficacy of human actions, seems to be the most typically Indian. The concept of *atman,* not altogether absent in Western thought, corresponds, in a certain sense, to the Western concept of a transcendental or absolute spirit self—important differences notwith-standing. The concept of *moksa* as the concept of the highest ideal has likewise been one of the concerns of Western thought, especially during the Christian Era, though it probably has never been as important as for the Hindu mind.

Most Indian philosophies assume that *moksa* is possible, and the "impossibility of *moksa*" (*anirmoksa*) is regarded as a material fallacy likely to vitiate a philosophical theory. In addition to *karma,* the lack of two other concerns further differentiates Indian philosophical thought from Western thought in general. Since the time of the Greeks, Western thought has been concerned with mathematics, and, in the Christian era, with history. Neither mathematics nor history has ever raised philosophical problems for the Indian. In the lists of *pramanas*, or ways of knowing accepted by the different schools, there is none that includes mathematical knowledge or historical knowledge. Possibly connected with their indifference toward mathematics is the significant fact that Indian philosophers have not developed formal logic.

The theory of the syllogism (a valid deductive argument having two premises and a conclusion) is, however, developed, and much sophistication has been achieved in logical theory. Indian logic offers an instructive example of logic of cognitions (*jnanani*) rather than of abstract propositions—logic not sundered and kept isolated from psychology and epistemology, because it is meant to be the logic of man's actual striving to know what is true of the world.

There is, in relation to Western thought, a striking difference in the manner in which Indian philosophical thinking is presented as well as in the mode in which it historically develops. Out of the pre-systematic age of the

Vedic hymns and the *Upanisads* and many diverse philosophical ideas current in the pre-Buddhistic era, there emerged with the rise of the age of the *sutras* (aphoristic summaries of the main points of a system) a neat classification of systems (*darsanas*), a classification that was never to be contradicted and to which no further systems are added. No new school was founded; no new *darsana* came into existence. But this conformism, like conformism to the Vedas, did not check the rise of independent thinking, new innovations, or original insights.

There is, apparently, an underlying assumption in the Indian tradition that no individual can claim to have seen the truth for the first time and, therefore, that an individual can only explicate, state, and defend in a new form a truth that had been seen, stated, and defended by countless others before him: hence the tradition of expounding one's thoughts by affiliating oneself to one of the *darsanas*. If one is to be counted as a great master (*acarya*), one has to write a commentary (*bhasya*) on the *sutras* of the *darsana* concerned, or one must comment on one of the *bhasyas* and write a *tika* (sub commentary). The usual order is *sutra–bhasya–varttika* (collection of critical notes)–*tika*. At any stage, a person may introduce a new and original point of view, but at no stage can he claim originality for himself. Not even an author of the *sutras* could do that, for he was only systematizing the thoughts and insights of countless predecessors. The development of Indian philosophical thought has thus been able to combine, in an almost unique manner, conformity to tradition and adventure in thinking.

The role of the sacred texts in the growth of Indian philosophy is different in each of the different systems. In those systems that may be called *adhyatmavidya*, or sciences of spirituality, the sacred texts play a much greater role than they do in the logical systems (*anviksikividya*). In the case of the former, Sankara, a leading Advaita Vedanta philosopher (*c.* 788–820), perhaps best laid down the principles: reasoning should be allowed freedom only as long as it does not conflict with the scriptures. In matters regarding supersensible reality, reasoning left to itself cannot deliver certainty, for, according to Sankara, every thesis established by reasoning may be countered by an opposite thesis supported by equally strong, if not stronger, reasoning. The sacred scriptures, embodying as they do the results of intuitive experiences of seers, therefore, should be accepted as authoritative, and reasoning should be made subordinate to them.

Whereas the sacred texts thus continued to exercise some influence on philosophical thinking, the influence of mythology declined considerably with the rise of the systems. The myths of creation and dissolution of the universe persisted in the theistic systems but were transformed into metaphors and models. With the Nyaya (problem of knowledge)–Vaisesika (analysis of nature) systems, for example, the model of a potter making pots determined much philosophical thinking, as did that of a magician conjuring up tricks in the Advaita (non dualist) Vedanta. The *nirukta* (etymology) of Yaska, a 5th-century- B.C. Sanskrit scholar, tells of various attempts to interpret difficult Vedic mythologies: the *adhidaivata* (pertaining to the deities), the *aitihasika* (pertaining to the tradition), the *adhiyajna* (pertaining to the sacrifices), and the *adhyatmika* (pertaining to the spirit). Such interpretations apparently prevailed in the *Upanisads*; the myths were turned into symbols, though some of them persisted as models and metaphors.

The issue of theism vis-à-vis atheism, in the ordinary senses of the English words, played an important role in Indian thought. The ancient Indian tradition, however, classified the classical systems (*darsanas*) into orthodox (*astika*) and unorthodox (*nastika*). *Astika* does not mean "theistic," nor does *nastika* mean "atheistic." Panini, a 5th-century-B.C. grammarian, stated that the former is one who believes in a transcendent world (*asti paralokah*) and the latter is one who does not believe in it (*nasti paralokah*). *Astika* may also mean one who accepts the authority of the Vedas; *nastika* then means one who does not accept that authority. Not all among the *astika* philosophers, however, were theists, and even if they were, they did not all accord the same importance to the concept of God in their systems. The Samkhya system did not involve belief in the existence of God, without ceasing to be *astika,* and Yoga (a mental-psychological-physical meditation system) made room for God not on theoretical grounds but only on practical considerations. The Purva-Mimamsa of Jaimini, the greatest philosopher of the Mimamsa school, posits various deities to account for the significance of Vedic rituals but ignores, without denying, the question of the existence of God.

The Advaita Vedanta of Sankara rejects atheism in order to prove that the world had its origin in a conscious, spiritual being called Isvara, or God, but in the long run regards the concept of Isvara as a concept of lower order that becomes negated by a metaphysical knowledge of Brahman, the absolute, nondual reality. Only the non-Advaita schools of Vedanta and the Nyaya-Vaisesika remain zealous theists, and of these schools, the god of the Nyaya-Vaisesika school does not create the eternal atoms, universals, or individual souls. For a truly theistic conception of God, one has to look to the non-Advaita schools of Vedanta, the Vaisnava, and the Saiva philosophical systems. Whereas Hindu religious life continues to be dominated by these last-mentioned theistic systems, the philosophies went their own ways, far removed from that religious demand. S.N. Dasgupta, a 20th-century Indian philosopher, has divided the history of Indian philosophy into three periods: the prelogical (up to the beginning of the Christian era), the logical (from the beginning of the Christian era up to the 11th century ad), and the ultralogical (from the 11th century to the 18th century).

What Dasgupta calls the pre-logical stage covers the pre-Mauryan and the Mauryan periods (*c.* 321–185 B.C.) in Indian history. The logical period begins roughly with the Kusanas (1st–2nd centuries ad) and finds its highest development during the Gupta era (3rd–5th centuries ad) and the age of imperial Kanauj (7th century ad). In its early prelogical phase, Indian thought, freshly developing in the Indian subcontinent, actively confronted and assimilated the diverse currents of pre-Aryan and non-Aryan elements in the native culture that the Aryans sought to conquer and appropriate. The marks of this confrontation are to be noted in every facet of Indian religion and thought: in the Vedic hymns in the form of conflicts, with varying fortunes, between the Aryans and the non-Aryans; in the conflict between a positive attitude toward life that is interested in making life fuller and richer and a negative attitude emphasizing asceticism and renunciation; in the great variety of skeptics, naturalists, determinists, indeterminists, accidentalists, and no-soul theorists that filled the Ganges Plain; in the rise of the heretical, unorthodox schools of Jainism and Buddhism protesting against the Vedic religion and the Upanisadic theory of *atman*; and in the continuing confrontation, mutually enriching and nourishing, that occurred between the Brahmanic (Hindu priestly) and Buddhist logicians, epistemologists, and dialecticians.

The Aryans, however, were soon followed by a host of foreign invaders, Greeks, Sakas and Hunas from Central Asia, Pushtans (Pathans), Mongols, and Mughals (Muslims). Both religious thought and philosophical discussion received continuous challenges and confrontations. The resulting responses have a dialectical character: sometimes new ideas have been absorbed and orthodoxy has been modified; sometimes orthodoxy has been strengthened and codified in order to be preserved in the face of the dangers of such confrontation; sometimes, as in the religious life of the Christian Middle Ages, bold attempts at synthesis of ideas have been made.

Nevertheless, through all the vicissitudes of social and cultural life, Brahmanical thought has been able to maintain a fairly strong current of continuity. In the chaotic intellectual climate of the pre-Mauryan era, there were skeptics (*ajnanikah*) who questioned the possibility of knowledge. There were also materialists, the chief of which were the Ajivikas (deterministic ascetics) and the Lokayatas (the name by which Carvaka doctrines—denying the authority of the Vedas and the soul—are generally known).

Furthermore, there existed the two unorthodox schools of *yadrchhavada* (accidentalists) and *svabhavavaha* (naturalists), who rejected the supernatural. Kapila, the legendary founder of the Samkhya school, supposedly flourished during the 7th century B.C. Pre-Mahavira Jaina ideas were already in existence when Mahavira (flourished 6th century B.C.), the founder of Jainism, initiated his reform. Gautama the Buddha (flourished 6th–5th centuries B.C.) apparently was familiar with all of these intellectual ideas and was as dissatisfied with them as with the Vedic orthodoxy. He sought to forge a new path—though not new in all respects—that was to assure blessedness to man. Orthodoxy, however, sought to preserve itself in a vast *Kalpa-* (ritual) *sutra* literature—with three parts: the *Srauta-*, based on *sruti* (revelation); the *Grhya-*, based on *smrti* (tradition); and the *Dharma-*, or rules of religious law, *sutras*—whereas the philosophers tried to codify their doctrines in systematic form, leading to the rise of the philosophical *sutras*. Though the writing of the *sutras* continued over a long period, the *sutras* of most of the various *darsanas* probably were completed between the 6th and 3rd centuries B.C. Two of the *sutras* appear to have been composed in the pre-Maurya period, but after the rise of Buddhism; these works are the *Mimamsasutras* of Jaimini (*c.* 400 B.C.) and the *Vedanta-sutras* of Badarayana (*c.* 500–200 B.C.).

The Maurya period brought, for the first time, a strong centralized state. The Greeks had been ousted, and a new self-confidence characterized the beginning of the period. This seems to have been the period in which the epics *Mahabharata* and *Ramayana* were initiated, though their composition went on through several centuries before they took the forms they now have. Manu, a legendary lawgiver, codified the *Dharma-sastra;* Kaumilya, a minister of King Chandragupta Maurya, systematized the science of political economy (*Arthasastra*); and Patanjali, an ancient author or authors composed the *Yoga-sutras*. Brahmanism tried to adjust itself to the new communities and cultures that were admitted into its fold: new gods—or rather, old Vedic gods that had been rejuvenated—were worshipped; the Hindu trinity of Brahma (the creator), Vishnu (the preserver), and Shiva (the destroyer) came into being; and the Pasupata (Shaivite), Bhagavata (Vaisnavite), and the Tantra (esoteric meditative) systems were initiated.

The *Bhagavadgita*—the most famous work of this period—symbolized the spirit of the creative synthesis of the age. A new ideal of *karma* as opposed to the more ancient one of renunciation was emphasized. Orthodox notions were reinterpreted and given a new symbolic meaning, as, for example, the *Gita* does with the notion of *yajna* ("sacrifice"). Already in the pre-Christian era, Buddhism had split up into several major sects, and the foundations for the rise of Mahayana ("Greater Vehicle") Buddhism had been laid. The logical period of Indian thought began with the Kusanas (1st–2nd century).

Gautama (author of the *Nyaya-sutras*; probably flourished at the beginning of the Christian era) and his 5th-century commentator Vatsyayana established the foundations of the Nyaya as a school almost exclusively preoccupied with logical and epistemological issues. The Madhyamika ("Middle Way"), or Sunyavada ("Voidist") school of Buddhism, arose and the thought of Nagarjuna (*C.* 200), the great propounder of Sunyavada (dialectical thinking), reached great heights. Though Buddhist logic in the strict sense of the term had not yet come into being, a logical style of philosophizing was in existence in such schools of thought.

During the reign of the Guptas, there was a revival of Brahmanism of a gentler and more refined form. Vaisnavism of the Vasudeva cult, centring on the prince-god Krishna and advocating renunciation by action, and Saivism prospered, along with Buddhism and Jainism. Both the Mahayana and the Hinayana ("Lesser Vehicle"), or Theravada ("Way of the Elders"), schools flourished. The most notable feature, however, was the rise of the Buddhist Yogacara School, of which Asanga (4th century ad) and his brother Vasubandhu were the great pioneers. Toward the end of the 5th century, Dignaga, a Buddhist logician, wrote the *Pramanasamuccaya*

("Compendium of the Means of True Knowledge"), a work that laid the foundations of Buddhist logic. The greatest names of Indian philosophy belong to the post-Gupta period from the 7th to the 10th century. At that time Buddhism was on the decline and the Tantric cults were rising, a situation that led to the development of the tantric forms of Buddhism. Saivism was thriving in Kashmir, and Vaisnavism in the southern part of India. The great philosophers Mimamsakas Kumarila (7th century), Prabhakara (7th–8th centuries), Mandana Misra (8th century), Salikanatha (9th century), and Parthasarathi Misra (10th century) belong to this age.

The greatest Indian philosopher of the period, however, was Sankara. All of these men defended Brahmanism against the "unorthodox" schools, especially against the criticisms of Buddhism. The debate between Brahmanism and Buddhism was continued, on a logical level, by philosophers of the Nyaya school—Uddyotakara, Vacaspati Misra, and Udayana (Udayanacarya). Muslim rule in India had consolidated itself by the 11th century, by which time Buddhism, for all practical purposes, had disappeared from the country. Hinduism had absorbed Buddhist ideas and practices and reasserted itself, with the Buddha appearing in Hindu writings as an incarnation of Vishnu. The Muslim conquest created a need for orthodoxy to readjust itself to a new situation. In this period the great works on Hindu law were written. Jainism, of all the "unorthodox" schools, retained its purity, and great Jaina works, such as Devasuri's *Pramananayatattvalokalamkara* ("The Ornament of the Light of Truth of the Different Points of View Regarding the Means of True Knowledge," 12th century ad) and Prabhachandra's *Prameyakamalamartanda* ("The Sun of the Lotus of the Objects of True Knowledge," 11th century ad), were written during this period.

Under the Cola (Chola) kings (*c.* 850–1279) and later in the Vijayanagara kingdom (which, along with Mithila in the north, remained strongholds of Hinduism until the middle of the 16th century), Vaisnavism flourished. The philosopher Yamunacarya (flourished ad 1050) taught the path of *prapatti,* or complete surrender to God. The philosophers Ramanuja (11th century),

Madhva, and Nimbarka (*c.* 12th century) developed theistic systems of Vedanta and severely criticized Sankara's Advaita Vedanta. Toward the end of the 12th century, creative work of the highest order began to take place in the fields of logic and epistemology in Mithila and Bengal. The 12th–13th-century philosopher Gangesa's *Tattvacintamani* ("The Jewel of Thought on the Nature of Things") laid the foundations of the school of Navya-Nyaya ("New-Nyaya"). Four great members of this school were Paksadhara Misra of Mithila, Vasudeva Sarvabhauma (16th century), his disciple Raghunatha Siromani (both of Bengal), and Gadadhara Bhattacaryya.

Religious life was marked by the rise of great mystic saints, chief of which are Ramananda, Kabir, Chaitanya, and Guru Nanak, who emphasized the path of *bhakti*, or devotion, a wide sense of humanity, freedom of thought, and a sense of unity of all religions. Somewhat earlier than these were the great Muslim Sufi (mystic) saints, including Khwaja Mu'in-ud-Din $asan, who emphasized asceticism and taught a philosophy that included both love of God and love of humanity.

The British period in Indian history was primarily a period of discovery of the ancient tradition (*e.g.*, the two histories by Radhakrishnan, scholar and president of India from 1962 to 1967, and S.N. Dasgupta) and of comparison and synthesis of Indian philosophy with the philosophical ideas from the West. Among modern creative thinkers have been Mahatma Gandhi, who espoused new ideas in the fields of social, political, and educational philosophy; Sri Aurobindo, an exponent of a new school of Vedanta that he calls Integral Advaita; and K.C. Bhattacharyya, who developed a phenomenologically oriented philosophy of subjectivity that is conceived as freedom from object.

All "orthodox" philosophies can trace their basic principles back to some statement or other in the Vedas. The Vedanta schools, especially, had an affiliation with the authority of *sruti*, and the school of Mimamsa concerned itself chiefly with the questions of interpreting the sacred texts. The Hindu tradition regards the Vedas as being *apauruseya*—

i.e., as not composed by any person. Sayana, a famous Vedic commentator, said that this means an absence of a human author. For Sayana, the eternality of the Vedas is like that of space and time; man does not experience their beginning or end. But they are, in fact, created by Brahma, the supreme creator. For the Advaita Vedanta, because no author of the Vedas is mentioned, an unbroken chain of Vedic teachers is quite conceivable, so that the scriptures bear testimony to their own eternality. The authoritative character of *sruti* may then be deduced from the fact that it is free from any fault (*dosa*), or limitation, which characterizes human words.

Furthermore, the Vedas give knowledge about things—whether *dharma* (what ought to be done) or Brahman (the absolute reality)—which cannot be known by any other empirical means of knowledge. The authority of the Vedas cannot, therefore, be contradicted by any empirical evidence. Later logicians of the "orthodox" schools sought to give these arguments precision and logical rigour. The Vedic hymns (*mantras*) seem to be addressed to gods and goddesses (*deva,* one who gives knowledge or light), who are personifications of natural forces and phenomena (Agni, the fire god; Indra, the rain god; Vayu, the wind god).

But there are gods not identifiable with such phenomena (*e.g.,* Aditi, the infinite mother of all gods; Mitra, the friend; Varuna, the guardian of truth and righteousness; Visvakarman, the all-maker; *sraddha,* faith). Also, the hymns show an awareness of the unity of these deities, of the fact that it is one God who is called by different names. The famed conception of *rta*—meaning at once natural law, cosmic order, moral law, and the law of truth—made the transition to a monistic view of the universe as being but a manifestation of one reality about which the later hymns continue to raise fundamental questions in a poignant manner, without, however, suggesting any dogmatic answer. All "orthodox" philosophies can trace their basic principles back to some statement or other in the Vedas. The Vedanta schools, especially, had an affiliation with the authority of *sruti,* and the school of Mimamsa concerned itself chiefly with the questions of interpreting the sacred texts.

The Hindu tradition regards the Vedas as being *apauruseya*—*i.e.*, as not composed by any person. Sayana, a famous Vedic commentator, said that this means an absence of a human author. For Sayana, the eternality of the Vedas is like that of space and time; man does not experience their beginning or end. But they are, in fact, created by Brahma, the supreme creator. For the Advaita Vedanta, because no author of the Vedas is mentioned, an unbroken chain of Vedic teachers is quite conceivable, so that the scriptures bear testimony to their own eternality. The authoritative character of *sruti* may then be deduced from the fact that it is free from any fault (*dosa*), or limitation, which characterizes human words. Furthermore, the Vedas give knowledge about things—whether *dharma* (what ought to be done) or Brahman (the absolute reality)—which cannot be known by any other empirical means of knowledge. The authority of the Vedas cannot, therefore, be contradicted by any empirical evidence. Later logicians of the "orthodox" schools sought to give these arguments precision and logical rigour.

The Vedic hymns (*mantras*) seem to be addressed to gods and goddesses (*deva*, one who gives knowledge or light), who are personifications of natural forces and phenomena (Agni, the fire god; Indra, the rain god; Vayu, the wind god). But there are gods not identifiable with such phenomena (*e.g.*, Aditi, the infinite mother of all gods; Mitra, the friend; Varuna, the guardian of truth and righteousness; Visvakarman, the all-maker; *sraddha*, faith). Also, the hymns show an awareness of the unity of these deities, of the fact that it is one God who is called by different names. The famed conception of *rta*—meaning at once natural law, cosmic order, moral law, and the law of truth—made the transition to a monistic view of the universe as being but a manifestation of one reality about which the later hymns continue to raise fundamental questions in a poignant manner, without, however, suggesting any dogmatic answer. The hymns may, in general, be said to express a positive attitude toward human life and to show interest in the full enjoyment of life here and hereafter rather than an anxiety to escape from it.

The idea of transmigration and the conception of the different paths and worlds traversed by good men and those who are not good—*i.e.*, the world of Vishnu and the realm of Yama—are found in the Vedas. The chain of rebirth as a product of ignorance and the conception of release from this chain as the greatest good of the spiritual life are markedly absent in the hymns. The *Upanisads* answer the question "Who is that one Being?" by establishing the equation Brahman = *atman*. Brahman—meaning now that which is the greatest, than which there is nothing greater, and also that which bursts forth into the manifested world, the one Being of which the hymn of creation spoke—is viewed as nothing but *atman*, identifiable as the innermost self in man but also, in reality, the innermost self in all beings. Both the words gain a new, extended, and spiritual significance through this identification. *Atman* was originally used to mean breath, the vital essence, and even the body. Later etymologizing brought out several strands in its meaning: that which pervades (*yad apnoti*), that which gives (*yadadatte*), that which eats (*yad atti*), and that which constantly accompanies (*yacca asya santato bhavam*).

Distinctions were made between the bodily self, the vital self, the thinking self, and the innermost self, whose nature is bliss (*ananda*), the earlier ones being sheaths (*kosas*) covering the innermost being. Distinctions were sometimes drawn between the waking (*jagrat*), dreaming (*svapna*), and dreamless-sleep (*susupti*) states of the self, and these three are contrasted with the fourth, or transcendent (*turiya*), state that both transcends and includes them all. The identification of the absolute reality underlying the universe with the innermost being within the human person resulted in a spiritualization of the former concept and a universalization of the latter. This final conception of Brahman or *atman* received many different explications from different teachers in the *Upanisads*, some of which were negative in character (*neti neti*, "not this, not this") while others positively affirmed the all-pervasiveness of Brahman.

But there were still others who insisted on both the transcendence and immanence of Brahman in the universe.

Brahman is also characterized as infinite, truth, and knowledge and as existence, consciousness, and bliss. Though the objective and the subjective, the macrocosm (universal) and the microcosm (individual), came to be identified according to their true essences, attempts were made to correlate different macrocosmic principles with corresponding microcosmic principles. The manifested cosmos was correlated with the bodily self; the soul of the world, or Hiranyagarbha, with the vital self; and Isvara, or God as a self-conscious being, with the thinking self. The transcendent self and the Brahman as bliss are not correlates but rather are identical. Buddhism was not a completely new phenomenon in the religious history of India; it was built upon the basis of ideas that were already current, both Brahmanic and non-Aryan.

Protests against the Brahmanic doctrines of *atman, karma,* and *moksa* were being voiced in the 6th century B.C., prior to the Buddha, by various schools of thought: by naturalists, such as Purana ("The Old One") Kassapa, who denied both virtue and vice (*dharma* and *adharma*) and thus all moral efficacy of human deeds; by determinists, such as the Ajivika Makkhali Gosala, who denied sin and freedom of will; and by materialists, such as Ajita Kesakambalin, who, besides denying virtue, vice, and afterlife, resolved man's being into material elements, Nigantha Nataputta, who believed in salvation by an ascetic life of self-discipline and hence in the efficacy of deeds and the possibility of omniscience, and, finally, Sanjaya Belathiputta, the skeptic, who, in reply to the question "Is there an afterlife?" would not say "It is so" or "It is otherwise," nor would he say "It is not so" or "It is not not so."

Of these six, the Jaina tradition identifies Nigantha with Mahavira; the designation "Ajivika" is applied, in a narrow sense, to the followers of Makkhali and in a loose sense to all nonorthodox sects other than the Jainas—the skeptics and the Lokayatas. Buddhism, Jainism, and the Ajivikas rejected, in common, the sacrificial polytheism of the *Brahmanas* and the monistic mysticism of the *Upanisads*. All three of them recognized the rule of natural law in the universe. Buddhism, however, retained the Vedic notions of *karma* and *moksa,* though rejecting the other fundamental concept of *atman*. In such an intellectual climate Gautama the Buddha taught his four noble truths:

1. *Dukkha* (generally but misleadingly translated as "suffering");
2. The origination of *dukkha* (*dukkhasamudaya*);
3. The cessation of *dukkha*; and finally
4. The way leading to the cessation. Although the word *dukkha* in common parlance means suffering, its use by Gautama was meant to include both pleasure and pain, both happiness and suffering. There are three aspects of this conception: *dukkha a* as suffering in the ordinary sense; *dukkha a* arising out of the impermanence of things, even of a state of pleasure; and *dukkha* in the sense of five aggregates meaning that the "I" constituted by any individual is nothing but a totality of five aggregates—*i.e.*, form, feeling, conception, disposition, and consciousness.

In brief, whatever is noneternal—*i.e.*, whatever is subject to the law of causality—is characterized by *dukkha*; for Gautama, this is the human situation. One who recognizes the nature of *dukkha* also knows its causes. *Dukkha* arises out of craving (*trsna*), craving arises out of sensation (*vedana*), and sensation arises out of contact (*sparsa*), so that man is faced with a series of conditions leading back to ignorance (*avidya*)—a series in which the rise of each succeeding member depends upon the preceding one (*pratityasamutpada*). The four noble truths follow the golden mean between the two extremes of sensual indulgence and ascetic self-torture, both of which Gautama rejected as spiritually useless. Only the middle path consisting in the eight steps—called the eightfold path—leads to enlightenment and to Nirvana. The eight steps are:

1. Right views,
2. Right intention,
3. Right speech,
4. Right action,

5. Right livelihood,
6. Right effort,
7. Right mindfulness, and
8. Right concentration. Of these eight, steps 3, 4, and 5 are grouped under right morality (*sila*); steps 6, 7, and 8 under right concentration (*samadhi*); and steps 1 and 2 under right wisdom (*prajna*).

Two key notions, even in early Buddhism, are those of *anatman* (Sanskrit: "no-self"; Pali *anatta*) and Nirvana. The Buddha apparently wanted his famed doctrine of *anatman* to be a phenomenological account of how things are rather than a theory. In his discourse to the wandering monk Vacchagotta, he rejected the theories of both eternalism (*sasvatavaha*) and annihilationism (*ucchedavada*). The former, he stated, would be incompatible with his thesis that all laws (*dharmas*; Pali *dhammas*) are selfless (*sabbe dhamma anatta*); the latter would be significant only if one had a self that is no more in existence. Thus, by not taking sides with the metaphysicians, the Buddha described how the consciousness "I am" comes to constitute itself in the stream of consciousness out of the five aggregates of form, feeling, conception, disposition, and consciousness. The doctrine of "no-self" actually has two aspects: as applied to *pudgala*, or the individual person, and as applied to the *dhammas*, or the elements of being. In its former aspect, it asserts the fact that an individual is constituted out of five aggregates; in its latter aspect it means the utter insubstantiality of all elements.

Intuitive realization of the former truth leads to the disappearance of passions and desires, realization of the latter removes all misconceptions about the nature of things in general. The former removes the "covering of the passions" (*klesavarana*); the latter removes "the concealment of things" (*jneyavarana*). Together, they result in Nirvana. Both negative and positive accounts of Nirvana are to be found in the Buddha's teachings and in early Buddhist writings. Nirvana is a state of utter extinction, not of existence, but of passions and suffering; it is a state beyond the chain of causation, a state of freedom and spontaneity. It is in addition a state of bliss. Nirvana is not the result of a process; were it so, it would be but another perishing state. It is the truth—not, however, an eternal, everlasting substance like the *atman* of the *Upanisads*, but the truth of utter selflessness and insubstantiality of things, of the emptiness of the ego, and of the impermanence of all things. With the realization of this truth, ignorance is destroyed, and, consequently, all craving, suffering, and hatred is destroyed with it.

The great epic *Mahabharata* represents the attempt of Vedic Brahmanism to adjust itself to the new circumstances reflected in the process of the aryanisation (integration of Aryan beliefs, practices, and institutions) of the various non-Aryan communities. Many diverse trends of religious and philosophical thought have thus been synthesized in this work. In its philosophical views, the epic contains an early version of Samkhya (a belief in real matter and the plurality of individual souls), which is prior to the classical Samkhya of Isvarakrsna, a 3rd-century philosopher. The chapter on "Moksadharma" in Book 12 of the *Mahabharata* is full of such proto-Samkhya texts. Mention is made of four main philosophical schools: Samkhya-Yoga, taught by Kapila (a sage living before the 6th century B.C.); Pancaratra, taught by Vishnu; the Vedas; and Pasupata ("Lord of Creatures"), taught by Shiva.

Belonging to the Pancaratra School, the epic basically attempts to accommodate certain presystematic Samkhya ideas into the Bhagavata faith. Samkhya and Yoga are sometimes put together, sometimes distinguished. Several different schemata of the 25 principles (*tattva*s) of the Samkhya are recorded. One common arrangement is that of eight productive forms of *prakrti* (the unmanifest, intellect, egoism, and five fine elements: sound, smell, form or colour, taste, and touch) and 16 modifications (five organs of perception, five organs of action, mind, and five gross elements: ether, earth, fire, water, and air), and *purusa* (man). An un-Samkhyan element is the 26th principle: Isvara, or the supreme Lord. One notable result is the identification of the four living forms (*vyuhas*) of the Pancaratra School with four Samkhya principles: Vasudeva with spirit, Samkarsana with individual soul, Pradyumna with mind, and Aniruddha with the ego-sense. Besides the Samkhya-Yoga, which is in the foreground of the epic's philosophical portions, there are Vedanta texts emphasizing the unity of spirits and theistic texts emphasizing not only a personal deity but also the doctrine of avatar (*avatara*), or incarnation. The Vasudeva-Krishna cult characterizes the theistic part of the epic.

In the *Santi Parvan* of the *Mahabharata*, there is also a notable account of the origin of kingship and of *rajadharma*, or the *dharma* (law) of the king as king. Bhisma, who is discoursing, refers with approval to two different theories of the origin of kingship, both of which speak of a prior period in which there were no kings. According to one account, this age was a time characterized by insecurity for the weak and unlimited power for the strong; the other regards it as an age of peace and tranquility. The latter account contains a theory of the fall of mankind from this ideal state, which led to a need for institutionalized power, or kingship; the former account leads directly from the insecurity of the pre-kingship era to the installation of king by the divine ruler for the protection and the security of mankind. Kingship is thus recognized as having a historical origin. The primary function of the king is that of protection, and *dandaniti*, or the art of punishment, is subordinated to *rajadharma*, or *dharma* of the king. Though it recognizes a quasi-divinity of the king, the *Mahabharata* makes the *dharma*, the moral law, superior to the king.

The *Bhagavadgita* ("Divine Song" or "Song of the Lord") forms a part of *Mahabharata* and deserves separate consideration by virtue of its great importance in the religious life and thought of the Hindus. Not itself a *sruti*, it has, however, been accorded the status of an authoritative text and is regarded as one of the sources of the Vedanta philosophy. At a theoretical level, it brings together Samkhya metaphysics, Upanisadic monism, and a devotional theism of the Krishna-Vasudeva cult. In its practical teaching, it steers a middle course between the "path of action" of the Vedic ritualism and the "path of renunciation" of the Upanisadic mysticism, and it accommodates all the three major "paths" to *moksa*: the paths of action (*karma*), devotion (*bhakti*), and knowledge (*jnana*). This synthetic character of the work accounts for its great hold on the Hindu mind. The Hindu tradition treats it as one homogenous work, with the status of an *Upanisad.*

Neither performance of the duties prescribed in the scriptures nor renunciation of all action is conducive to the attainment of *moksa.* If the goal is freedom, then the best path to the goal is to perform one's duties with a spirit of nonattachment without caring for the fruits of one's actions and without the thought of pleasure or pain, profit or loss, or victory or failure, with a sense of equanimity and equality.

The Kantian ethic of "duty for duty's sake" seems to be the nearest Western parallel to Krishna's teaching at this stage. But Krishna soon went beyond it, by pointing out that performance of action with complete nonattachment requires knowledge (*jnana*) of the true nature of the self, its distinction from *prakrti,* or Matter (the primeval stuff, not the world of matter perceived by the senses), with its three component elements (*sattva – i.e.,* tension or harmony; *rajas – i.e.,* activity; and *tamas – i.e.,* inertia), and of the highest self (*purusottama*), whose higher and lower aspects are Matter and finite individuals, respectively.

This knowledge of the highest self or the supreme lord, however, would only require a devotional attitude of complete self-surrender and performance of one's duties in the spirit of offering to him. Thus, *karma-yoga* (yoga of works) is made to depend on *jnana-yoga* (yoga of knowledge), and the latter is shown to lead to *bhakti-yoga* (yoga of devotion).

Instead of looking upon Krishna's teaching as laying down alternative ways for different persons in accordance with their aptitudes, it would seem more logical to suppose that he taught the essential unity and interdependence of these ways. How one should begin is left to one's aptitude and spiritual makeup. In the *Tripitaka* (Pali: "The Three Baskets"; Sanskrit *Tripitaka*), collected and compiled 300 years after the Buddha's *mahaparinirvana* (attainment of Buddhahood), at the council at Pataliputra (3rd century B.C.), both the canonical and philosophical doctrines of early Buddhism were codified. *Abhidamma pimaka*, the last of the *Tripitaka*, has seven parts: *DhammAsangani*, which gives an enumeration of *dhammas*, or elements of existence; *Vibhanga*, which gives further analysis of the *dhammas*; *Dhatukatha*, which is a detailed classification, following many different principles, of the elements; *Puggalapannatti*, which gives descriptions of individual persons according to stages of their development; *Kathavatthu*, which contains discussions and refutation of other schools (of Buddhism); *Yamaka*, which derives its name from the fact that it deals with pairs of questions; and *Patthana*, which gives an analysis of relations among the elements.

The key notion in all this is that of the *dhammas*. Because Buddhist philosophers denied any permanence, whether in outer nature or in inner life, they felt compelled to undertake a detailed, systematic, and complete listing and classification of the different elements that constitute both the external world and the mental, inner life. Each of these elements except for the three elements that are not composed of parts (*i.e.*, space, or *akasa*, and the two cessations, Nirvana and a temporary stoppage, in states of meditation, of the flow of passions, or *apratisamkhyanivodha*), is momentary.

The primary object of this exhaustive analysis was an understanding not so much of outer nature as of the human person (*pudgala*). The human person, however, consists in material (*rupa*) and mental (*nama*) factors, which led to an account of the various elements of matter. The primary interest, nevertheless, is in man, who is regarded as an aggregate of various elements. The analysis of these components, together with the underlying denial of an eternal self, was supposed to provide the theoretical basis for the possibility of a good life conducive to the attainment of Nirvana.

The individual person was analyzed into five aggregates (*skandhas*): material form (*rupa*); feeling (*vedana*); conception (*samjna*); disposition (*samskara*); and conscious-ness (*vijnana*). Of these, the last four constitute the mental; the first alone is the material factor. The material is further analyzed into 28 states, the *samskara* into 50 (falling into three groups: intellectual, affectional, and volitional), and the *vijnana* into 89 kinds of states of consciousness. Another principle of classification leads to a list of 18 elements (*dhatus*): five sense organs, five objects of those senses, mind, the specific object of mind, and six kinds of consciousness (visual, auditory, olfactory, gustatory, tactual, and purely mental). A third classification is into 12 bases (*ayatanas*), which is a list of six cognitive faculties and their objects.

The Buddhist analysis of matter was in terms of sensations and sense data, to which the sense organs were also added. The analysis of mind was also in terms of corresponding modes of consciousness and their objects.

HINDU IDEALISM

There are currents of idealism in classical Hindu philosophy. Idealism and materialism are the principal monist ontologies. A related branch is the Buddhist concept of consciousness-only. Idealist notions have been supported by the Vedanta and Yoga schools opposed by dualist Samkhya, the atomist Vaisheshika, the materialist Nyaya and Mimamsa as well as the atheist Carvaka schools.

Like Platonic idealism, Hindu idealism is essentially monotheist, espousing the view that consciousness, which at its root emanates from God (Brahman, Purusha or Svayam bhagavan), is the essence or meaning of the phenomenal reality.

The presence of idealist concepts in Indian thought has been emphasized by Rupert Sheldrake and Fritj of Capra. These ideas have also been developed by P.R. Sarkar and advanced by his disciple Sohail Inayatullah, notably in the theory of Microvitum.

The essence of Hindu Idealism is captured by such modern spiritual teachers as Sri Nisargadatta Maharaj, Sri Aurobindo and Sri Anandamurti, also known as P.R. Sarkar. Sri Nisargadatta advocated discovery of the *real self*. By establishing oneself in the earnestness of spiritual pursuits, it is possible to transcend the temporal self, limited by desires, fears, memories and mental constructs, and gain blissful immersion in the *pure* consciousness of God.

Sarkar went further by emphasising that liberation was best achieved through service to self and society, exemplified by his socio-spiritual movement Ananda Marga, or the "Path of Bliss".

4

The Elementary Education and its Genesis

Education is important not only for the full development of one's personality, but also for the sustained growth of the nation. Elementary education in India, therefore, is the foundation on which the development of every citizen and the nation as a whole hinges. But making primary education available for all in India has also been one of the major challenges for the government. Moreover, the quality of elementary education in India has also been a major cause of worry for the government. In fact, making elementary education in India accessible, universal and relevant has been a goal since the eighth five year plan.

Elementary education in India means eight years of schooling from the age of six. The government has made elementary education compulsory and free. But, the goal of universal elementary education in India has been very difficult to achieve till now. Therefore it has introduced innovative ways of universalizing elementary education in India. After the District Primary Education Programme (DPEP) of 1994, the govt. has now launched the "Sarva Shiksha Abhiyan" or SSA. Sarva Shiksha Abhiyan was launched in 2001 to universalize and improve the quality of elementary education in India through community ownership of elementary education.

In order to effectively decentralize the management, it has involved Panchayati Raj institutions, School Management

Committees, Village and Urban Slum Level Education Committees, Parents' Teachers' Associations, Mother Teacher Associations, Tribal Autonomous Councils and other grassroots level structures. SSA, apart from being a programme with clear time frame for Elementary Education, also offers opportunities to the states to develop their own vision of elementary education.

It has set 2007 as the deadline for providing primary education in India and 2010 as the deadline for providing useful and relevant elementary education to all children in the 6 to 14 age group. In order to improve the quality of elementary education in India, the SSA has emphasized on improving the student teacher ratio, teachers training, academic support, facilitating development of teaching learning material and providing textbooks to children from special focus groups etc. Despite all the efforts of the government of India, universalisation of elementary education in India remains a distant dream.

This is because of the persistent poverty and various prejudices prevailing in the Indian society. While the growth in female literacy is increasing at a faster rate than male literacy, the gap in the male-female literacy has been a major hindrance in the universalisation of elementary education in India. While the total literacy rate is 65.38% according to 2001 census, the female literacy rate is only 54.16%. Another area of concern is to reduce the gap between the rural and urban literacy rate.

While 80.3% urban people are literate, only 59.4% of the rural population is literate according to 2001 census data. Thus reduction in poverty, promotion of female education, emphasis on rural education, providing incentives for retaining the children from weaker sections of the society would have to go together so that it can achieve the goal set by the Sarva Shiksha Abhiyan and also the Millennium Development goal by 2015 set by the UNESCO.

INDIAN STRATEGIES TO ACHIEVE UNIVERSALISATION

Four and a half decades ago, we in India had taken a pledge through our Constitution that within a period of ten years from 1950, free and compulsory elementary education would be provided to all children up to 14 years of age. Since 1950, determined efforts were made towards the achievement of this goal. Over the years, there have been very impressive increases in the number and spread of institutions as well as enrolment.

Today, India has about 574,000 primary schools (classes I-V) and 156,000 upper primary schools (classes VI-VIII), the number of teachers in them being 1.705 million and 1.082 million respectively. The enrolment at the primary and upper primary stages is 109 million and 40 million respectively. The Indian elementary education system is thus one of the biggest such systems in the world, providing accessibility within 1 km to over 825,000 habitations covering 94 per cent of the country's population.

During the past one decade the enrolment rate has grown close to 100 per cent at the primary stage. However, universalisation of elementary education (UEE) in its totality is still an elusive goal and much ground is yet to be covered. Drop-out rates continue to be high (36.3 per cent in classes I-V and 53 per cent in classes VI-VIII), retention of children in schools is poor, achievement levels are low, and wastage is considerable. Despite increased participation of girls, disparity still exists, more particularly among scheduled castes (SCs) and scheduled tribes (STs).

In the National Policy on Education (NPE) 1986, with revised modifications in 1992, we resolved to achieve the goal of UEE by the turn of the century, emphasising three aspects: universal access and enrolment, universal retention up to 14 years of age, and a substantial improvement in the quality of education. The resolve is spelt out unequivocally and emphatically in the programme of action (POA) 1992, which gave unqualified priority to UEE.

One is therefore pinning great hopes on the new innovations and alternative strategies which are being applied to ensure that the shortcomings and inadequacies, which did not allow us to realise this goal so far, are overcome, and the new resolve will not have to be extended further. The Education for All (EFA) Summit of the nine high-population countries held in New Delhi in December 1993, which an offshoot of the World Conference on Education for All was held in Jomtien, Thailand, in March 1990, culminated in a policy declaration and framework of strategies for its implementation. The policy declaration called for providing basic education facilities for every child and consolidating efforts towards basic education for children, youth and adults.

In the context of an integrated approach of basic education for all people, literacy and adult education programmes are to be improved and extended, eliminating disparities of access and improving the quality and relevance of basic education. It can be said that the Indian NPE 1986 and its POA 1992, while resolving to ensure free and compulsory education of satisfactory quality to all children up to 14 years of age by the year 2000, adumbrated the policy statement made at the EFA Summit. The purpose of this chapter is to briefly describe some of the new innovations and strategies that are being applied in India today to achieve UEE by the turn of this century.

New Innovations and Alternative Strategies

Some of the major initiatives and strategies are:

- Disaggregated target setting and decentralised micro-planning, which will provide the framework of universal access and community participation.
- Strengthening alternative channels of schooling such as the non-formal education (NFE) system for those who cannot avail of conventional full-time schooling.
- Introduction of minimum levels of learning (MLLs) at primary and upper primary stages to improve learner's achievement.

- Improvement of school facilities by revamping the scheme of Operation Blackboard (OB) and connecting it to the MLL strategy.
- Establishing linkages between programmes of early childhood care and education (ECCE), primary education, literacy and UEE.
- Addressing the more difficult aspects of access, particularly to girls, disadvantaged groups and out-of-school children.
- Restructuring of teacher training in view of the changed strategies and programmes.
- Availing of external financial support for basic education.
- Launching the National Elementary Education Mission (NEEM).

DECENTRALISED MICROPLANNING

Our experience with UEE encompasses the entire Third World experience. On the one hand, we have States like Kerala, which have achieved universal literacy as well as UEE in terms of school participation with social indicators as good as those of the best among the Third World countries. On the other, we have States like Bihar and Madhya Pradesh, with indicators as bad as those of the Sub-Saharan countries. One of the new strategies to achieve UEE is adoption of disaggregated target setting and decentralised planning. Our long experience with the pursuit of UEE has established that UEE is contextual. The contextuality varies widely across the country. Even in a State like Kerala, where participation is near universal, much requires to be done in respect of quality and achievement. In such states, the pursuit of UEE would be mainly in the areas of quality, facilities and achievement, while in other states participation and demand aspects would need more attention. Therefore, the attempt would be to prepare district-specific and population-specific plans for UEE within the broad strategy frame of micro-planning through people's participation.

Micro-planning has been defined as a family-wise and child-wise design of action to ensure that every child regularly attends a school or an NFE centre and completes 8 years of schooling at a pace suitable to him or her and attains an essential level of learning. Guidelines for operationalising micro-planning have been prepared and distributed to the state governments. The concepts of micro-planning and local level capacity building have been given currency and efforts launched to decentralise educational planning and management. Micro-planning exercises have already been undertaken in several states to ensure that all children receive primary education of satisfactory quality either through formal schools or through part-time NFE centres. To operationalise the strategy for UEE through disaggregated target setting and decentralised planning, a new scheme titled District Primary Education Programme (DPEP) has been evolved. The concept of DPEP is a beachhead for effecting improvements and full-scale development of the entire elementary education sector. The overall goal of the programme is the reconstruction of primary education as a whole in the districts instead of piecemeal implementation of the various schemes. The fundamental principle of DPEP is capacity building at all levels to evolve further strategies which are replicable and sustainable.

The specific objectives of the programme are:

- to reduce differences in enrolment, drop-out and learning achievement among gender and social groups to less than 5 per cent.
- to reduce the overall primary drop-out rate to less than 10 per cent.
- to raise average achievement levels by at least 25 per cent over measured baseline levels and ensure achievements of basic literacy and numeracy competencies and a minimum of 40 per cent achievement levels in other competencies by all primary school children.
- to provide, according to national norms, access for all children to primary education classes (I-V), i.e., primary schooling wherever possible or its equivalent non-formal education.

The programme would strengthen the capacity of national, state and district institutions and organisations for the planning, management and evaluation of primary education. NEEM has recently been set up to oversee, among other things, the implementation of this programme throughout the country.

ALTERNATIVE CHANNELS OF EDUCATION

Non-formal education has become an accepted alternative channel of education for children who cannot attend full-time schools due to various socio-economic constraints. To reach this large segment of marginalised children, we in India have been running, since 1979-80, a programme of NFE for children in the 6-14 age groups, who have remained outside the formal system.

These include drop-outs from formal schools, children from habitations without schools, working children, children who have to remain at home to do domestic chores and girls who are unable to attend formal schools for a variety of reasons. The enlarged and modified version of the NFE programme now in operation visualises NFE as a child-centred, environment-oriented and flexible system to meet the diverse educational needs of the geographically and socio-economically deprived sections of society. Non-formal education is designed to overcome the shortcomings of the formal school and make education a joyful activity. Decentralised community participation through village education committees (VECs) in planning, running and overseeing the programme has been considered crucial for its success. Although the focus of the programme is on the educationally backward states, it also covers urban slums and hilly tribal and desert areas in other states as well. Today, the programme is being implemented in 20 states and union territories through the state governments and voluntary organisations. While there are more than 226,000 NFE centres in the state sector, there are about 29,000 run by voluntary agencies. About 44 per cent of all the NFE centres are exclusively for girls, who are the main victims of socio-cultural and socio-economic factors.

The estimated enrolment capacity is about 6.3 million children. Under the NFE programme, efforts are now being made to further improve quality, allow greater flexibility to implementing agencies and relocate NFE centres on the basis of micro-planning/area survey. The NFE programme is being linked to ground realities, allowing for continuous experimentation. Development and scaling-up of effective NFE models that can help the learners to learn at their own pace is a major thrust area.

MINIMUM LEVELS OF LEARNING (MLL)

The need to lay down minimum levels of learning (MLL) emerged from the basic concern that irrespective of caste, creed, location or sex, all children must be given access to education of a comparable standard. The MLL strategy is an attempt to combine quality with equity. It lays down learning outcomes in the form of competencies or levels of learning for each stage of elementary education. The strategy also prescribes adoption of measures that will ensure achievement of these levels by children both in formal schools and in NFE centers. The focus of the MLL strategy is development of competency-based teaching and learning. Preliminary assessment of the existing levels of learning achievements has revealed that they are quite low across several districts.

Minimum levels of learning in respect of three subjects, namely language, mathematics and environmental studies, have already been laid down for the primary stage. It has been stressed that the emphasis should be on concept formation rather than on content. The burdens of non-comprehension and overload of content are forcing children to resort to rote memorisation.

The issues of content versus concept, understanding versus rote memorisation, unachievable content load versus achievable set of competencies, have been integrated into the new MLL approach. Minimum levels of learning have been specified in terms of competencies expected to be mastered by every child by the end of a particular class. The programme has been initiated throughout the country with the help of voluntary agencies, research institutions and others concerned. Minimum levels of learning for the upper primary stage are now being finalised.

THE SCHEME OF OPERATION BLACKBOARD (OB)

Recognising the unattractive school environment, unsatisfactory condition of school buildings, inadequate physical facilities, and insufficiency of instructional materials in primary schools, which function as demotivating factors for enrolment and retention, a scheme symbolically called Operation Blackboard was introduced in 1987-88 to bring all existing primary schools in the country to a minimum standard of physical facilities. Under this scheme, each school is provided with:

i. At least two reasonably large all-weather rooms along with separate toilet facilities for boys and girls;
ii. At least two teachers (one male and one female); and
iii. Essential teaching and learning materials including blackboards, maps, charts, a small library, toys and games, and some equipment for work experience.

External evaluation of the scheme indicated the lack of training of teachers in using the teaching materials, specification of a large number of uniform facilities to be provided without modification according to local needs, and lack of provision for breakage of equipment. Effective steps have since been taken to remove these drawbacks. The scheme of Operation Blackboard has also been modified and expanded to provide a third room and a third teacher to primary schools where enrolment exceeds 100, and it has been extended to upper primary schools. The scheme is concentrating on rural areas and SC/ST areas, and girls' schools are being given the first priority.

ESTABLISHING LINKAGES

Early childhood care and education (ECCE) is viewed as a crucial input in the strategy of human resource development, as a feeder and support programme for primary education, and as a support service for working women of the disadvantaged sections of society.

Since the age-span covered by ECCE is from conception to 6 years, emphasis has been given to a child-centered approach and play-way and activity-based learning in place of formal methods of teaching including introduction of the 3 Rs. Keeping in mind the role of ECCE as a support service in UEE, it is deliberately directed to the most underprivileged groups, those who are still outside the mainstream of formal education. The aim of ECCE is that every child should be assured access to the fulfillment of all basic needs. It involves the total development of the child in every aspect including the physical, psychomotor, cognitive, language, emotional, social and moral.

The present ECCE programmes include:

- The integrated child development service (ICDS)
- The scheme of assistance to voluntary organisations for running early child education (ECE) centers
- *Balwadis* and day-care centers run by voluntary agencies with government assistance
- Pre-primary schools run by state governments, municipal corporations and other agencies
- Maternal and child health services through primary health centers, sub-centers and other agencies

The ICDS is today the biggest programme of early childhood development, serving about 15 million children and 3 million mothers. Appropriate linkages are being established between ECCE programmes, primary schools, NFE centers and other related schemes of UEE.

PROMOTION OF ACCESS

As with all educational indicators, gender disparities are conspicuous in regard to enrolment and retention. Over the past 25 years, enrolment of girls at the primary stage has grown from 5 million to 47 million and at the upper primary stage, from 0.5 million to 16 million. But disparities persist. Today girls account for only 46 per cent of the enrolment at the primary stage and 38 per cent at the upper primary stage. The drop-out rates of girls at the primary and upper primary stages are higher than those of boys. Regional disparities are also conspicuous.

The very low female literacy (20 to 29 per cent) in some of the major north Indian states causes grave concern. The rural girls are doubly disadvantaged by non-availability of educational facilities and by their domestic chores.

Concerted efforts are now on to reach out to the girl child in rural and remote areas and urban slums by designing special NFE programmes with a view to getting them back into the formal stream. The NFE programmes are being dovetailed into the total literacy campaigns (TLC) to reach out to the girls in the 10-20 age groups. Programmes for continuing education are being designed to ensure that neo-literates and school-going girls have access to reading materials. An important constraining factor for female education is the lack of women teachers in rural areas. Therefore, special efforts are being made to recruit women teachers and to augment teacher training facilities for women so that adequate numbers of qualified women teachers are available. Co-ordinated efforts are also on to provide the necessary support services to enhance their participation and performance.

We in India are unambiguous about removal of disparities and attainment of equality of education opportunities for SCs, STs and other backward sections including girls. A number of strategies aimed at accelerating their rate of enrolment and retention have been detailed and are being implemented. Because of the affirmative policies of the government, the enrolment of these categories has increased considerably at the primary stage. The participation of SCs and STs at the primary level is more or less in proportion to their share in the population. Drop-outs, though declining, continue to be significantly large [primary stage (classes I-V), SC 49 per cent, ST 64 per cent; upper primary stage (classes VI-VIII), SC 68 per cent, ST 79 per cent]. Gender disparities are conspicuous among SCs and STs.

To ensure universal access and enrolment of SC children in rural areas, priority is given to the needs of SC habitations and hamlets in opening primary and upper primary schools. For SC children access and enrolment are assured primarily in the formal schools. Where they are not able to attend these, provision is made for non-formal and distance education centers. Every ST habitation is being provided with a primary school or other suitable institution. In tribal areas, the educational plan is being implemented in an integrated manner. Pre-school education, non-formal education, elementary education and adult education are being organically linked and integrated to ensure achievement of total literacy of the entire population.

Adequate incentives are given to the children of SC, ST and other backward sections in the form of scholarships, uniforms, textbooks, stationery and midday meals. All schools, NFE centers, and pre-school centres in SC/ST habitations are being equipped with necessary infrastructural facilities in accordance with the norms lay down for Operation Blackboard and for achieving MLL. Operation Blackboard has already covered almost all schools in tribal areas. Indigent SC/ST families are given incentives to send their children, particularly girls, to school.

RESTRUCTURING OF TEACHER TRAINING

Teacher performance is the most crucial input in the field of education. In the ultimate analysis, the national policies on education have to be interpreted and implemented by teachers as much through their personal example as through teaching-learning processes. With a view to improving the quality and competence of teachers, a centrally sponsored scheme of Restructuring and Reorganisation of Teacher Education (RRTE) was launched in 1987. During the period 1987-90, nearly 1.8 million teachers were trained under the programme of mass orientation of school teachers (PMOST). Most of them were primary and upper primary teachers. The main objective of the programme was to orient teachers in the main priorities and directions envisaged in the NPE 1986 and to improve their professional competence.

Among the other main components of the RRTE, as far as elementary education is concerned, are:

1. Setting up of District Institutes of Education and Training (DIETs) in all districts to provide good quality pre-service and in-service training to elementary school teachers and adult education/non-formal education personnel and to provide resource support to these systems.
2. Organising Special Orientation Programmes for Primary Teachers (SOPT) with a view to providing training to teachers in the use of OB materials and orienting them towards MLL strategy with a focus on teaching of language, mathematics and environmental studies.

More than 300 DIETs have already become operational and have started conducting training programmes.

The SOPT launched in 1993-94 is now going on in almost all states and more than 115,000 teachers have already been trained. A National Council for Teacher Education (NCTE) was set up in 1993 with statutory status for the effective implementation of all teacher education and training programmes and to achieve planned and co-ordinated development of the entire teacher education system throughout the country. The regulation and proper maintenance of norms and standards in the teacher education system is the responsibility of the NCTE.

AVAILING OF EXTERNAL FINANCIAL SUPPORT

As a matter of policy and principle, India had not been seeking financial support from external agencies to implement its programmes of basic education. This situation changed in 1991-92, when a conscious and strategic decision was taken to avail of external assistance to achieve the goal of Education for All (EFA). Today a number of agencies including the World Bank, UNESCO, UNICEF, Swedish International Development Agency (SIDA), International Development Association (IDA), and the British Overseas Development Agency (ODA) are sharing our concerns in this area. A new phase has, therefore, emerged – a phase of partnership between the inherent potential of the country and financial and other support from external agencies.

THE NATIONAL ELEMENTARY EDUCATION MISSION (NEEM)

With the objective of mobilising all the resources – human, financial and institutional – necessary for achieving the goal of UEE by the year 2000, a National Elementary Education Mission (NEEM) was set up in August 1995 with the District Primary Education Programme (DPEP) as its core. This Mission will monitor and implement all the meticulously formulated strategies based on micro-planning, and will ensure that free and compulsory education of satisfactory quality is provided to all children up to 14 years of age by the turn of the century.

The educational system in India has faced a basic dilemma ever since its introduction by the British. The essence of this problem was summed up by Mahatma Gandhi in his historic statement at Chatham House, London, in 1931. The British administrators when they came to India, instead of taking hold of things as they were, began to root them out.

They scratched the soil and began to look at the root and left the root like that and the beautiful tree perished. The village schools were not good enough for the British administrator so he came out with his own programme. Every school must have so much paraphernalia, building and so forth. Well, there were no such schools at all – ancient schools have gone by the board – and the schools established after the European pattern were too expensive to fulfill a programme of compulsory primary education of these inside of a century. This very poor country of mine is ill able to sustain such an expensive method of education.

Free India did not have the will to fulfill Mahatma Gandhi's dream of reviving the ancient tradition of the village schoolmaster, supported by the community, his status and survival as a *guru* being embedded within the culture and ecology of his immediate environment. Instead the government chose to continue with efforts to educate the masses through a vast, centralised machinery and superstructure of staff, infrastructure and resources. Successive efforts at universalisation of primary education, ranging from Operation Blackboard to DPEP (now funded by the World Bank and other international agencies) and Education For All, have only reinforced the strength of the challenge posed by Mahatma Gandhi in his statement at Chatham House. The Adult Literacy Campaign and, more recently, the investment thrust on primary education to produce the literate child, carries within itself the hidden suspicion that the goal of universal education for the masses may even be quietly set aside one day, planners having perhaps finally realised that the goal is unattainable within the present system.

As pointed out by the Mahatma, the success of this system depends solely on expenses and affordability. It thus gives rise to a situation where a mass of underprivileged and under-educated children face a largely urban elite population of privileged schoolchildren. Needless to say, it is the latter that get into the universities. While the tax-payer pays for both government schools as well as universities, the poor man pays for both but benefits from neither. The per capita public cost of university education is exorbitant when compared with school education. In the words of Ivan Illich, School is a perfect system of regressive taxation where the privileged graduates ride on the back of the entire paying public. Every poor Indian who can manage to make both ends meet thus strives to join the ranks of far better (and more expensive) schools, because only these can form the gateway to subsidized higher education.

The past two decades have seen a phenomenal growth of two types of private schools outside the system of government schools (which have also, incidentally, grown by leaps and bounds, despite resource constraints). These are the so-called elite schools where education is sold to the highest bidder, and the plethora of petty teaching shops against which it is fashionable for the educated elite to occasionally raise a hue and cry. In between there exist a large number of institutions, often run by charitable or religious organisations, which seek to make as many compromises as possible within the given system. It is not surprising that the government of a democratic state would also be compelled to join this race for providing more expensive schools for quality education. The Kendriya Vidyalayas, Sainik Schools, Railway Schools, Tibetan Schools and (more recently) Navodaya Vidyalayas are responses to the basic dilemma facing the existing system.

The KVs and NVs together run about 1,200 schools. The KVs, which were set up to cater to children of government servants having All-India transfer liability, have now increasingly opened their doors to the children of upwardly mobile, less privileged urban families. While 'political pressure' is ostensibly to blame, the trend basically reflects a sensible popular response of the underprivileged. In the public perception, the system of mass government-sponsored education appears to have failed to deliver the goods, increasing expansion having led apparently to decreasing quality. Hence the upwardly mobile social classes are aggressively latching on to whatever better education is available at public cost. As regards rural India, it needed a statesman like Rajiv Gandhi to visualise that the day was not far off when the rural elite would also grow restive and clamour for expensive quality education at par with quality schools set up in urban areas serving predominantly urban populations.

Hence Navodaya Vidyalayas were set up as residential schools with 75 per cent reservations for rural candidates, all candidates being selected on the basis of a nation-wide talent test. No doubt the Navodaya system has made the best possible compromises within the given contradictions of the existing social system. There is a 30 per cent reservation for girls and reservation for scheduled castes and scheduled tribes commensurate with their population strength in the district. Elitism of merit is the hallmark of the system. While the talent test is open to all rural children studying in class V of rural schools, the admissions are also structured so as to ensure that all geo-economic regions within the district are proportionately and equitably represented and no single region dominates. Navodaya Vidyalayas have sometimes been sarcastically described as the Doon School alternative for rural areas. But this can mean different things to different people. From the urban point of view it is often a derisive comment implying that by the very nature of the socio-economic set-up of the country, Doon Schools can hardly be relevant for country bumpkins. For the rural elite it is viewed as an optimistic statement, since they would naturally like to have the best for themselves, the urban elite invariably furnishing the role model. There is a third point of view put forth by planners and educationists who feel that these rural elite schools are being set up at the cost of improvements in mass universal education. Such expensive schools set up in the rural environment only bring into focus the deprivation suffered by the rural masses.

Setting aside expenditure on construction, which is quite heavy (each school complex costing over Rs. 4 crores), the average cost per Navodaya student (including all administrative and other expenses) comes to about Rs. 9,900 per annum. Is such heavy investment on as few as 500-odd students per district justified? These are the questions raised by the Acharya Ramamurti Report, as also by the CPI (M) government of West Bengal, which has steadfastly refused to introduce the Navodaya Vidyalaya Scheme in its state purely for ideological reasons. The Acharya Ramamurti Report indicts the NV Scheme on the grounds that it is very costly; it caters to a microscopic minority of the total school population and perpetrates an exclusive system inconsistent with the 'long cherished common school system of public education'. These educationists, however, seem to have overlooked the main problem pointed out by Mahatma Gandhi with the 'cherished system of public education', namely, that if at all schools are to be established after the European pattern they will inevitably be too expensive for the people.

If rural areas are not to follow the pattern of more and more exclusive and expensive schooling mushrooming in urban areas, rural talent will never get a chance to compete for higher education unless it migrates to the urban environment.

This is a hard fact of life which this point of view does not face but which could be realised. By initiating the Navodaya Vidyalaya Scheme, government simply brought the process of handling contradictions inherent within the system to its logical climax. To the urban elite, however, what is sauce for the goose is definitely not sauce for the gander. In the trend towards exclusive and increasingly expensive education the residential school stands at the apex of the school system and is sought to be duplicated for educationally underprivileged and rural children by the Navodaya Vidyalayas.

As regards day schools, it is no secret that home tuition is embedded in the system of even the best public schools today. Both schools as well as parents find themselves unable to cope with the existing syllabus as well as an increasingly competitive environment without the aid of home tuitions, which today comprise a flourishing business. In government schools the underprivileged may also suffer since the temptation to earn more as a side business tends to retard optimum contribution of government teachers within school. Thus even the expensive day school has ended up in total dependence on a parallel and equally expensive system of home coaching.

A recent development in the private sector has now led to the opening of even more exclusive elite schools which restrict the number of students per class. While sixty students are replaced by twenty students only in these super schools, the costs of sixty are naturally paid for by the twenty privileged families. School has, therefore, become a flourishing and money-guzzling industry. Children exist for schools, not schools for children, and this is as true for private paying schools as it is for government schools. While the seeds of spiralling expenses have grown into monstrous weeds, the seeds of alienation spread in a more subtle manner. The residential school is an apt symbol of alienation not only from its cultural and social environment but also from society itself. It stands at the apex of a system which rests on this artificial separation that seeks to inculcate values of exclusivity and elitism.

Within the day schools the system alienates the teacher from the taught through the weight of sheer numbers and the cumulative burden of learning and measuring up to academic standards. It also alienates the student community as a whole from the socio-cultural matrix which surrounds it. The accent on competition and the constant stress on the individual as against the group and the community further alienate children from one another. Seeds of alienation are embedded in the examination system, which lays a premium on a system of marking that is the sole determinant of individual achievement, the costs of which are paid for by the under-achievers. In its mildest form the under-achievers pay for it by being relegated to 'non-ability' as against 'ability' sections in public schools, alienation from one's immediate peers being thus glorified and institutionalised. At its worst the system is scarred by student suicides.

Universities like Taxila and Nalanda flourished and attained international acclaim. In the ancient systems of learning the *guru* invariably utilised the older boys to teach the younger ones. Their roles were supportive, not exploitative. How unlike the system of public schools where the exploitation of younger boys by older boys is dubbed respectably as 'ragging'. While the school tie and similar indicators of superior status may still hold them together at school, these tenuous bonds no longer operate in the universities. University students in India in particular are in essence a mob, whether it be a passive mob or a mob on the rampage. There are often deaths of students in which their peers are indirectly or directly involved through ragging. It is not a mere coincidence that these incidents have generally occurred in professional institutions for engineering or medical students.

While at first glance this phenomenon may appear to be incomprehensible, once the seeds of alienation present in the whole system are exposed it could also be seen as an offshoot of the system itself. The idea and essence of peace and universal harmony, of oneness with nature and association with the earth, of education as a pursuit in the arts of living in an interconnected universe is entirely missing from the system. Instead to the fore are values of individual achievement, branding and typing young persons as bright, mediocre, elite, poor, and under-privileged. Divisive forces predominate over harmony. Products dominate over people. Competition dominates over brotherhood. That this system is giving rise to problems entirely of our own making is being realised in many parts of the world. Radical thinkers, sociologists and educationists have raised voices in protest.

Everett Reimer in *School Is Dead* and Ivan Illich in *Deschooling Society* have asked some of the profoundest questions about education today. They have recognised that most countries in the world can only afford to give their children the barest minimum of education while the costs of schooling are rising everywhere faster than enrolments and faster than national incomes. While regarding schools as institutional props for privilege for most people, Everett Reimer also recognises the fact that they are at the same time major instruments of social mobility. But he questions the cost in terms of true learning, true creativity and true democracy. The search for alternatives in education has already begun. Some, like Everett Reimer, search for alternatives in terms of content, organisation and finance.

At the other end of the spectrum, *Letter to a Teacher*, written by eight young Italian village boys from the school of Barbiana, is a minor classic which reveals with devastating clarity how the school system oppresses and marginalises the rural poor by divorcing them completely from their ecological base and their cultural environment. It also presents a radical alternative. In India today the government's and NGOs' search for alternatives has led to greater support and funding for non-formal schools, the most dramatic example being that of the Charvaha Schools of Bihar. However, this experiment suffers from all the general weaknesses of the state system. In Bihar there are other alternatives developed with more success, such as the model 'Sidh', started by Pawan Kumar

Gupta, an NGO, in and around about 15 villages surrounding Kempty, near Mussoorie.

Many other examples of rural-based education centres can be documented where the initiative for establishment and management has vested with communities themselves. Craft-oriented training and basic education have been outstanding successes of Dwarko Sundrani's Bodh Gaya Ashram, where schooling on the Gandhian pattern is made available to the poorest of the poor in Bihar.

These non-formal schools, being beyond the pale of the state boards, are also free from the usual bureaucratic supervision of school inspectors, but by their very nature they are limited to the class V level. The Yashpal Committee was set up specifically for suggesting ways to reduce the academic burden on students in recognised schools. The Committee strongly recommended toning down of individual competitiveness and introduction of group activity in schools. Simultaneously it advocated decentralisation of curriculum formation, textbook writing and much greater involvement of teachers in these processes, particularly textbook formation. In general the Yashpal Committee came out strongly against textbooks, syllabi and examinations which together form a system that inflicts upon the children the 'tyranny of rote memorisation.

The Department of Education has taken up these suggestions for serious review. The CBSE pattern of education will be set aside or modified in the near future. Sir Thomas Munro, who set in motion the process of establishment of schools after a new pattern in Madras Presidency in the 1820s, aptly summarised the aims of the new education as being 'to facilitate the acquisition of wealth or rank'. As long as society accepts these as the aims of schooling, the CBSE syllabus and the emphasis on science and commerce streams (putting incalculable strain on the students) will continue regardless of the Yashpal Committee report or any other similar reports. There are a few notable public schools (like Rishi Valley of the J. Krishnamurti Foundation, Banasthali Vidyapeeth of Rajasthan, and the Netarhat residential school experiment of

Bihar) which have departed from the mainstream and yet retained eminence within the general delivery system.

The difficulties of innovating within over three hundred and seventy government residential schools such as the Navodaya Vidyalayas would be apparent to any educational administrator. Being wholly funded by government, there is an even greater compulsion for these schools to deliver and perform as per the marks-oriented examination system laid down by the CBSE. Not only do residential schools allow for more investment in time, but the Vidyalayas themselves, with their resource pool of talented rural students, stand Janus-like between two worlds – with one hand they can reach out to grasp the best of scientific and technical skills, while with the other they can gather easily the ancient wisdom of the east enshrined in the oral tradition and rituals of their immediate cultural environment.

Hence the Samiti has started a small venture to give schooling a human face through a carefully planned programme of Art in Education, based firmly on the indigenous *guru-shishya* tradition of learning. Workshops in theatre, folk music, folk arts, epics and ballad singing can very easily slip into the groove of consumerism and assembly-line production that has come to characterise our school system. Again, overemphasis on achievement and the accent on the individual could vitiate the cathartic experience, the flowering of creativity, the realisation of a deep harmony between man and nature which these workshops should generate. Hence every workshop in Navodaya Vidyalayas is designed around an activity with a cluster of groups working on the theme in accordance with their own particular talent. Thus a Pandawani workshop held in Durg was not just an exercise to locate another Teejan Bai amongst the students and project her on the stage.

It was an experience in which the literary group interviewed Teejan Bai, wrote up reports and poems, while the visual art group was busy drawing and painting the scenes she depicted. Those who had talent for dramatic performances learnt the art and performed on the stage, but it was a holistic experience through which the Chhattisgarhi children of Durg moved towards a joyous self-attainment, a recognition of an abiding and ancient identity which was derived from sources that stand apart from and are superior to their school and their schoolmasters. The richness of rural roots and traditions gave them a sense of pride and psychological reassurance which no success in examinations could ever give. By honouring notable rural artists in this fashion the Samiti was able to bridge the gulf between teachers and taught, urban and rural, so-called literate and so-called illiterate.

To put it in the works of Dharampal, the present system "has kept most educated Indians not only ignorant of the society they live in, the culture which sustains this society and their fellow beings, but yet more tragically, for over a century it has induced a lack of confidence and loss of bearing amongst people of India in general". It is a tribute to the children that they could very easily grasp the essence of the programme best summed up in a poem written by one girl who exclaimed "Aha! Look at her! She has not been to school even for a single day and yet what greatness she has achieved. Look at us, who go to school everyday, it is for us to get inspired and learn from her!" It is ultimately left to each one of us in the educational field to move one small step forward towards this transformation of vision towards reorientation of values and objectives of education. Not only in India, but in the entire world, education places an overriding value on products over people, on achievement over harmony. Ivan Illich has expressed this need in moving terms, quoting from Yevtushenko's poems.

We now need a name for those who love people more than products,

Those who believe that

No people are uninteresting

Their fate is like the chronicle of planets.

Nothing in them is particular and planet is dissimilar from planet.

We need a name for those who love the earth on which each can meet the other.

And if a man lived in obscurity

Making his friends in that obscurity

Obscurity is not uninteresting.

NATIONAL POLICY ON EDUCATION (NPE) AND PROGRAMME OF ACTION (POA)

The National Policy on Education (NPE), 1986 along with its Revised Policy Formulation and the Programme of Action (POA) evolved as a result of widespread deliberations, consultation and consensus were last reviewed and updated in 1992. The POA envisages that given the rich diversity of our nation, it would be in the fitness of things, if each State and Union Territory formulates a State POA in accordance with their situational imperatives as well as with the POA 1992. The National Policy on Education (NPE), 1986, as updated in 1992, envisages improvement and expansion of education in all sectors, elimination of disparities in access and laying greater stress on improvement in the quality and relevance of education at all levels, including technical and professional education.

It also emphasises that education must play a positive and interventionist role in correcting social and regional imbalances, empowering women and in securing a rightful place for the disadvantaged, linguistic groups and minorities. The Nation is firmly committed to providing Education for All, the priority areas being free and compulsory primary education, covering children with special needs, eradication of illiteracy, vocationalisation, and education for women's equality, special focus on the education of SCs/ STs and Minorities. The task of implementing the NPE and POA lies with the States and Union Territories, and the Centre is to monitor the implementation. Accordingly, the POA 1992 stands circulated in 1993 to all States and Union Territories to draw up their own State Programme of Action (SPOA).

CENTRAL ADVISORY BOARD OF EDUCATION (CABE)

The Central Advisory Board of Education (CABE), the highest advisory body to advise the Central and State governments in the field of education, was first established in 1920 and dissolved in 1923 as a measure of economy. It was revived in 1935 and the extended tenure of the last CABE expired in March 1994. Despite the fact that in the past, important decisions had been taken on the advice of CABE and it had provided a forum for widespread consultation and examination of issues relating to educational and cultural development, it was unfortunately not reconstituted after the expiry of its extended tenure in March, 1994. CABE has a particularly important role to play at the present juncture in view of the significant socio-economic and socio-cultural developments taking place in the country and for the review of the National Policy on Education which is also due. It is a matter of importance therefore, that the Central and State governments, and educationists and people representing all interests, should increase their interaction and evolve a participative process of decision making in education, which enhances the federal structure of our polity.

The National Policy on Education, 1986 (as modified in 1992) also envisages that the CABE will play a pivotal role in reviewing educational development, determining the changes required to improve the system and monitoring implementation, and will function through appropriate mechanisms created to ensure contact with, and coordination among, the various areas of human resource development. Accordingly, the CABE has since been reconstituted by the Government in July 2004. The Board consists of nominated members representing various interests in addition to representatives of the Government of India, State Governments and UT Administrations, elected members from the Lok Sabha and the Rajya Sabha, etc.

The functions of CABE are: a) to review the progress of education from time to time; b) to appraise the extent and manner in which the education policy has been implemented by the Central and State Governments, and other concerned agencies, and to give appropriate advice in the matter; c) to advise regarding coordination between the Central and State governments/UT Administrations, State Governments and nongovernmental agencies for educational development in accordance with the education policy; and d) to advise, suo moto, or on a reference made to it by the Central Government or any State Government or Union Territory Administration on any educational question.

The first meeting of the re-constituted Central Advisory Board of Education was held on August 10-11, 2004, during which some critical issues emerged, needing detailed deliberation. It was decided to set up Committees of CABE to examine in detail these critical issues. Accordingly, seven Committees of the Central Advisory Board of Education (CABE) have been set up to look into some of the critical issues faced by the Education Sector in the country, as indicated below: 1. CABE Committee on Free and Compulsory Education Bill and other issues related to Elementary Education under the Chairmanship of Shri Kapil Sibal, MOS Science and Technology.

1. The terms of reference are:
   - To suggest a draft of Legislation envisaged in Article 21A of the Constitution.
   - To examine other issues related to elementary education for achieving the objectives of free and compulsory basic education.
2. CABE Committee on Girls Education and the Common School System under the chairmanship of Shri Tarun Gogoi, Chief Minister, Assam. The terms of reference are:
   - To examine existing schemes, incentives and special measures aimed at reducing gender disparity and increasing the participation and retention of girls, in all sectors of education.

- To make the provision in the NPE and POA regarding the Common School System, a reality.
- To examine ways of promoting inclusive education and the education of all children with disabilities/ special needs.

3. CABE Committee on Universalisation of Secondary Education under the chairmanship of Shri Ghanshyam Tiwari, Education Minister, Rajasthan. The term of reference is to prepare a blueprint for the universalisation of secondary education consequent upon the attainment of universalisation of elementary education.
4. CABE Committee on Autonomy of Higher Education Institutions under the chairmanship of Shri Kanti Biswas, Education Minister, West Bengal. The terms of reference are:
   - To suggest measures for enhancing the autonomy of higher education institutions, especially those with potential for excellence.
   - To institutionalise regulatory provisions for promoting autonomy and accountability of higher education institutions.
5. CABE Committee on Integration of Culture Education in the School Curriculum under the chairmanship of Prof. U. R. Ananthamurthy. The terms of reference are:
   - To suggest ways of enhancing the quality of cultural awareness among school-going children;
   - To suggest ways of introducing both in curricular and extra-curricular ways, the learning of our traditional, folk, classical and contemporary art forms;
   - To suggest ways of helping the students to appreciate the world of arts, music and literature;
   - To suggest ways of introducing a capsule on the appreciation of arts in the curriculum of teacher education;
   - To suggest ways of introducing art appreciation as an elective subject in the universities;

- To help understand the status of art and music schools and colleges in the country.

6. CABE Committee on Regulatory Mechanism for the Text Books and parallel text books taught in schools outside the Government system co-chaired by Prof. Zoya Hassan, JNU, New Delhi and Prof. Gopal Guru, JNU, New Delhi. The terms of reference are:
   - To study and report on text books in Government schools not using the CBSE syllabus;
   - To study the text books and curriculum of schools outside the Government system, including those run by the religious and social organisations;
   - To suggest an appropriate regulatory mechanism for institutionalising the issue of preparation of text books and curricular material. While reviewing the textbooks, the Chairpersons of the Committee may co-opt subject matter/language specialists.
7. CABE Committee on Financing of Higher and Technical Education under the chairmanship of Prof. Bhalchandra Mungeker, Member Education, Planning Commission. The terms of reference are:
   - To examine the adequacy of investments in Higher/Technical Education and to find ways of augmenting the resource flow in Higher Education;
   - To examine the question of a fair share of 6 per cent of GDP for Education;
   - To suggest the ways of encouraging and regulating private participation and investments in Higher/Technical Education.

EDUCATION MINISTERS' CONFERENCE

A meeting of the Education Ministers of all States/UTs dealing with School Education was held on October 28, 2004, at Vigyan Bhawan under the chairmanship of the Minister of Human Resource Development.

Bharat Shiksha Kosh

In order to facilitate donations including smaller amounts from India and abroad for implementing projects/programmes connected with the education sector, the Government has constituted "Bharat Shiksha Kosh" as a Society registered under the Society Registration Act, 1860. The Kosh was officially launched on January 9, 2003, during the celebration of Pravasi Bharatiya Diwas. The Kosh will receive donations/contributions/endowments from individuals and corporate, Central and State Governments, nonresident Indians and people of Indian origin for various activities across all sectors of education.

NATIONAL INSTITUTE OF EDUCATIONAL PLANNING AND ADMINISTRATION

The National Institute of Educational Planning and Administration (NIEPA) is an autonomous organisation set up and fully funded by the Department of Secondary and Higher Education, Ministry of Human Resource Development. The objectives of the Institute are to undertake, promote and coordinate research in educational planning and administration; to provide training and consultancy services in this field; to train and orient key level functionaries as well as senior-level administrators from the Centre and the States; to collaborate with other agencies, institutions and organisations, to provide facilities for training and research to other countries, particularly of the Asian region in the field of educational planning and administration; to prepare print and publish papers, periodicals and books, to share experience and expertise in the area of educational planning and administration with other countries; and to conduct comparative studies for the furtherance of these objectives. During 2004-2005, 40 training programmes had been organised till December, 2004.

The faculty provided consultancy and professional support to National, State and institutional-level bodies like Ministry of Human Resource Development, University Grants Commission, State Education Departments, State Councils of Higher Education, SCERTs, SIEMATs besides International

Agencies such as UNESCO, UNICEF, World Bank and SIDA. The Institute has a well stocked Library/Documentation Centre on Educational Planning and Administration and Inter Disciplinary subjects. It can claim to have one of the richest libraries in the field of Educational Planning and Management in the Asian Region. It serves the faculty, research scholars and the participants of the various programmes, and also other organisations through the Inter Library Loan system.

The Library reading room facilities are open to all. The Library has collection of over 55,961 volumes and subscribes to as many 390 periodicals and has a computerised catalogue of books and articles. An Outside Peer Review Committee under the Chairmanship of Subhash C. Kashyap, former Secretary General, Lok Sabha Secretariat, was set up to review the work and progress of NIEPA. The Review Committee has submitted its report and has recommended that NIEPA has done extremely well in fulfilling the objectives identified in its Memorandum of Association. Other recommendations of Review Committee are being considered by the Department.

SCHEME OF ASSISTANCE FOR STUDIES

The Scheme of Studies, Seminars, Evaluation, etc., for the implementation of Education policy is intended to provide financial assistance to deserving institutions and organisations, on the merits of each proposal, so as to finance a variety of activities having direct bearing on the management and implementation aspects of National Policy on Education. These include sponsoring of seminars, workshops, etc., conduct of impact and evaluation studies, and consultancy assignments in order to advise the Government on the best alternatives and models for making the system to work. The guidelines of the scheme have been revised during the year 1999-2000.

As per the revised guidelines, financial assistance under this scheme would cover remuneration and allowances/ payment of TA/DA to project staff, stationery and printing, hiring charges of accommodation/venue and other contingencies like postage, etc. Normally, the ceiling of assistance for Studies/Evaluation is Rs. 5 lakh. The ceiling of expenditure on National Conference/Seminar is Rs. 3 lakh and on International Conferences (or, with substantial International participants/members), it is Rs. 5 lakh. During 2004-2005, financial assistance was given for organising 23 seminars/conferences/studies/ evaluations, etc., till December 2004. The target for the year 2005-2006 is to give financial assistance for 50 seminars/conferences/workshops/ evaluations, etc.

STATISTICS UNIT

The Statistics Unit of the Department of Education is the nodal agency for the collection, compilation, processing and dissemination of educational statistics in the country. The national annual educational statistics brought out by the Ministry of Human Resource Development are collected from over 10 lakh institutions, covering all levels of education from preprimary to higher education through mailed questionnaires in collaboration with the State Education Departments. On the basis of data collected from States, the Statistics Unit brings out nine annual publications and some occasional publications. Efforts have been made to improve the quality of educational statistics and to reduce the time lag in their publication. The inherent bottlenecks in the system, however, still remain a handicap.

The recommendations of the National Statistical Commission to improve the system have also been taken up for implementation. In order to strengthen the State Education Departments with bare minimum infrastructure to supplement the existing structure available in the country for educational statistics, a scheme titled 'Strengthening of Statistical Machinery in States' is under formulation. This scheme would improve the efficiency of various schemes of the Ministry of HRD. India has continued to participate in the World Education Indicators Programme through the Joint Pilot Project organised by Organisation for Economic Cooperation and Development (OECD)/United Nations Educational Scientific and Cultural Organisation (UNESCO). Necessary support in the form of supply of national statistics is being provided to the international institutions like UNESCO/ OCED every year.

PLANNING AND MONITORING UNIT ANNUAL PLANS AND FIVE YEAR PLANS

Formulation of Annual Plans and Five-Year Plans, review of programmes and schemes, timely monitoring of Plan expenditure vis-à-vis outlays in Budget Estimates, and analysis of actual expenditure as per the targets fixed are the important activities of the Unit. The approved Tenth Plan (2002-07) outlay was Rs. 43,825 crore: Rs. 13,825 crore for the Department of Secondary and Higher Education and Rs. 30,000 crore for the Department of Elementary Education and Literacy. The approved Annual Plan outlay (2004-05) is Rs. 6,000 crore for the Department of Elementary Education and Literacy and Rs. 2,225 crore for the Department of Secondary and Higher Education. Budget documents from various States/UTs were received and the data compiled, analysed and published in the Analysis of Budgeted Expenditure on Education for 2001-02 to 2003-04. The Unit liaised with the Planning Commission during quarterly review of Plan expenditure. The Unit also liaised with various Divisions of the Ministry, Planning Commission, Ministry of Finance, etc., on various matters relating to Plan Schemes.

Area Officers Scheme

The Area Officers Scheme was started in the Department in 1999 as a mechanism for regular and effective review, monitoring and coordination of various Central sectors and Centrally Sponsored Schemes. As per the original scheme, an officer of the rank of Deputy Secretary and above is made in-charge of a State/UT.

NATIONAL COUNCIL OF EDUCATIONAL RESEARCH & TRAINING

The last two decades of the twentieth century witnessed a global initiative to extend the outreach venture of universal elementary education to each and every human being who was yet outside the fold of education. It was total quality, utility and relevance of education, not mere literacy, that mattered in a comprehensive manner.

This focus is going to be crucial in the future too. Besides, the quality of elementary education on the one hand, and the quality of teacher education on the other have also recently emerged as areas meriting special attention. Teacher, the key factor in all educational development needs to be professionally equipped with teaching competencies, commitment and determination to perform at their best. The world needs more teachers, better teachers and more committed teachers, and India is no exception. Reforms in school education and teacher education are an irreversible phenomenon; strategies, approaches and technologies would, however, vary. The policy initiatives in 1968 and 1986 were meant to shape educational strategies and programmes.

After the *National Policy on Education, 1986* (revised in 1992), there has been no policy change. In consonance with these policy documents, the NCERT developed curriculum frameworks for school education in 1975, 1988 and in 2000. Curriculum frameworks for teacher education were also developed in 1978, 1988 and 1998. While the first two were prepared by the National Council for Teacher Education as a non-statutory body, located in the Teacher Education Department of the NCERT, the last one was developed by the statutory National Council for Teacher Education (NCTE). The latest *National Curriculum Framework for School Education* (NCFSE)-2000 has given rise to a national debate on various aspects of school education. Some of its related issues also came up for discussion in the Parliament and a debate in the Supreme Court of India. In its landmark judgment delivered on 12th September, 2002, the Hon'ble Supreme Court endorsed the approach of the NCERT. The NCERT, then, developed detailed syllabi and new curricular materials for all the stages of schooling.

These books have been received with an astoundingly favourable response from their users. Notwithstanding its several newly initiated programmes for the preparation of resource persons in keeping with the spirit of the NCFSE-2000, the NCERT was fully conscious of its responsibility to develop a suitable response on teacher education. The NCFSE-2000 was finalised after nation wide consultation with all the stakeholders of education. In these deliberations at every stage, references were also made to teacher education and significant suggestions for making changes in this field came up quite frequently. The NCERT, in deference to these suggestions, initiated the project to develop a suitable blueprint of teacher education in keeping with the NCFSE-2000. An Advisory Committee was constituted for the purpose. The outcome of the meetings and the opinions of the expert educationists invited by the NCERT on various occasions led to a draft document which was put up for a national level consultation meeting in October 2002. It was restructured on the basis of several important suggestions made therein.

The curriculum document for teacher education as it emerged finally, is now being presented to the nation. Traditionally, teachers in India have overcome shortcomings and inadequacies of various types through their resourcefulness and commitment. That makes it all the more important that the teacher education institutions become better equipped in infrastructure and also receive greater professional support on a continuous basis. The school - community mutuality has to be re-established in the changing context. Fully conscious of the existing realities, this curriculum framework takes a pragmatic view of things and suggests changes within the various parameters of implementation. Resources have to be channelised and the professionals in teacher education motivated to convert challenges into opportunities. A perusal of the content herein would indicate enhanced contextualisation of teachers' role and also the expectations from them.

The thrust areas generally overlap through all stages but need to be sharply delineated for the specific groups of teachers, hence the need to identify stage specific roles and prepare teachers accordingly. Issues of management have become very important as a consequence of large scale expansion and advent of new techniques and technologies. The critical areas like focus on work education, vocationalisation of education, education of learners with special needs, in-service orientation and recurrent in-service education of serving teachers deserve a fresh look as new complexities are emerging practically in each area. As the crucial objectives of education are globally identified as enabling learners to learn how to live together and how to achieve social cohesion, teacher education cannot ignore its obligations to strive for communal harmony, national integration and establishment of peace. Both teacher education and school education have to gather knowledge from various other disciplines and areas of knowledge generation and research.

Converting the existing institutions into quality institutions with clear objectives and missions remains the prime goal before the stakeholders in teacher education. The NCERT has over the last four decades worked as an academic advisor in the field of school education and teacher education. It collaborates with various state level agencies and other national level institutions. In addition, it is constantly in touch with school teachers and teacher educators who participate in its various consultation processes. The ideas generated out of such consultations have immensely helped the NCERT in developing the present curriculum framework. This curriculum framework, with all the ideas it contains, is for perusal in teacher education institutions and by educational planners and policy makers so that the requisite changes in pre-service and in-service teacher education programmes may be planned and implemented more pragmatically. That is the critical point to ignite change in teacher education institutions. The contents of this book are based on this premise and it is hoped that it would certainly contribute to teachers' personal and professional development.

5

National Policy on Education

Educational policy and progress have been reviewed in the light of the goal of national development and priorities set from time to time. In its Resolution on the National Policy on Education in 1968, an emphasis on quality improvement and a planned, more equitable expansion of educational facilities and the need to focus on the education of girls was stressed. About a decade ago and a half later, the National Policy on Education (NPE-1986) was formulated which was further updated in 1992. The NPE 1986 provides for a comprehensive policy framework for the development of education up to the end of the century and a Plan of Action (POA) 1992, assigning specific responsibilities for organising, implementing and financing its proposals.

POLICY FRAMEWORK

India's commitment to the spread of knowledge and freedom of thought among its citizens is reflected in its Constitution. The Directive Principle contained in Article 45 enjoins that the State shall endeavour to provide within a period of ten years from the commencement of this Constitution, for free and compulsory education for all children until they complete the age of fourteen years. Article 29 (i) provides that any citizen having a distinct language, script, special care of the economic and educational interests of the underprivileged sections, particularly, the Scheduled Castes and Scheduled Tribes is laid down as an obligation of the State under article

46. Though education is in the concurrent list of the Constitution, the State Governments play a very major role in the development of education particularly in the primary and the secondary education sectors.

STRUCTURE AND PROGRESS

The focus is in on the broad dimensions and magnitude of the structure, organisation and progress in education. Further it also highlights growth and priority areas in education in India that point to the challenges of the future. There are about 888 thousands educational institutions in the country with an enrolment of about 179 millions. Elementary Education System in India is the second largest in the World with 149.4 millions children of 6-14 years enrolled and 2.9 million teachers. This is about 82% of the children in the age group.

STRUCTURE OF SCHOOL EDUCATION

A uniform structure of school education, the 10+2 system has been adopted by all the States and Union Territories of India. However, within the States and the UTs, there remains variations in the number of classes constituting the Primary, Upper Primary, High and Higher Secondary school stages, age for admission to class I, medium of instruction, public examinations, teaching of Hindi and English, number of working days in a year,academic session, vacation periods, fee structure, compulsory education etc.

STAGES OF SCHOOL EDUCATION

The Primary Stage consists of Classes I-V, i.e., of five years duration, in 20 States/UTs namely Andhra Pradesh, Arunachal Pradesh, Bihar, Haryana, Himachal Pradesh, Jammu & Kashmir, Madhya Pradesh, Manipur, Orissa, Punjab, Rajasthan, Sikkim, Tamil Nadu, Tripura, Uttar Pradesh, West Bengal, Andaman & Nicobar Islands, Chandigarh, Delhi and Karaikal and Yanam regions of Pondicherry. The primary stage consists of classes I-IV in Assam, Goa, Gujarat, Karnataka, Kerala, Maharashtra, Meghalaya, Mizoram, Nagaland, Dadra &

Nagar Haveli, Daman & Diu, Lakshadweep and Mahe region of Pondicherry.

The Middle Stage of education comprises Classes VI-VIII in as many as 18 States.Uts viz., Arunachal Pradesh, Bihar, Haryana, Himachal Pradesh, Jammu & Kashmir, Madhya Pradesh, Manipur, Punjab, Rajasthan, Sikkim, Tamil Nadu, Tripura, Uttar Pradesh, West Bengal, Andaman & Nicobar Islands, Chandigarh, Delhi and Karaikal region of Pondicherry; Classes V-VII in Assam, Goa, Gujarat, Karnataka, Kerala, Maharashtra, Meghalaya, Mizoram, Dadra & Nagar Haveli, Daman & Diu, Lakshadweep and Mahe region of Pondicherry and Classes VI-VII in Andhra Pradesh, Orissa and Yanam region of Pondicherry. In Nagaland Classes V - VIII constitute the upper primary stage.

The Secondary Stage consists of Classes IX-X in 19 States/ UTs. Viz., Arunachal Pradesh, Bihar, Haryana, Himachal Pradesh, Jammu & Kashmir, Madhya Pradesh, Manipur, Nagaland, Punjab, Rajasthan, Sikkim, Tamil Nadu, Tripura, Uttar Pradesh, West Bengal, Andaman & Nicobar Islands, Chandigarh, Delhi and Karaikal region of Pondicherry. The High School stage comprises classes VIII to X in 13 States/ UTs viz., Andhra Pradesh, Assam, Goa, Gujarat, Karnataka, Kerala, Maharashtra, Meghalaya, Mizoram, Orissa, Dadra & Nagar Haveli, Daman & Diu, Lakshadweep and Mahe & Yanam regions of Pondicherry. However, the Higher Secondary/ Senior Secondary stage of school comprising classes XI-XII (10+2 pattern) is available in all the States/UTs though in some States/UTs these classes are attached to Universities/Colleges.

AGE RESTRICTION FOR ADMISSIONS

The minimum age for admission to class I of the Primary School stage is generally 5+ or 6+ years. In 22 States/UTs the minimum age for admission to Class I is 5+ years and in 7 States/UTs the minimum age for admission is 6+ years. There is no age restriction in the case of Mizoram. In Gujarat, the minimum age for admission is 5+ years (voluntary) and 6+

years (compulsory). In Lakshadweep, the minimum age for admission is 5 ½ years.

Medium of Instruction

Mother tongue or regional language is the medium of instruction at the primary stage of education in most of the States/UTs. Facilities for studying in a medium other than regional language vary considerable in different States and Union Territories.

Teaching of Hindi

Apart from Hindi speaking States, teaching of Hindi is compulsory in most of the non-Hindi speaking States/UTs, though the classes from which the teaching of Hindi is compulsory differ from State to State. Teaching of Hindi is not compulsory in the States of Tamil Nadu, Tripura and Karaikal region of Pondicherry.

Teaching of English

Teaching of English is compulsory in all the States/UTs, except Bihar. However, the classes in which teaching of English is compulsory differs from State to State. In general, it is compulsory in Classes VI-X in most of the States/UTs.

Public Examinations

In all the States/UTs Public Examinations are conducted at the end of X an XII Classes by the respective State Boards of Secondary and Higher Secondary Education. The minimum age for the Secondary School Examination varies from 14+ to 16+ years in Andhra Pradesh, Arunachal Pradesh, Assam, Bihar, Gujarat, Jammu & Kashmir, Karnataka, Kerala, Maharashtra, Manipur, Orissa, Punjab, Tamil Nadu, Tripura, West Bengal, Andaman & Nicobar Islands, Delhi, Lakshadweep and Pondicherry. In Mizoram, the minimum age for secondary school examination is 13+ years. Other States/UTs either do not have age restriction or have not prescribed any age restriction.

The minimum age for higher Secondary School Examination varies from 16+ to 18+ years in Arunachal Pradesh, Bihar, Gujarat, Jammu & Kashmir, Kerala, Maharashtra, Punjab, Tamil Nadu, Tripura, Andaman & Nicobar Islands, Delhi, Lakshadweep and Pondicherry. In other States/UTs, either there is no age restriction prescribed or if it exists, it has not been indicated. In some of the States/UTs, the first Public Examination is also conducted at the Middle stage of School Education.

Number of Working Days

The number of working days of School Education in a year is generally more than 200 days in all the States/UTs. Academic Session

The academic session begins from different months of the year in the different States and Union Territories. However, in most of the States, the long vacation periods are availed in the summer season while in some of the hilly States, this fall in the winter months.

Compulsory Education

Compulsory education has been enforced in four States and Union Territories at the primary stage of education while in eight States/UTs there is compulsory education covering the entire elementary stage of education. As many as 20 States/ UTs have not introduced any measure of compulsion up to the year 1997-98.

Free Education

A majority of States and Union Territories have introduced free education in Classes I-XII of their schools.

Tution Fees per Annum per Child

In the States/UTs where education is not free for classes IX and above, the annual fee varies considerably from the highest level of Rs. 360/- for classes XI and XII in the case of Meghalaya to the lowest at Rs. 48/- in the case of Assam.

FINANCING OF EDUCATION

From 1968 onwards, goal has been to set apart 6% of National Income on education. In spite of resource constraints as well as competing priorities, the budgetary expenditure on education by Centre & States as percentage of Gross National Product has steadily increased from 0.8% in 1951-52 to 3.3% in 1994-95. Para 11.4 of NPE, 1986 states that the investment on education be gradually increased to reach a level of 6% of the National Income as early as possible. Since the actual level of investment has remained far short of that target, it is important that greater determination is shown now to find the funds for the programmes laid down in this policy. While actual requirements will be computed from time to time on the basis of monitoring and review, the outlay on education will be stepped up to ensure that during the 8th Five year Plan and onwards it will uniformly exceed 6% of the national income.

The total budgetary expenditure on Education by the Education Departments of the Centre and States has increased from Rs. 644.6 millions in 1951-52 to Rs. 300,000millions in 1995-96. In terms of its share in total budgetary expenditure, it has increased from 7.9% in 1951-52 to 11.1% in 1995-96. There are, at present 130 plan schemes in the Department with a total Eighth Plan outlay of Rs. 74430 Millions. The total plan outlay of the Department for the year 1996-97 is Rs. 33827 millions. There are 18 Centrally Sponsored Schemes which account for 65.7% of the total plan outlay. Mid-Day-Meal Scheme is the major Centrally Sponsored Scheme with 1996-97 outlay of Rs.14,000 millions. Other major Centrally Sponsored Schemes are Operation Blackboard, Non-formal Education, Teacher Education, Post Literacy and Continuing Education and Vocational Education with 1996-97 Outlay of Rs. 2790 millions, Rs. 1582.5 millions, Rs. 1170 millions, Rs. 755 millions and Rs. 820 millions respectively.

No coherent policy on education, says Arun Nigavekar INDIA has no coherent national policy on higher education, said former University Grants Commission (UGC) chairman

Arun Nigavekar, speaking at the fourth Foundation Day of the Symbiosis International University on Friday. Delivering a lecture on the topic Deemed Universities: Opportunities and challenges, Nigavekar highlighted the constraints plaguing modern Indian education system today. The last time a national policy was formulated was during the Rajiv Gandhi government in 1986, and now, 20 years later, that policy is no longer relevant, he said, adding that although new policies are formulated, they change when new governments

Uganda: Open Distance Learning Policy in Offing STAKEHOLDERS in the education sector trying to formulate the Open Distance Learning (ODL) policy to focus on quality assurance, costing and financing of the education system. The state minister for higher education, Gabriel Opio, said once the policy is in place, it would enable the country to explore opportunities of achieving the national educational goals. While opening a three-day consultative forum on ODL at Hotel Africana, Opio said, we have a challenge of increasing access to education in all sectors and levels.

Prime Minister Helen Clark has given Education Minister Trevor Mallard a public rebuke over his comments about National's foreign policy. Mr. Mallard made a botched attempt last week to link National with American interests provoking a backlash which is perceived as having damaged Labour's election campaign. Helen Clark said on TV One's Breakfast programme today: I think what Trevor has drawn from that is he had better stick to education. Mr. Mallard claimed last week that National's policies were written in Washington and his remark provoked a statement from the United States Embassy in Wellington saying it had never sought.

NCERT DEVIATING FROM EDUCATION POLICY

The Shiksha Bachao Andolan Samiti (SBA) on Monday registered its protest over the National Council of Educational Research and Training (NCERT) engineering a deviation from the National policy of Education, 1986. The SBA, a forum of 14 cultural groups, during its interaction with NCERT director Krishna Kumar, pointed out total absence of reference to value education, dilution of content in social sciences, marginalisation of Sanskrit and several other things in the Draft National Curriculum Framework (NCF) for schools. The Human Resource Development Ministry under Arjun Singh has proposed to present the draft before the Central Advisory Board of Education (CABE).

QUALITY CONCERNS

This is how the Education Commission described the role of education in social and economic transformation of India. While the development planners rightly recognized that expansion of educational facilities has to be accompanied with significant improvements in quality and relevance of education at all levels, the outcome is quite disappointing. At the international level, the development experience in social sectors shows that a literate society has enormous gains over an illiterate society and no illiterate society has ever been able to modernize and progress. We are now transiting to a knowledge society where the quality and relevance of education would play a crucial role in economic development. Poor quality of teaching learning and systemic level inefficiencies affect the learners as well the society in many ways. The long-term implications include lower productivity levels of the perspective workforce, resistance to modernization and perpetuation of inefficient production systems where cost benefit ratio adversely affect the economic sustainability of production processes.

CONCERNS FOR QUALITY OF EDUCATION

As far as the provision of access and coverage is concerned, India today boasts of its educational system being the second largest in the world. It consists of nearly 610 thousand primary and 185 thousand upper primary schools, about a quarter million non-formal education centers, about 1.87 million teachers and 110 million students study in primary classes in the recognized schools (1997-98). As per 1991 Census estimates there were about 115.6 million children in primary school going age group in the country. The latest educational statistics indicate a GER of 89.7

percent for primary classes (81.2 percent being for girls and 97.7 percent for boys). The number of students in primary classes in India is larger than the total population of the neighbouring Bangladesh. No doubt, the system can claim it to be one of the largest, but it can not make similar claims for efficiency, quality and achievement of learners? Various five years plans incorporated programs and strategies based on periodic assessment of the progress of education by the Ministry of Education, Commissions and the destiny of India is now being shaped in her classrooms. Education Commission, 1964-66.

CONCERNS FOR QUALITY OF EDUCATION

As far as the provision of access and coverage is concerned, India today boasts of its educational system being the second largest in the world. It consists of nearly 610 thousand primary and 185 thousand upper primary schools, about a quarter million nonformal education centers, about 1.87 million teachers and 110 million students study in primary classes in the recognized schools (1997-98). As per 1991 Census estimates there were about 115.6 million children in primary school going age group in the country. The latest educational statistics indicate a GER of 89.7 percent for primary classes (81.2 percent being for girls and 97.7 percent for boys). The number of students in primary classes in India is larger than the total population of the neighboring Bangladesh. No doubt, the system can claim it to be one of the largest, but it can not make similar claims for efficiency, quality and achievement of learners? Various five years plans incorporated programs and strategies based on periodic assessment of the progress of education by the Ministry of Education, Commissions and Committees appointed by the central and state governments.

The National Policy on Education (NPE), 1986 and the revised NPE, 1992, reiterated the urgency to address the quality concerns in schools education on priority basis. Quality can not improve by itself. It requires reforms in teacher training; improvements in the facilities and infrastructure in schools; teachers' motivation; and a change in the style of teaching to make it attractive to the students. However, in actual practice, there has always been a trade-off between quality and quantity, in favor of the latter. This not only affected the internal efficiency of the educational system but also resulted in a situation where only a few graduates of the school and higher education system could attain the expected skills and competencies. The labor market policies and predominance of public sector employment opportunities did not put enough pressure on the educational systems to change as the degree was more important than the acquired knowledge and skills.

The gap between the planned and the realized goals of education continues be so large that even the basis of educational planning and underlying assumptions can be easily challenged. The basic educational planning models have gone off the trajectory both at the central as well in the states. Bringing it back on the tracks remains a serious challenge for the development planners. The inter-state and intra-state variations in school facilities, quality of teachers and learning outcome are large and so are social and economic conditions of the areas where the primary schools operate.

While indicators to measure the access, retention and internal efficiency of the educational system in terms of participation rate, accessibility, repetition rates, promotion rates, dropout rates and input-output ratio have been developed, but little information is available about the learners' achievement of cognitive and non-cognitive competencies. Under the no detention policy, followed by most of the states, a child is not even tested on the learning outcomes for many years after entering the school. The no detention policy prohibits the use of examinations in first few years of schooling. The proposed system of continuous and comprehensive evaluation is yet to be implemented on sustainable basis. Reforms in the quality of education have not received serious attention of many states.

DEFINING QUALITY OF EDUCATION

Assessment may be defined as 'any method used to understand the current knowledge that a student possesses.

The idea of current knowledge implies that what a student knows is always changing and that we can make judgment about student achievement through comparison over a period of time. Good assessment techniques provide accurate estimates of student performance and enables teachers and decision-makers to make appropriate decisions. The current debate about the determinants of student achievement, specifically the contributing effect of teacher variables, has its origin primarily in the findings of the Coleman Report (1966). In developing countries, the examination results are often used as a proxy for the quality of education. However, such a method is fraught with great problems, as the examination system is limited in scope and coverage as far as learning is concerned. The research has established that acquiring both cognitive and non-cognitive competencies are necessary for a child's overall development. However, most of the research in learning achievement has focused on the assessment of cognitive skills acquired by the students.

An equally reliable measure of quality of education is whether pupils are learning effectively, improving their knowledge, skills and abilities; widening their experience and growing socially and morally or not. Ability to work with others, readiness to accept responsibility and to work for public good are highly praised characteristics among school leavers. But assessment tools do not test for such skills. While there is no consensus among educationists regarding the definition of the quality in education but there are several ways of measuring quality in education. In the context of school effectiveness, the concept of quality is linked to the efficiency of teaching learning processes. Quality is a relative concept and not something that is absolute. One useful approach could be to select a range of educational indicators that are explicit and measurable representing various facets of quality.

The quality of education and its determinants remain a topic of interest since the beginning of formal education. It is possible to develop indicators to measure learning along important dimensions, closely related to the curriculum, both in standardized assessment instruments and in alternative for ms of assessment. Non standardized assessment refers to the traditional form of assessment by teachers on regular basis through classroom interaction, questions, assignment of homework and other such techniques. The results of such assessment may be accurate or faulty, depending upon the teachers' skill as a judge of various indicators and their applicability in a given situation. Standardized tests have proved useful in comparing, generalizing and indicating levels of attainment based on pre-defined standards. It is assumed that levels of learners' achievement are assessed at best through standardized achievement tests.

Since the beginning of sixties, the measurement of students' academic performance on regular basis has been an ongoing effort in the advanced countries. Based on these results policy level interventions are made so that the deficiencies in learners' achievement can be overcome. In India, the large scale achievement studies were conducted only in the recent years for primary education. The methods and tools for assessing learning outcome at other levels of education are yet to be put in place. The country is yet to evolve a policy for periodic collection and analysis of learners' achievement data and using it for monitoring the quality of education at various levels. Considerable research is needed to improve the achievement testing methodology, achievement tests and tools of analysis. The analysis and feedback from achievement studies must be used for curriculum reforms and for restructuring of teacher training contents and methodology of training.

In the last few years, international organizations like the World Bank, UNICEF, UNESCO and UNDP have produced valuable studies on educational assessment and measurement. The Fourth Survey on Research in Education in India identified many studies, essentially at the M.Phil and Ph.D. level, addressed to the achievement of primary school children. These researches are more of conceptual nature and their use in policy planning was practically nil. Recently, Shukla (1994) conducted another study on about 66,000 students to find out the level of attainment of primary school children in 25 states/UTs. Among other things, the study showed different patterns of educational attainment in different states. Pupil's achievement was related to the education of the father and the facility for learning and educational environment at home.

Considerable research evidence is available on the factors affecting the learning outcomes. While a study by Heyneman and Loxley (1982) showed that 90 percent of variance in students science achievement is explained by school and teacher variables and only a small proportion by home related factors, the study by Kingdon (1998) shows that home background and school influence are both important to students achievement in India. Jangira (1994), while synthesizing the results of Baseline Assessment Studies of the DPEP states found that student's performance in reading and arithmetic was low.

There was a marked difference in achievement levels among states and between schools. In a study conducted in Karnataka, covering 2,598 class IV learners and 442 teachers, it was observed that the learning achievements are not significantly different between rural and urban schools. However, a significant difference was observed among the schools belonging to different management agencies. Similar studies were also conducted in many states as a part of the DPEP baseline learners' studies. The findings of the study on Kerala covering 3,089 class IV learners and 502 teachers suggests that the type of management of the school is not an influencing factor in learning achievement. The study found that the level of school infrastructure and variations in the availability of teaching-learning materials is not clearly related to learning achievement.

LEARNERS ACHIEVEMENT AND QUALITY OF EDUCATION

The interest among developing and developed countries to compare information and experience about achievement in terms of both the standards which are prescribed and the standards that are actually achieved by the learners is indicated by the growing number of countries participating in the cross-national comparative studies on learning achievement. At the international level, the International Evaluation Agency (IEA) has developed achievement tests which are administered across the participating countries and used for establishment and comparison of learning outcome of children of specified age groups in developed and developing countries. The OECD has a long tradition of assessing achievement level in various countries and providing comparative statistics. In addition to the international studies, many countries have also adopted a unique approach for assessing learning outcomes at various levels on regular basis.

In France, for example, the focus of external assessment is to provide information on the attainment of individual pupils so that teachers can respond effectively to specific weaknesses or strengths as revealed through assessment studies. In United States, assessment studies have been conducted for a long time and have been used for national assessment and international comparison of learning outcome of American pupils with other developed countries. In England and Wales, all students are assessed at the end of ages 7, 11 and 14. The information on achievement of pupils is made available to the schools and public. It is considered essential that the public has the right to know about the performance of schools and be able to make comparative judgements between schools.

In Ontario, Canada, all grade 3 pupils (8-9 year olds) are assessed on various literacy and numeracy tasks in a comprehensive testing programme. The programme is designed to set benchmarks for achievement at this level. In Australia, some states such as Victoria and New South Wales test all students of a similar age. The information on performance of pupils is made available to the pupils and schools and not to the public. New South Wales conducted state-wide tests in literacy and numeracy at years 3 and 5 for many years. The common element of all these tests has been to help teachers improve their programmes. From Target to Action, published by the Department of education (UK) provides examples how schools have used the assessment results to monitor the effectiveness of their teaching learning strategies and to set targets for improving their students achievement.

REVIEW OF EMPIRICAL RESEARCH ON ACHIEVEMENT

The review of empirical research on learners' assessment shows that there are two distinct phases. The period up to 1990 is characterised as the first phase and the researches and empirical studies undertaken after 1990 fall into the other category.

A main characteristic of the empirical studies in the first phase was that these were mainly academic in nature and the administrators did not use their findings for policy reforms. The present chapter examines the studies undertaken after 1990. There was a significant departure during nineties as far as assessment and measurement of learners' achievement is concerned.

Earlier studies were confined to small samples and each followed a different sampling design and achievement tests. Therefore the findings were not strictly comparable. Moreover, most of the studies were cross-sectional in nature and at no point of time temporal comparisons were made. Temporal analysis is necessary to understand the dynamics of policy formulation and educational reforms in teaching learning processes. In early nineties, a major initiative to achieve universal primary education came in the form of District Primary Education Programme (DPEP) which has now emerged as a major vehicle for bringing about a qualitative change in primary education. The DPEP model has also been replicated on a large scale through many innovative projects.

LEARNING ACHIEVEMENT LEVELS IN DELHI

Recently, a study on learning achievement for primary schools in Delhi was conducted by the author. The study covered all types of primary schools/sections in Delhi and was based on a sample of 169 schools. Besides other aspects, the achievement levels in language and mathematics were assessed through competency based tests developed by the NCERT. The overall mean score based on Class I competencies was 80.2 percent for Language and 78.2 percent for Mathematics. The mean score for English and Hindi medium schools was statistically different in mathematics. The mean score for the SC children was 8-10 percent points lower than those of the children belonging to general category.

The differences in mean achievement scores due to gender were reflected both in language and mathematics. However, the girls scored much lower in mathematics as compared to the boys. The achievement scores based on class IV competencies were very low as compared to class I mean achievement scores.

The gap was large in mathematics as compared to language. The mean score in mathematics for Hindi medium schools was 40.46 percent as compared to 56.5 percent for the mean score in language. The gap between mean score in mathematics and language is considerable and statistically significant. In view of the low achievement scores, the underachievers are large in number. About 50 percent of learners in Hindi medium schools failed to obtain more than 40 percent score in mathematics. The corresponding share of learners in language was 23 percent.

The differences in achievement become more pronounced as one examines disaggregated scores for gender, caste, management and related attributes. Children with pre-primary education in Hindi medium schools achieved 8-10 percentage points more than those who did not have pre-primary education. This corroborates the impression that SC children are deficient in learning outcomes. Significant differences (15-18 percentage points) in the mean achievement score were also observed between different types of management. The schools managed by MCD reported the lowest mean scores. More than 20 percent children were reportedly scored less than 20 percent in MCD schools. The poor performance of MCD schools is thus a cause of concern.

The large differences in the achievement scores between class I and Class IV points to a gap in the quality of teaching, learning and classroom interaction processes.

While Class I achievement score is based on oral test, the class IV scores were based on the written test. Even within the class IV tests, the performance was poorest in mathematics as compared to language. It appears that children could understand and express orally but have difficulties in written communication. This has significant bearing on the teaching of language and expression in the form of written text. The achievement levels of children studying in English medium schools were analyzed separately. The mean score was 47.8 percent in mathematics as compared to 49.7 percent for language. About 38 percent of children failed to score more than 40 percent in mathematics and 24 percent failed to cross this threshold in language. Therefore, the general impression that all is well with English medium schools is not correct. While it is true that their performance is far better than the government schools, but the extent of underachievement is also very high.

Within the language, the underachievement is more serious in reading comprehension. This is a clear reflection on the poor quality of classroom teaching learning processes. Based on the detailed analysis presented above, the following issues were identified as far as provision of primary education in Delhi is concerned:

- Inadequate/absence of access to a comparable quality of education.
- Overcrowding in the existing government schools.
- Mismatches between demand and supply of schooling facilities.
- Dilapidated condition of class rooms, particularly those running in rented buildings. Repairs of rented buildings can not be undertaken under Rent Control Act.
- Lack of sanitation and water facilities in old school buildings.

- Excessive reliance on centrally sponsored schemes has also created its own problems. The states seldom initiate programs of educational development at their own initiatives and wait for central government initiatives.
- The educational planning for UEE in the urban context requires special emphasis. The traditional methods of removing supply side constraints would not succeed in achieving UEE objectives.

Assessment of Learners Achievement in DPEP Districts

The large-scale studies for the DPEP project were conducted in 46 districts covering eight states in 1993/94. Some unique features of achievement studies conducted under DPEP were:

- A common national framework for the design and data collection of baseline and mid-term studies in all districts.
- Use of nationally developed standardised achievement tests in all the states.
- The period of data collection was same for baseline and mid-term assessment studies for all the 42 districts belonging to phase I of the project.
- Provided inputs for the curriculum revision, preparation of new textbooks, teachers' guides and supplementary teaching learning materials.
- Provided inputs for the restructuring of teacher training curriculum as well as the training methodologies.
- The studies brought about awareness about research based interventions.

Achievement tests were conducted for assessing the levels of learner's achievement of students at the end of Class I and the penultimate class of primary education cycle in mathematics and language based on Class I and Class IIII/IV curriculum. Class II tests were oral in nature. The tests developed by the NCERT for the Primary Education Curriculum Renewal Project were used for DPEP achievement studies. Class IV/V standardised tests were developed by the TSG/NCERT. A total of 24,504 students of class IV/V, 23,056 students of class II and 5,114 teachers were covered under the baseline studies for the phase I districts. The period of reference was 1993-94 academic session. The study suffered from one limitation that it was confined to government schools only. Thus it was not possible to compare the differences in achievement level between children from the private and public schools. Such an analysis is necessary in the present context when the demand for private schooling is increasing exponentially even in smaller rural habitations.

The results of the learning assessment studies conducted under DPEP were quite revealing. Letter and word reading are basic skills which require 100 percent mastery for developing further skills. But surprisingly, none of the districts even achieved 80 percent in either of the tests. Like students teachers also found it difficult to handle mathematics questions. A mathematics test conducted on 42 teachers showed that most of them could not even correctly do a question on LCM while 64 percent could not give a correct title to a paragraph in the language comprehension test. The studies also identified that supervision was the weakest link in educational administration. Two third of teachers reported that they did not receive any type of assistance or help from their head teachers and the same proportion mentioned that there was no supervision by the Block education Officers.

In Karnataka study, it was found that a significantly large number of teachers were themselves first generation learners. Many teachers covered under the survey were not even properly qualified and did not attend any in-service programme during the five years preceding the survey *Trends in Learning Achievement.* The second round of studies was conducted as a part of the mid-term assessment (MAS) for the 42 phase-I districts. While the MAS used tests different from the one used at the time of BAS, an effort was made to compare the results of the 1993/94 and 1997/98 studies.

The MAS data covered 66,831 students, 6,221 teachers and 2068 schools spread over 42 districts belonging to phase I of the DPEP. The important findings of MAS were:

- A comparison of learners' mean score in language (class

I competencies) for the BAS and the read ministered test under MAS had revealed a mixed picture. In 28 of 42 districts the gains were positive and ranged between 0-36 percent. However, for the remaining 14 districts, the mean score in language was lower by 0-18 percent. In the case of mathematics, 33 out of 42 districts showed positive gains and the remaining nine districts showed a significant decline in mean scores.

- A similar analysis for class III competencies showed that 13 districts out of a total of 15 districts showed positive gains in language test. The decline in the remaining two districts was not significant. The mathematics results indicated that mean score for 11 out of 15 districts showed significant gains.
- The analysis of data for Class IV competencies indicated that the mean scores in language for 18 out of 27 districts showed gains, of them 15 showed statistically significant gains. The decline was more pronounced in some districts of Madhya Pradesh. Similar trends were observed in the case of mean scores for mathematics.
- The analysis also confirms the general trend that the performance of students in Class I both in language and mathematics was better than their counterparts in class III and IV. This is a matter which has to be seriously examined. This confirms the decline in educational standards as the students move from lower to the higher classes. It also signifies the issues related with the transition from oral to written mode of evaluation. Are the students well prepared for this transition?
- The DPEP goal of reducing the difference in mean achievement score between boys and girls have been accomplished in 40 out of 42 districts in language and 31 out of 42 districts in mathematics. However, similar objectives for the SC/ST population are yet to be achieved.
- The study confirms a moderate effect of teacher training on mean achievement scores. Students' achievement stands positively related to the availability of competency

based teaching learning materials.

Inter-district Variations in Mean Achievement Scores: Class I perhaps a striking finding of the achievement studies was the large differences in average achievement score between the best performing and the worst performing districts. The mean percentage score in language varied from 44.5 percent for Rewa district in Madhya Pradesh to 85.5 percent for Belgaum district in Karnataka.

The minimum and maximum achievement score in mathematics also followed a similar pattern i.e. it varied between 36.5 percent for Guna district to 87.5 percent for the Belgaum district. Thus the mean score for the best district was roughly twice that of the districts having the minimum score. There was a positive association between the mean percentage score in language and mathematics. The correlation between the two being 0.73.

Thus the districts with high achievement level in mathematics also depict high achievement level in language. Therefore, sustained efforts will be required in improving competencies in both the subjects in low performing districts. Many districts belonging to Madhya Pradesh fall in the category of low achievement districts both in language as well as in mathematics.

It is important to note that many of these districts are characterized by high degree of deprivation. The share of SC and ST population in some of these districts is very large. For example, the districts with the second lowest mean score in language had more than 60 percent of its population classified as SC and ST. *Inter-district Variations in Mean Achievement Scores: Class III/IV* The dispersion with regards to achievement scores was similar to that of Grade I competencies. The achievement score in language varies from 30.9 percent for Satna to 67.6 for Raisen district. Similarly, the mathematics means score varies from 20.6 for Sehore to 61.3 percent for Dhubri districts.

For 32 out of a total of 42 districts, the average score in mathematics was lower than that of language. How does one explain such a lower performance in mathematics as compared to language? The mean score in language and mathematics are consistently lower in Class III/IV than the corresponding mean score in Class I. Why should the scores decline as pupils move to higher classes? This is particularly intriguing, as the phenomenon is true for both the subjects. One possible reason could be that class II tests were oral and classes III/IV were written. To what extent the difference could be attributed to the transition from oral to written form of examination? It is generally believed that girls are more deprived than the boys. This is well reflected in the historically obtained patterns of educational attainment and levels of literacy. Data has also suggested that the DPEP districts have registered higher growth rate of enrolment for girls as compared to boys.

The analysis of enrolment and retention data for the DPEP districts has shown that most of the districts, the Index of Gender Equity was more than 95, thus showing the near absence of gender related inequities. Is this also true of learning achievement? The analysis shows that differences in achievement of boys and girls were not very striking. The distribution of districts into various classes for mean achievement scores for class III/IV between boys and girls. While the overall levels of achievement continue to be low both for the boys and girls, the differences in achievement patterns were not very significant excepting for a few districts. The average score was lower for mathematics than for language. The rural urban differences in achievement scores were more striking as compared to gender disparities. In the case of language, the rural students seem to be performing better than the boys. It is the other way round for mathematics.

This phenomenon needs to be examined in detail. The performance of the rural children in mathematics was very low as 32 out of the 42 districts had mean score of less than 40 percent-an exceptionally low performance of the pupils with rural background. Thus, the position with respect to teaching of mathematics is very unsatisfactory in class III/IV. These findings have serious implications for the planning and management of DPEP for the next few years. Will DPEP be able to prepare a framework for the universalisation of primary education in a manner that all children not only attain the objectives of DPEP but also able to cross the threshold by which 80 percent of the competencies are attained by 80 percent of the students. *Extent of Under Achievement in Various Classes* A detailed analysis of the underachievement patterns is attempted in this section.

The cutoff for the underachievers can be defined in many ways. For the purpose of this study, it is considered that any child who scores less than 40 percent should be considered as underachiever and the children who attain more than 80 percent should be considered as high achievers. The mean achievement score is highest for class I, followed by class III and lowest for class IV learners. Thus there is clear evidence that as children progress through various grades, their performance deteriorates.

Although this finding is not based on the same set of students who are observed over a period of time, yet the sample is large enough and cross-section data reflects the likely trends which would have been obtained over a period of time. The extent of underachievement (less than 40 percent) in language varies from 21.8 percent in class I to 36.2 percent in class III and 66.3 percent in class IV. Thus, nearly two third children of class V should not have been there as their competency levels were too low in language. By pushing them to higher grades, the underachievement is rewarded.

The extent of underachievement in mathematics is much higher than that of language. It is estimated that 19.8 percent of class I students fall within the category of underachievers as compared to 59 percent for class III and 72.2 percent for class IV. Translated in absolute numbers, this implies that 14,371 class IV learners out of a total of 19,894 got 40 percent or fewer score in mathematics. More than half (52. 1 percent) pupils could not score more than 30 percent. How does one reconcile such poor levels of performance where nearly three fourth children fail to acquire even 40 percent score, what to talk of 80 percent score for all the children? Let us consider the high achievers, especially in class III/IV. In language, 1.9 and 0.3 percent children were able to achieve mastery level (more than 80 percent). In mathematics, 2.3 and 1 percent of children were able to achieve mastery level competencies in classes III and IV. How to attain the intended target of achievement of 80 percent for 80 percent of students?

The NCERT studies have not examined the correlates of learning. While the data was collected on these aspects, the analysis and findings have not been released. The NCERT study does mention that the schools having competency based instructional materials faired well as compared to others. Similarly, it has been pointed out that parents' educational qualification is positively related to their achievement score.

Despite significant efforts, all is not well with the educational system. It is not only that many children do not have access to proper schooling facilities, but the internal efficiency of the educational system is also very low. This is reflected in high proportion of children leaving the school system without completing the primary cycle of education and low achievement among those who continue to stay in the system.

The concern for quality of education has been voiced from time to time in India. The National Policy on Education (NPE), 1986 and the revised NPE, 1992, again highlighted the urgency to address the quality concerns on priority basis. Quality can not improve by itself. It requires multi-pronged and strategic reforms in teacher training; improvements in the facilities and infrastructure in schools; teachers' motivation; and a change in the style of teaching to make it attractive to the students.

The policy also recommended that a system of continuous and comprehensive evaluation would be established. Besides the state level schemes to improve access and quality of education, a number of Centrally Sponsored Schemes and externally funded projects, undertaken in the recent years, are experimenting with various models of bringing about increased coverage, retention and improvement in quality. It is demonstrated by many researches that a solid foundation in mathematics and language is necessary for primary school children to navigate the information in technological age.

Students with strong grasp in mathematics have an advantage in academics as well as in the job markets. In the recent years, a number of new approaches have been developed to assess the achievement levels. In India, some of these methods have yet to be tried to establish their applicability.

In the simplest of the terms, it may be mentioned that assessment should be viewed as a tool for improving educational standards, provide information to educators to determine which practice has resulted in desired outcomes and to what extent.

The study has raised many issues that have serious implication for quality improvement in primary education. Some of these issues are discussed below.

a. There is a clear evidence to suggest that achievement levels tend to decline as the children move along the educational hierarchy. This is true of both the English and mathematics test. This shows that schools are not able to cope with the teaching learning load as the pupils' progress through various grades.
b. The temporal comparison of learners' performance has shown some gains in the first few years of DPEP. While this welcome outcome and confirms the broader direction of reforms, it also raised many questions about the negative/decline in achievement level in certain other districts. While the contextuality of the district is an important parameter of planning, the implementation processes should also be reviewed to isolate the factors, which have facilitated/impeded the trends in learning outcome.
c. The students from privately managed schools perform better as compared to the students from government and aided schools, although the evidence is limited. It is also

clear that despite better performance, even the private schools are far away from achieving the goals set up by the MLLs.

d. There are no mechanisms for assessing the achievement levels for children studying through non-formal and alternative schools. Since these systems are more of informal and flexible, it is important to establish their credentials through effective monitoring and evaluation.

e. The overall scores of class V learners based on class IV competencies are low for both mathematics and language. The low achievement in mathematics is indeed a matter of concern.

   The long term effect of low achievement in mathematics is revealed by the secondary and senior secondary examination results where most of the children fail in mathematics and the overall result stays around 50 percent. It is therefore important to evaluate the mathematics curriculum and related instructional materials.

f. The teachers are at the centre stage of the educational system. There is no system to identify teacher training needs. The teacher training packages do consult the teachers but once finalised, their content is same for all the teachers. Is it possible to identify the level of competencies attained by teachers in language and mathematics so that a proper module on their capacity building is developed?

g. Upgrade curriculum periodically, integrate technology and high quality instructional materials and to help students in learning the applications of mathematics in real life. Teachers should be encouraged to develop and use locally relevant instructional materials.

h. Underachievement, even if it defined at 40 percent level, is very high in classes III and IV. The extent of underachievement among class V learners was 66 percent in language and 72 percent in mathematics. Those achieving mastery level competencies constituted a small fraction of the total students. The prescribed norms are that 80 percent children should be able to learn 80 percent competencies. Thus, there are miles to go before the target of MLLs can be achieved.

i. The class II tests were oral in nature and class III/IV was written. The sudden drop in the level of mean achievement scores also points to another phenomenon i.e. the transition from oral to written mode of examination. Are the students well prepared for this transition? Perhaps at no point of time, the students are taught about this transition. This aspects need to be examined by the pedagogists.

j. A national testing agency or a research cell in the national/state institutions should be established to undertake continuous and comprehensive analysis of learners' achievement at primary and upper primary stage. The cell should assists the state governments to meet the challenging mathematics standards at primary stage, work closely with teachers unions and other NGOs for upgrading the skills of teachers on continuous basis. Educational administrators needs assessment information that will help them remove barriers to learning by telling schools to decide on what works well and what does not. Enable teachers to identify students learning needs early, before the problem becomes too big. The school administrators should also ensure that that the dialogue between the schools and children is better informed; giving parents a better picture of the progress of their children and the effectiveness of the schools.

k. In the Indian context, there is no mechanism for the training of head teachers of primary and upper primary schools in school leadership. In most countries, such training is a part of the capacity building exercise. Review of the professional development strategies for the teachers and head teachers stressing both subject matter expertise and pedagogical mastery is thus necessary.

l. As more and more data becomes on students achievement, it needs to be organised systematically so that the researchers and can have access to these database for testing of various types of alternative hypotheses. In conclusion, it is pertinent to note that the assessment studies undertaken in the recent years have brought to focus many issues which require immediate attention. These efforts will go a long way in developing local specific strategies and help the system to develop an integrated model of UEE, where the focus is not only on removing supply side constrains by providing more teachers, facilities, instructional materials etc., but also in identifying the critical inputs that optimise the learning outcomes in a given situation.

6

Non-Government Organizations and their Role

Importance of education cannot be overemphasized in the present day context as it is the single most important means for individuals to improve personal endowments, build capability levels, overcome constraints and, in the process, enlarge their available set of opportunities and choices for a sustained improvement in well-being. Education is now widely valued not only for its intrinsic value in enriching the lives of individuals but also for its functional value in the development of the human capital of a nation. Educational investments in children have shown to have high private and social returns. The private returns are associated with increased productivity and earnings in adulthood, and with further non-pecuniary gains arising from the greater efficiency with which educated individuals are able to acquire and process information. One of the Millennium Development Goals (MDGs) agreed in September 2000 at a UN summit of world leaders is the achievement of universal primary school attendance for boys and girls.

This, of course, requires a 100% primary school completion rate, that is, that all students entering grade 1 are retained until grade 5. It also implies a complete closing of the gender gap in educational attainments. The MDG couched in these terms reflects recognition of the importance of basic (primary/elementary) education. This is particularly pertinent in India where primary education has historically been neglected by the state, with educational expenditures being concentrated on the tertiary sector. Though, the situation has started to change lately as major chunk of educational budget is now directed towards elementary education. As a result of the historical neglect, there are vast inequalities in educational attainment in India, a remarkable degree of illiteracy coexisting with frontier research in science and technology. India is also marked for being one of the groups of countries in South Asia and Northern Africa where outcomes tend systematically to be better for boys than for girls, suggesting gender discrimination or at least undesirable gender differentiation. A further reason that India offers an interesting case study is that it exhibits striking diversity in educational indicators across its states.

INDICATORS OF EDUCATIONAL ATTAINMENT

Literacy is a person's first step in learning and knowledge building and, therefore, literacy indicators are essential for any measurement of human development. There can be many indicators such as literacy rate for population as a whole or a part of the population, including, those for adults, females, the deprived and the backward. Other indicators like enrolment, attendance and dropout rates of the school going children or the girl child; or the proportion of population having higher and technical qualification, etc. could also be used to capture the level of educational attainment in a society. Each of these indicators, however, focuses on a particular aspect of the education and, to that extent, captures only a limited dimension of educational attainment. For instance, adult literacy rate (that has frequently been used as an indicator to reflect educational development in human development indices) may measure only a superficial capacity to read and write one's name or a simple sentence and, hence, may not be a good indicator for capturing educational attainment of a society, particularly when it is a result of mass adult literacy program and not an outcome of a formal education system.

For a developing country like India, where literacy levels are comparatively low, where there are critical gaps in educational attainments across regions, population segments and, more importantly, there are significant returns to education – economic, social and political – to be reaped – investing in education is therefore probably the best social investment.

EDUCATION SYSTEM

The Constitution of India is the ultimate document which guides State policy in all sectors, including Education. Some of the important constitutional provisions pertaining to education are as follows:

- Provision of free and compulsory education to all children up to the age of fourteen years.
- Education, in general, is the concurrent responsibility of the Union and the States.
- Local authorities (*Panchayati Raj* Institutions, Municipalities, etc.) are to be assigned a suitable role in education (especially School, Adult and Non-Formal Education) through individual State legislations.
- State Governments and Local Authorities are expected to provide facilities for instruction in the mother tongue at the primary stage of education.

Before 1976, education was the exclusive responsibility of the States. The Constitutional Amendment of 1976, which included education in the Concurrent List, was a far-reaching step. The substantive, financial and administrative implication required a new sharing of responsibility between the Union Government and the States. While the role and responsibility of the States in education remained largely unchanged, the Union Government accepted a larger responsibility of reinforcing the national and integrated character of education, maintaining quality and standards including those of the teaching profession at all levels, and the study and monitoring of the educational requirements of the country. The Central Government continues to play a leading role in the evolution and monitoring of educational policies and programs, the most notable of which are the National Policy on Education (NPE), 1986 and the Program of Action (POA), 1986 as updated in 1992.

The policy envisages a National System of Education to bring about uniformity in education, making adult education programs a mass movement, providing universal access, retention and quality in elementary education, special emphasis on education of girls, vocational orientation of secondary education, starting more Open Universities in the States and adoption of an effective evaluation method, etc. Besides, a decentralised management structure had also been suggested to ensure popular participation in education. The POA lays down a detailed strategy for the implementation of the various policy parameters by the implementing agencies. The National System of Education as envisaged in the NPE is based on a national curricular framework, which envisages a common core along with other flexible and region-specific components. While the policy stresses widening of opportunities for the people, it calls for consolidation of the existing system of higher and technical education. It also emphasises the need for a much higher level of investment in education of at least 6% of the national income, which is currently hovering at less than 4%.

The NPE talks about the reconstitution of Central Advisory Board of Education (CABE), which was first formed in 1920. It is the highest advisory body to advise the Central and State Governments in the field of education. The NPE also envisages that the CABE will play a pivotal role in reviewing educational development, determining the changes required to improve the system and monitoring implementation, and will function through appropriate mechanisms created to ensure contact with, and coordination among, the various areas of human resource development. Accordingly, the CABE has been constituted by the Government in July 2004. The Board consists of nominated members representing various interests in addition to elected members from the Lok Sabha and the Rajya Sabha, and the representatives of the Government of India, State Governments and UT Administrations.

ORGANIZATION OF THE MINISTRY OF HUMAN RESOURCE DEVELOPMENT (MHRD)

All levels of education, from primary to higher education, are overseen by the MHRD, and heavily subsidized by the Indian government, though there is a move to make higher education partially self financing. The MHRD is headed by the union Cabinet Minister, who is currently assisted by two Ministers of State. At the executive level, the Ministry has two departments:

- Department of School Education and Literacy
- Department of Higher Education

All aspects of education pertaining to elementary, secondary, adult education and literacy are overseen by the Department of School Education and Literacy. Department of Higher Education primarily looks after university, technical and higher education. At present, work of the Department is divided into six bureaus as follows:

- University and Higher Education, Minorities Education, Book Promotion and Copyrights
- Technical Education
- Distance Education and Scholarships
- Planning
- International Cooperation, Administration, Coordination, Policy, Statistics, and Languages
- Integrated Finance Division

The Indian educational system is divided into preprimary (or nursery), primary, secondary (or high school), and higher levels. Preprimary is usually composed of Lower Kindergarten and Higher Kindergarten, where primary reading and writing skills are developed. Primary school includes children of ages six to eleven, organized into classes one through five.

Secondary school pupils aged eleven through fifteen are organized into classes six through ten, and higher secondary school students ages sixteen through seventeen are enrolled in classes eleven through twelve.

STRUCTURE OF INDIAN EDUCATION SYSTEM

In some States, there is a concept called Middle schools (upper primary) for classes between six to eight. In such cases, classes nine to twelve are classified under high school category. Higher Education in India provides an opportunity to specialize in a field and includes technical schools (such as the Indian Institutes of Technology), colleges, and universities. In India, the main types of secondary and higher secondary schools are those controlled by:

- The Central Board of Secondary Education (CBSE) board.
- The Council for the Indian School Certificate Examinations (CISCE) board.
- The state government boards.
- National Open School.

MAIN PLAYERS IN THE HIGHER EDUCATION

Central Government is responsible for major policy relating to higher education in the country. It provides grants to the University Grants Commission (UGC), which is responsible for coordination, determination and maintenance of standards as well as release of grants to the universities and institutions of higher education.

The Central Government is also responsible for declaration of Educational Institutions as 'Deemed to be University' on the recommendation of the UGC. Professional Councils are responsible for recognition of courses, promotion of professional institutions and providing grants to undergraduate programs and various awards.

The statutory professional councils are:

- All India Council for Technical Education (AICTE)
- Distance Education Council (DEC)

- Indian Council for Agriculture Research (ICAR)
- Bar Council of India (B.C.I)
- National Council for Teacher Education (NCTE)
- Rehabilitation Council of India (RCI)
- Medical Council of India (MCI)
- Pharmacy Council of India (PCI)
- Indian Nursing Council (INC)
- Dentist Council of India (DCI)
- Central Council of Homeopathy (CCH)
- Central Council of Indian Medicine (CCIM)

STATUS OF EDUCATION

India's educational development is a mixed bag of remarkable successes and glaring gaps. In the post independence period, the pace of educational development was unprecedented by any standards. At the same time, perhaps, the policy focus and public intervention in the provisioning of educational services was not adequately focused or, even misplaced, to the extent that even after over five decades of planned effort in the sector, nearly one-third of the population or close to 300 million persons in age-group 7 years and above are illiterate.

There are critical gaps in the availability of infrastructural facilities and qualitative aspects of education including, teachers training, educational curricula, equipments and training materials, particularly, in the publicly funded schooling system of the country. The attainments, as also the failures have not been uniform across all regions. Though, the regional differences are indeed striking, there has been a significant reduction in inequalities in educational attainments across gender and population segments by income levels and the rural-urban divide.

LITERACY RATE

The Census of India defines the literacy rate as proportion of literates to total population in age group 7 years and above.

It was merely 18.3% (for the age group 5 years and above) in 1951, 43.6% in 1981 and is 65.3% as per the Census 2001 In the decade 1991-2001 the number of illiterates declined, for the first time since the Census of 1951, by almost 23 million in absolute terms, from 329 million in 1991 to 306 million in 2001. There are, however, large inter-State variations in literacy rates in the country. At one end, proportion of literates was the highest in Kerala, at over 90%, and at the other it was less than 50% in Bihar for the year 2001.

REGIONAL AND GENDER DISPARITIES

The regional variations in literacy rates have declined since 1991, though the disparities become more pronounced if one takes into account rural-urban differences or the differences between male and female literacy rates. The literacy rate in rural areas increased from about 36% in 1981 to 59% in 2001. The corresponding rates in urban areas were about 67% and 80%, respectively. Thus, rural-urban gap has declined from about 31 to 21 percentage points Literacy rate for males increased from about 56% in 1981 to nearly 76% in 2001. The corresponding change in female literacy rate has been from around 30% to 54%. Overall, the decline in gender gap, which peaked in 1981 at 26.6 percentage points, and was 21.7 percentage points in 2001, is less impressive than the decline in rural-urban gap. For rural areas, gender gap declined from 28 to 24 percentage points, whereas in case of urban areas the decline was from 20 percentage points 13 percentage points.

The inter-State variations in literacy rate for males were much lower in comparison to females. Of the larger States, while Kerala is among the best performers in terms of literacy rate – both for males and females – Bihar continues to be at the bottom. The State of Mizoram which had reported the lowest gap in male female literacy during 1991 with 7.01 percentage points has further narrowed it down to 4.56 in 2001, to lead all the States/ UTs in the country. Mizoram is followed by Meghalaya with a gap of 5.73 percentage points and Kerala with 6.34 percentage points. The highest improvement in male literacy rate during 1991-2001 has been observed in Rajasthan with an improvement 21.47 percentage points. It is followed by Chhattisgarh, Dadra & Nagar Haveli, Andhra Pradesh and Uttar Pradesh, which show an improvement of 19.79, 19.76, 15.72 and 15.41 percentage points respectively.

Kerala has the minimum increase of 0.58 percentage points, as it has already reached a saturation level. In female literacy rates, the highest decadal improvement has been made by Chhattisgarh recording an increase of 24.88 percentage points followed by Rajasthan with 23.90 percentage points. Kerala has similarly shown the least increase of 1.69 percentage points in the female literacy rate. Notwithstanding the disparities in attainments on literacy across States, regions and population segments, there is a definite transition taking place in respect of literacy rates across States in India. For instance, in 1991, there were number of States with literacy rate less than 50%, but in 2001, it is only in case of Bihar that literacy rate is less than 50%.

ENROLMENT IN SCHOOLS

The enrolment of children in schools depicts the current flow or the spread of education. Among the more commonly used measures, gross enrolment ratio, age-specific enrolment ratio, net enrolment ratio, dropout rates and school attendance rates, are relevant for capturing the flow aspect of the educational attainment of the population.

Gross Enrolment Ratio (GER) refers to enrolment at a specified level of schooling, irrespective of the age of student enrolled, to the population of children in the age group expected to be at that level of schooling. This ratio is indicative of the general level of participation at a given school level. It captures, to some extent, accessibility and capacity of the education system to enroll students. According to the Planning Commission, GER at primary and upper primary levels improved significantly between 1950-51 and 1999-2000 from 42.6% to 94.9% for primary and from 12.7% to 58.8% for upper primary (classes VI-VIII) during the period. The boys-girls differential in GER at the primary and upper primary levels declined significantly from 28.5 and 29.6 percentage points in 1990-91 to 22 and 18 percentage points in 1999-2000.

The Net Enrolment Ratios (NER), which are obtained by disregarding underage and overage children enrolled in grades I-V and VI-VIII, were significantly lower than GER in case of both boys and girls. The NER for boys and girls was 78% and 64% respectively at primary level in 1997-98. The overall NER at primary level was 71%, which suggests that at least 29%of children of the specific 6-10 age group continued to remain out of school in 1997-98.

Dropout Rate is the percentage of students dropping out of a class/classes in a given year. Though a substantial number of children get enrolled, dropout rate is very high and many leave before completing secondary education. Poverty is the prime reason for high dropout rate as whatever resources poor families have; it is used for their mere subsistence. Moreover, many poor children can attend school only when they are not working for a livelihood. According to Annual Report 2006-07 of MHRD, the dropout rate at the primary level, though declined from 39% in 2001-02, was still very high at 28.49% in 2004-05. A National Sample Survey Organization (NSSO) survey for the year 1995-96 showed that drop out rate increases cumulatively with level of education.

Among reasons for dropping out from schools, it was found that one-third of the drop outs were because either the children or their parents were not interested and nearly as many were on account of economic considerations, such as the compulsion to work for wages or looking after younger siblings. About 26% cited, school and teaching curricula related factors such as unfriendly atmosphere in schools, doubts about the usefulness of schooling and inability to cope with studies as reasons for their dropping out. Among girls in rural areas, these factors accounted for over 75% of the dropouts. With such a magnitude of drop out rates and, often, poor attendance rates in some schools as well, the use of school enrolment rates as indicators to capture the flow or spread of education in the country may not be accurate in capturing the current educational attainment of people. A child may be reported as enrolled in a certain class, but he/she may not attend school on a regular basis and in some cases when attending may be dropping out before the end of the year. It is only when the enrolled students are retained over successive classes that the indicator on enrolment becomes useful from the point of capturing the current educational progress of a society.

Non-government Initiatives and Public-Private Partnership (PPP) Non-government Initiatives and PPP in a vast and populous country like India, the government alone cannot provide education for all. Thus, private initiatives and community based programs become imperative for achieving the goal of Universal Elementary Education (UEE). Non-government organizations (NGOs), mostly non-profit agencies, are implementing non-formal education programs to meet the educational needs of out-of-school children. Many of them focus on socially and economically backward areas and marginalized sections of the society and on education of girls. A large number of voluntary agencies are providing education, health and nutrition to children in urban slums and for working children. For running their programs, non-profit organizations and communities mostly seek donations and sponsorships from individuals, corporate bodies and international organizations such as UNICEF, World Bank etc. The non-profit organizations are also coming in a big way to collaborate with the Government in implementing various educational programs.

NGOs associated with the various education projects of the Government such as DPEP, SSA and NLM have been instrumental in mobilizing community resources for basic education. The Government of India has been extending the requisite grants-in-aid for its Centrally Sponsored Schemes, which are routed through the State Governments. The public-private-partnership brings in greater professionalism to bear on this association through introducing meaningful concepts. There is, nevertheless, scope of further expanding its coverage and also involve the private corporate sector in this endeavor. SSA, which is the flagship educational initiative of the Government of India, emphasizes decentralization and community ownership of schools. The community based approach is adopted for planning at habitation level and monitoring of school activities.

Participation of the community is sought effectively through a series of school-based activities that open up the school as a social institution to the community. Funds for the program flow through local community based bodies for all school related expenditures, which constitutes more than 50% funds for SSA. SSA also encourages computer aided learning (CAL) methodology in Elementary Schools. Under this program Public-Private Partnership is encouraged. The main objective of this initiative is to make schools attractive for children at elementary level in the age group of 6-14 years by introducing interesting and joyful learning through contents with multimedia effect. This is basically to reduce dropout and increase retention rates. Private and public computer firms are selected by the State Government through competitive bidding or negotiation.

Tamil Nadu has undertaken this program for Upper Primary level. It has been introduced in Class VI and would gradually be extended to Classes VII and VIII in subsequent years. Over 200 firms have been engaged on a lease arrangement, which includes supply of hardware, software, training, operations and maintenance. Each firm has been allocated an area of operation, allocating a number of schools. 40 hours of learning per child on computers is provided for, which includes computer literacy skills, subject based learning and student evaluation. In Karnataka, CAL is being implemented in collaboration with Azim Premji Foundation (APF) in 135 five schools. APF has developed e-learning material (education software) on CDs in different languages including English, Kannada, Hindi and Telugu. The foundation is using solar panels for running of computers in areas without electricity. Infrastructure and computer hardware have been made available by the Government through SSA funds.

The States of Andhra Pradesh, Rajasthan, Orissa, Uttar Pradesh, Bihar, Nagaland and Assam have adopted a BOOT (Build on Operative and Transfer) model for the CAL project. Private firms have been given the responsibility to install hardware/software and provide approved e-learning material and teachers training for a fixed period, mutually agreed upon. The E&Y Foundation has offered to voluntary support the pilot phase of Delhi's efforts to introduce a complete set of animated learning and study material called CALtoonZ. This has helped for innovative learning and teaching practices in the schools of Delhi. During 2006-07, more than 27,000 primary/upper primary schools covering 5.8 million children have benefited under CAL component of SSA.

NON GOVERNMENT INITIATIVES

A classic example of successful and prolific non government educational initiative is Pratham, which was started in 1994 in the slums of Mumbai. The organization works toward universalization of primary education. Pratham network has spread to 14 states in India since its inception. It served 2,400 children in 1994 where as it served 3 million children in 2004. The organization was fostered by UNICEF for the first three years and is now parented by ICICI Bank. Pratham is based on a triangular partnership between the government, the corporate sector and the citizens. Its extensive network in the slum area enables Pratham to layer other activities, such as health and computer education, at a minimum additional cost of delivery. Some of the innovative educational programs run by pratham are: *Balwadi Pre-School Program* targets pre-school children in the age group of 3-5 years from low-income families to provide them early childhood education. Such schools are located either at a municipal school, community space, place of worship, or a teacher's home.

Each class has around 18 children with instructor from the local community and runs for 2-3 hours a day. *Bridge Course Program* targets children in the age group of 6-12 years who have never attended school or have dropped out, and prepares them to enter or re-enter the formal school system. Classes generally start in the community and move to the local municipal school building if space is available and comprise of around 15-20 children with a teacher from the local community. *Balsakhi Remedial Education Program* targets municipal school children from grade II-IV bordering on illiteracy with the aim to help these students achieve literacy and numeric skills. This program helps children who are identified by their class teachers as lagging behind academically. Balsakhis (child's friends) are sent to schools on request to help such children and work under the guidance of school teachers.

A Balsakhi works with 20-30 children. *Akhar Setu Program* mainstreams children who are working to support their parents economically and are, therefore, unable to attend school. Children are formally registered in a nearby government schools and regular classes are held in the community itself by Balsakhis. Children are allowed to participate in all extra curricular activities of the school and the headmaster of the school is required to visit this class randomly and verify attendance once a month. International Collaboration International Collaboration In a nation as sprawling and diverse as India, offering even a few years of education to all boys and girls is a daunting prospect, but one that the government is confronting with the aid of the international community. International organizations like the World Bank, European Commission and specialized agencies of the United Nations (UNICEF, UNESCO, etc.) have been collaborating with the Government and the private sector as well for promotion of education in the country.

UNICEF

UNICEF is an active partner in SSA, the National Program for Universal Elementary Education, which aims to provide quality education for children between the ages of 6 and 14 years by 2010. UNICEF supports the national program in its objective to ensure that all children complete five years of school and have access to good quality education. UNICEF strategy is built around three inter-linked themes: access, quality and equity in basic education. This includes the implementation of a 'quality package' in 14,000 schools across 14 states. The package aims to improve the quality of teacher education, curricula, learning assessments and the classroom environment; it advocates gender-sensitive and child-centered processes along with interactive learning to make teaching and learning a motivating experience. UNICEF is also working to strengthen effectiveness of school-based interventions focusing on HIV/AIDS prevention.

In order to help eliminate gender and social disparities in primary education, UNICEF supports the provision of equal opportunities for disadvantaged children, especially girls, the urban poor, Scheduled Castes and Scheduled Tribes, and working children. UNICEF is working closely with the Government's recently launched National Program on Girls' Education at the Elementary Level (NPEGEL) to further accelerate progress in girls' education. UNICEF also supports alternative learning strategies, such as bridging courses and residential camps for adolescent girls who are out of school. The effort is to ensure that these girls emerge motivated to continue their education. In addition, as part of efforts to strengthen education planning and monitoring, UNICEF supports the District Information System for Education (DISE) to promote better collection, collation, and analysis of data, thereby improving educational statistics.

In Madhya Pradesh, UNICEF is the main UN agency which is partnering the state in improving quality of education under SSA. With UNICEF's support the state is implementing quality package in four districts - Guna, Shivpuri, Bhind and Jhabua. In 1999, in partnership with the government and other voluntary organisations, UNICEF initiated a project for girls' education in four blocks of Uttar Pradesh's Barabanki district, where female literacy was about 15 per cent. Alternative learning centres (ALCs) were established in villages that did not have a primary school within a one-kilometer radius with the active participation of communities. Instructors were selected in co-operation with *panchayats* and preference was given to local candidates. The number of ALCs increased from 50 in 1999 to 140 in 2001 when more than 4000 children were enrolled - a significant majority of which were out-of-school girls.

A one-year residential camp program for girls was also introduced to provide learning opportunities for older out-of-school girls. This is now being replicated under SSA across the state.

European Commission (EC)

The EC signed an agreement with the Government of India (GoI) in November 2001 to support the SSA. INR 9.6bn has been committed for seven years of implementation. The main objective of the EC grant is to reinforce India's own efforts to universalize elementary education. The EC grant to SSA is in the form of sectoral support, whereby the GoI will have the flexibility to deploy EC resources to implement its priorities.

EC funds are to be released against outcomes and progress towards the goals and objectives of SSA. Building on the good experience of the donor consortium that supported DPEP, efforts will be made to develop a similar approach for external financing for SSA, whereby major donors act in concert to support and jointly monitor a program to improve elementary education with the GoI.

World Bank

The District Primary Education Program (DPEP), launched in November 1994, was an ambitious attempt to provide a decisive thrust to universalize and transform the quality of primary education in India. While the World Bank has been the single largest contributor to this initiative, the program is also supported by many other donors, including the European Commission, UNICEF and the governments of the Netherlands and Sweden.

UNESCO

India is among the founding members of UNESCO, and the country has been playing an active role in promoting UNESCO's ideals and objectives. The Government of India had set up the Indian National Commission for Cooperation with UNESCO (INCCU) in 1949. The Commission consists of five Sub-Commissions in the fields of Education, Culture, Communication, Social Sciences and Natural Sciences. In India, UNESCO associates itself with various local and international NGOs in India to promote its education related objectives.

The INCCU operates a scheme of financial assistance to voluntary organizations, UNESCO Clubs and Associated Schools for undertaking activities in consonance with UNESCO objectives. UNESCO is running a project named Associated School Project (ASP net). Associated Schools are educational institutions, which are directly linked with UNESCO Secretariat for participation in the Associated Schools Project (ASP net) for undertaking activities relating to education for international understanding, cooperation and peace. On the recommendation of INCCU, 42 schools and Teacher Training Institutions from India have been enlisted with UNESCO under this project. There are 252 Clubs and 264 Associated Schools registered with INCCU.

With the concerted efforts of the Centre and State Governments, NGOs, local bodies and international organizations, the overall scenario of education sector in India has improved considerably over recent years.

While availability of elementary schools within a reasonable distance from habitations is now fairly universal, same cannot yet be said in regard to Secondary Schools and Colleges. Pockets still exist in many remote parts of the country where the nearest Secondary School or College is much too far for everyone to be able to attend. In spite of improvements in the enrolment ratios and dropout rates, participation rates at various levels of education are undoubtedly low, and need to be raised very substantially, for India to become a knowledge society. Participation rates in Education are poor largely because students from disadvantaged groups continue to find it difficult to pursue it. Even when they manage to participate, students suffering from disadvantages of gender, socio-economic status, physical disability, etc. tend to have access to education of considerably lower quality than the others, while the education system needs to provide them access to the best possible education so that they are able to catch up with the rest.

There is also the challenge of quality in Indian education, which has many dimensions:

- Providing adequate physical facilities and infrastructure,
- Making available adequate teachers of requisite quality,
- Effectiveness of teaching-learning processes,
- Attainment levels of students, etc.

Besides the need to improve quality of Indian educational institutions in general, it is also imperative that an increasing number of them attain world-class standards and are internationally recognized for their quality. There is a need to enhance the relevance of education in India by making it more skill-oriented – both in terms of life-skills as well as livelihood skills.

In sheer numerical terms, India has the manpower to substantially meet the needs of a world hungry for skilled workers, provided its education system can convert those numbers into a skilled work-force with the needed diversity of skills. The geographic vastness of India as well as huge diversity in socio-economic conditions across the country makes it difficult for the top tier of the Government to effectively administer all the programs and policies pertaining to education. Therefore, the management of Indian education needs to build in greater decentralization, accountability, and professionalism, so that it is able to deliver good quality education to all, and ensure optimal utilization of available resources.

EDUCATION AND ECONOMIC & HUMAN RESOURCE DEVELOPMENT

Education is a critical input in human resource development and is essential for the economic growth of the country. In an increasingly competitive international economic environment, investment in education becomes an indispensable instrument to help maintain India's comparative advantage.

Successful transitions from subsistence agriculture to modern agriculture, from basic industry to higher technology, from manufacturing to provision of services, all depend on the quality of human capital; and the quality of human capital depends to a large extent on investment in the social sectors, including education, health, and nutrition. The major indicators of socio-economic development viz., the growth-rate of the economy, birth rate, death rate, infant mortality rate (IMR) and literacy rate are interconnected but the literacy rate has been the major determinant of the rise or fall in the rate of other indicators.

The conclusion that literacy and education of women lead to a higher pace of population control and to greater economic productivity has awakened the world to the need to focus upon literacy and elementary education programmes not simply as a matter of social justice but more pertinently as a matter of economic growth, social well-being and social stability. There is enough evidence even in India to show that a high literacy rate, especially in the case of women, correlates with low birth-rate, low IMR and increase in the rate of life-expectancy. Investment in education especially in basic education, therefore, has a high rate of return – that is, the value of the benefits to the individual and to society exceeds the cost of the investment by a large margin. Experiences also clearly demonstrate that investment in basic education is a prerequisite for economic development, and that continuing investment in quality education at all levels together with development of appropriate skills for the workforce is a prerequisite for continuing economic growth, particularly in an era of rapid and revolutionary advances in Information and Communications Technology (ICT). Workforce skill development facilitates the shift to higher order technology, improves productivity, and helps to maintain economic competitiveness.

Higher education sharpens the cutting edge of development by fostering capacity for innovative research, strengthening higher-level management skills, and enhancing local research and development capacity. Continuing and adult education programmes allow individuals to pursue both professional and personal development over a lifetime. Our national leaders had recognized the significance of education, as an investment in socio-economic development, very early and they had, therefore, persistently struggled for universalisation of primary education as a part of the freedom movement. After independence, Article 45 of the Indian Constitution as well as several Committees and Commissions stressed education as the foundation of national reconstruction and up-gradation of the people's quality of life.

The National Policy on Education (NPE) (1992) has once again highlighted the importance of literacy and elementary education as an inescapable investment for human development. Provision of equality of opportunity through Universalisation of Elementary Education (UEE) as also the instrumentality of UEE for strengthening social cohesion and the democratic process, are now recognised as the most crucial aspects of educational action in all developing countries including India. Government of India has already made up its mind to make education a fundamental right of the citizens of the country and Parliament has recently unanimously passed the Legislative Bill to introduce requisite amendments in the Indian Constitution to translate the noble thinking into action and reality. It was the overall perspective of Education that guided the deliberations of the Steering Committee and the Working Group on Elementary and Adult Education constituted by the Planning Commission in the context of formulation of the Tenth Five Year Plan.

ELEMENTARY & ADULT EDUCATION

India's basic educational system today is in large part a consequence of its past. The literacy rate in India remained appallingly low at less than 10% among all adults as late as in 1931. The provision of free and compulsory education to all the children till they reached the age of 14 years was accepted as the responsibility of the State for the first time during early 1940s. The Post-war Plan of Education in India (1944) recommended the provision of free and compulsory education to all the children in the age group 6-14 years in a phased programme over a period of 40 years. However, national leadership was determined to telescope the process and a Committee under the chairmanship of B.G. Kher recommended that the goal should be achieved by 1960.

It was this recommendation that formed the basis of Article 45 of the Indian Constitution enjoining that the "State shall endeavour to provide within a period of 10 years from the commencement of the Constitution for free and compulsory education for all children until they complete the age of 14 years". The task of providing basic education for all, with concrete plans of action, however, gained greater momentum only after the National Policy of Education (NPE), which was announced in 1986 and revised in 1992. With the World Declaration on Education for All (EFA) adopted in Jomtein in 1990, basic education, in all its facets such as ECCE, elementary education, education for adolescents, adult education, gender equality and quality improvements, has been the focus of international attention. These international developments together with several positive developments within the country brought to the centre stage the need for recognizing basic education as a fundamental right of every citizen.

The Government of India in partnership with State Governments has made a number of attempts to fulfill the Constitutional obligation and national aspirations and has launched a variety of programmes towards this end. Though the significant improvements are observed in terms of various indicators, the ultimate goal of providing universal quality education for all but still remains to be achieved. An ever increasing population, financial and organizational constraints, socio-economic problems and finally the lack of political will appear to have been the main hurdles in achieving this goal. This Chapter presents a snapshot view of the present basic education scenario in the country.

GROWTH OF LITERACY

Over the decades, literacy rates have shown substantial improvement in India. The total literacy rate was only about 18 % in 1951, which rose to 52.21% in 1991. The provisional results of the census 2001 indicate that literacy rate has gone up to 65.38 %, 75.85 % for males and 54.16 % for females. For the first time, the number of illiterates has, in absolute terms, decreased by 31.9 million.

Number of literates on the other hand has increased by 203.6 million during the last decade. The female literacy rates during the last decade have increased by 14.87% as against 11.72% for males thus bridging the male-female literacy rates to 21.7 % as against the differential of 24.84% in 1991. It is significant to note that all States without exception have registered an increase in the literacy rates of both males and females.

ENROLMENT TRENDS

Considerable progress has been made in enrolment at primary and upper primary levels of education. Enrolment at primary level increased from 19.16 million in 1950-51 to 113.61 million in 1999-2000. Compared to primary level, the growth in enrolment at the upper primary level has been much more impressive and substantial although still not adequate to attain the goal of universal enrolment of children up to the age of 14 as enjoined by the Constitution of India. From a 3.12 million in 1950-51, enrolment at the upper primary level increased to 42.06 million in 1999-2000, indicating a 13.5 times increase as against six times at the primary level. The percentage share of girls to total enrolment, both at primary and upper primary levels, has increased considerably and consistently between 1950-51 (28.1 per cent) and 1999- 2000 (43.6 per cent). However, girls' share to total enrolment at the upper primary level (40.4 per cent) continues to be lower than their share at the primary level (43.6 per cent) in 1999- 2000.

ENROLMENT RATIOS

The Gross Enrolment Ratio (GER) at primary and upper primary levels improved significantly between 1950-51 and

1999-2000 i.e., GER has increased from 42.6 to 94.9 for primary and from 12.7 to 58.79 for upper primary during the period. The boys-girls differential in GER at the primary and upper primary levels has declined significantly from 28.5 and 29.6 percentage points in 1990-91 to 22 and 18 percentage points in 1999-2000. The Net Enrolment Ratios (NER), which are obtained by disregarding underage and overage children enrolled in grades I-V and VI-VIII, were significantly lower than GER in case of both boys and girls. The NER for boys and girls was 78 per cent and 64 per cent respectively at primary level in 1997-98. The overall NER at primary level was 71 per cent, which suggests that at least 29 per cent of children of the specific 6-10 age group continued to remain out of school in 1997-98. Educationally backward States, and within them backward districts, have lower NER than the all-India average of 71 per cent.

EDUCATIONAL FACILITIES

Availability of schooling facilities is measured by a set of indicators concerning access. As per norms, a habitation (cluster of households) is entitled to have a primary school, if it has a total population of 300 and more, and has no school within a distance of one kilometer. For upper primary schools, the corresponding norm is total population of 500 and more, and a distance of three kilometers. These norms are often relaxed in case of hilly and tribal areas, difficult terrains and border districts. During the period 1950-51 to 1999-2000, the number of primary schools has increased by more than 3 times from 2.10 lakhs in 1950-51 to 6.42 lakhs in 1999-2000 whereas the number of upper primary schools increased 15 times from 1, 36,000 in 1950-51 to 1, 98,000 in 1999-2000. In 1950-51, the ratio of upper primary school to primary schools was 1:15, which has come down to 1:3.2 in 1999-2000.

The total number of teachers increased from 6.24 lakh in 1950-51 to 32.17 lakh in 1999-2000, i.e., registering an increase of more than five times, while the number of female teachers increased from 0.95 lakh in 1950-51 to 11.52 lakh in 1999-2000, an increase of twelve times. The percentage of female teachers to total teachers which was 15.2% at primary level and 15.1% at upper primary level has increased to 35.6 and 36.1% respectively. However, the teacher-pupil ratio (TPR) has worsened over the years. During 1950-51, the TPR in primary schools was 1:24, and in middle schools it was 1:20. In 1999-2000, this ratio has increased to 1:43 in primary schools and 1:38 in upper primary schools. Despite increase in the number of habitations and population, both the percentage of habitations and rural population served by primary and upper primary schools/ sections within a distance of 1 and 3 kms. has increased significantly. Of the 10,61,000 rural habitations in the country, 52,800 (about 50 per cent) had a primary school/section each within the habitation itself in 1993-94.

About 83.4 per cent habitations had a primary school/ section within or at a walking distance of 1 kilometer. Presently, about 1, 00,000 habitations continue to remain unserved as per prescribed norms.

The alternative and innovative programme envisages opening of non-formal education centers in habitations where opening of a full-fledged school is not economically feasible or academically viable. Over a period of time, infrastructure and other facilities in schools have also improved significantly although a large number of primary and upper primary schools continue to suffer from deficiencies making it difficult for schools to function smoothly and preventing them from providing optimal conditions for teaching and learning.

The Ninth Five Year Plan regarded education as the most crucial investment in human development. Prime Minister's Special Action Plan gave emphasis to total eradication of illiteracy, equal access to and opportunity of education up to the school leaving stage, improvement in the quality of education at all levels from primary schools to universities, and the need for expansion and improvement of infrastructure facilities for education.

The thrust areas for educational development in the Ninth Plan included UEE, achievement of full adult literacy, raising the quality of education at all levels, improving learner achievement, upliftment of the educational status of disadvantaged groups including SC/ST, girls and disabled children, removal of regional disparities, vocationalisation of education, renewal of curriculum to meet emerging challenges in information technology and support for development of centers of excellence at the tertiary level. Elementary education was given the highest priority in sub-sectoral allocations within the education sector, indicating a strong reiteration of the country's resolve to achieve the goal of Education for All (EFA) during the plan period.

The goal was sought to be achieved through several measures, which included the following:

- Amendment of the Constitution to make elementary education a fundamental right;
- Decentralisation of planning, supervision and management of education through local bodies at district, block and village levels; Social mobilisation of local communities for adult literacy through campaigns and for promotion of primary education;
- Convergence of different schemes for UEE;
- Stronger partnership with NGOs and voluntary organisations;
- Advocacy and media campaign for UEE; and
- Provision of opportunities for non-formal and alternative education for out-of-school children in the most backward areas and for un-reached segments of the population in response to local needs and demands articulated at the grass-root level; and
- Universal participation and retention rather than universal enrolment.

The goal of UEE was enlarged to include provision of education of a satisfactory quality to all children.

INTERVENTION STRATEGIES

The intervention in the programmes of elementary education aim at providing schooling facilities within a walking distance of one km. for children of primary school ages and three kms.

for children of upper primary school and strengthening of the alternative mode of education, viz. non-formal education for school dropouts, working children and girls. This package has to be combined with the qualitative aspect of minimum levels of learning at primary and upper primary stages so as to achieve universal elementary education.

PROGRAMME OF MINIMUM LEVELS OF LEARNING (MLL)

The Programme of Minimum Levels of Learning (MLL) has been introduced in most States. The Programme aims at specifying competency levels which children are required to attain in language, mathematics and in environmental studies, in classes 1 to 5 and to reorient the teaching learning process to facilitate achievement of these.

Several States have successfully used the idea of MLL to launch a number of activities including revision of text books, change in curricula and teaching methodologies, as well as in the content of teachers training.

OPERATION BLACKBOARD

The Scheme of Operation Blackboard which aimed at improving class room environment by providing infrastructural facilities, additional teachers and teaching learning material to primary schools and by provision of a third teacher to such schools where the enrolment figure exceeded 100 has been extended to upper primary schools. 5.23 lakh primary schools and 1.27 lakh upper primary schools have been provided funds for development of academic infrastructure (teaching learning material). About 1.50 lakh posts of additional teachers for single teacher primary schools, 0.75 lakh posts of additional teachers at the upper primary stage and 0.83 lakh posts of third teachers have been sanctioned so far.

It is a matter of concern, however, that several States are reluctant to create the additional posts of teachers sanctioned under OBB due to the condition that recurring liabilities on account of salary of teachers would stand transferred to the States at the end of the year.

RESTRUCTURING AND REORGANIZATION OF TEACHER EDUCATION

The scheme of Restructuring and Reorganization of Teacher Education envisaged strengthening of the institutional base of teacher training and for taking up special programmes for training of teachers in specified areas and other non-institutional programmes for teacher training. The scheme also envisages setting up District Institutes of Education and Training (DIETs) in each district to provide academic and resource support to elementary education teachers and non-formal and adult education instructors; establishment of Colleges of Teacher Education (CTEs) and Institutes of Advanced Studies in Education (IASEs), to organize preservice and in-service training for secondary teachers; strengthening State Council of Educational Research and Training (SCERT) in States; orienting teachers in use of Operation Blackboard material; and implementation of Minimum Learning Level (MLL) strategy. Under this scheme 461 DIETs, 85 CTEs, 37 IASEs have been sanctioned so far.

More than 14.23 lakh teachers have been given training under the Special Orientation Programme of Primary Teacher (SOPT) in the use of OB material and implementation of MLL strategy. The scheme has recently been revamped with greater thrust on improving quality of teacher training institutions in partnership with States. The revised scheme provides for more assistance to States; MOU with States to improve efficiency of key resource institutes; widening the scope of Special Orientation Programme for school teachers; and enhancing capacities of existing personnel for management of teacher education programmes.

DISTRICT PRIMARY EDUCATION PROGRAMME (DPEP)

The District Primary Education Programme (DPEP) which is assisted by the World Bank and European Union aims at operationalising the strategies for achieving UPE/UEE through district specific planning and disaggregated target setting in low female literacy districts and builds on successful TLC campaigns which have created a favourable climate for universalisation. The project is funded 85% by external agencies through the Central budget and the remaining 15% by the concerned State Governments.

The programme components include construction of class rooms and new schools, opening of the non-formal/ alternative schooling centres, appointment of new teachers, setting up of early childhood education centres, strengthening of State Councils of Educational Research and Training/ District institutes of Educational Training, setting up of block resource centres/ cluster resource centres, teacher training, interventions, development of teaching-learning material, research and a thrust for education of girls, SC/ST etc.

A new initiative of providing integrated education to disabled children and distance education for teacher training has also been incorporated in the DPEP scheme. DPEP has opened 10,000 new formal schools and over 56,000 alternative schools covering 20 lakh children besides conducting 20,000 bridge courses. It has set up over 10,000 ECE centres and strengthened more than 50,000 pre-primary centres of Anganwadis. DPEP has provided training to over 3 million community members and about 1 million teachers. About 26,300 school buildings, 34, 200 class rooms and 11,100 resource centres have been completed or are in progress in DPEP districts. The programme now covers about 50 per cent of the children in primary stage in the country spread over 271 districts in 18 States.

SHIKSHA KARMI PROJECT AND LOK JUMBISH PROJECT IN RAJASTHAN

Two of the externally aided projects for basic education are the Rajasthan Shiksha Karmi Project (SKP) and Lok Jumbish Project (LJP) in Rajasthan which are also innovative projects aimed at universalisation of elementary education together with qualitative improvement in remote and socially backward villages with a primary focus on gender. The projects respond to some of the major obstacles in achieving UEE, namely, teacher absenteeism, high rate of dropouts, working children, uninteresting teaching methods, lack of contextual learning materials, low motivation and competence of teachers, a centralized and inflexible approach etc.

There is a special emphasis on community participation in these projects. Non Government Organizations (NGOs) and the community play a pivotal role in the implementation of the SKP. The Village Education Committee (VECs) have contributed a lot to the improvement of school environment, augmentation of infrastructure and facilities, larger enrolment of children through school mapping and micro-planning in the Shiksha Karmi Schools. There has been a seven-fold increase in the enrolment of children in the schools taken over by the project. SKP covers 2708 villages in 147 blocks spread over 31 districts. The Lok Jumbish Project (LJP) has been able to set up innovative management structures incorporating the principles of decentralization and delegation of authority as well as building partnerships with local communities and the voluntary sector.

LJP has also made a positive contribution to quality improvement through the development of improved MLL based textbooks from Classes I-IV, which are also being used in all schools in Rajasthan. LJP has conducted school mapping in 8921 villages, opened 2560 Sahaj Shiksha Centres covering 47,000 children and started 529 new primary schools and 268 upper primary schools.

The programme has also strengthened 239 pre-school centres of Anganwadis and formed over 7600 Mahila Groups.

MAHILA SAMAKHYA

Another externally assisted programme with a specific focus on gender is Mahila Samakhya, started in 1989 in 5 States, aims to promote women's education through empowerment. The Mahila Samakhya (MS) programme for women's education and empowerment of women in rural areas, particularly women in socially and economically marginalized groups, endeavours to create a learning environment where women can collectively affirm their potential, gain and strength to demand information and knowledge, and move forward to change and take charge of their lives.

MS has reached the poor and marginal women who have been able to overcome social barriers and are addressing social issues such as child marriage, child labour, and violence against women. A pool of aware women has been created through the Mahila Shikshan Kendras and there is an ever-increasing demand for literacy and the education for their daughters and grand daughters. This has had social implications in terms of delaying marriage of girls. The programme is currently implemented in over 9000 villages in 53 districts spread over 10 States.

MID-DAY MEAL SCHEME (MDM)

The National Programme of Nutritional Support to Primary Education commonly known as Mid-day Meal Scheme was launched in 1995. It aims to give a boost to universalisation of primary education by increasing enrolment, retention and attendance and simultaneously impacting upon nutritional status of students in primary classes. The scheme envisages serving cooked meals with calorie value equivalent to 100 gms. of wheat or rice per student per school day. The number of children covered under the programme has risen from 3.34 crore in about 3.22 lakh schools in 1995-96 to 10.51 crore in about 7.92 lakh schools spread over 576 districts in the country in 2000-2001. It is targeted to cover 10.72 crore children in 578 districts during 2001-02. Over 15 lakh tonnes of food-grains were lifted during 2000-01 compared to 14 lakh tonnes in the previous year.

Currently, only 6 States, namely Gujarat, Kerala, Orissa, Tamil Nadu, 174 tribal blocks in Chhattisgarh and Madhya Pradesh and U.T. of Pondicherry are providing hot cooked meals under the programme. In Delhi, ready-to-eat food is being distributed. The remaining States/ UTs are distributing food-grains (wheat/rice).

The initial impact of the scheme on enrolment and participation of children, especially on girls' enrolment has been favourable. Evaluation studies conducted in four States, i.e., Orissa, Tamil Nadu, Himachal Pradesh and Uttar Pradesh by the Planning Commission reveal that average attendance rate has increased and dropout rate has decreased in the post mid-day meal period compared to the pre-mid-day meal period. These studies have suggested that:

a. The teachers should be involved in the supervision and monitoring of mid-day meal programme, and
b. Basic infrastructure facilities like spacious kitchens are required in all the schools.

Another evaluation conducted by Operation Research Group in 10 States shows that in Assam, Madhya Pradesh, Uttar Pradesh and West Bengal, the programme has given a boost to the enrolment while in other States; it has made a positive impact on attendance and retention. Despite the fact that the scheme, as pointed out by the Evaluation Studies, has boosted the enrolment as well as retention of students, it has not been successful in achieving its ambitious targets for nationwide coverage. Some of the weaknesses of the programme are highlighted as below:

- Non-implementation of a cooked meal programme has impaired the objectives set in the Scheme.
- Enrolment data provided by the States each year and on the basis of which food-grains are allocated for 10 academic months is not available. This is evident in the fact that there is a mismatch between allocation and liftment of food-grains.
- Inability of States to arrange the delivery of food-grains in time has also eroded the utility of the scheme. In this context, the non-availability of funds with the implementing agencies to meet the initial expenditure on transportation charges to be reimbursed later from the Central Government has been stated to be a major hurdle in delivery of food grains in time, particularly in far flung

areas.

- Lack of awareness, advocacy etc., of the scheme has not been able to attract the community participation in its implementation.
- As the initial arrangement for MIS through National Informatics Centre (NIC) net did not start off, close monitoring and supervision of the programme was negligible, resulting in furnishing of erratic reports on utilization as well as beneficiaries covered under the scheme.

NON-FORMAL EDUCATION (NFE) AND EGS & AIE

The scheme of non-formal education (NFE) introduced in 1977-78 on a pilot basis and expanded in subsequent years focused on out-of-school children in age group of 6-14 years who have remained outside the formal system due to socio-economic and cultural reasons.

The scheme was initially limited to 10 educationally backward States with coverage of urban slums, hilly, tribal, desert areas. It is observed that the scheme was fraught with many lacunae - poor quality, lack of enthusiasm of teachers, poor quality of training, ambiguity in curriculum and textbooks, lack of community participation, weak management system, insufficient outlay, non emphasis on mainstreaming etc. Moreover, most of the NFE centers were in habitations already served by formal schools. The programme was revised under the name "Education Guarantee Scheme and Alternative and Innovative Education" (EGS & AIE) in the year 2000.

It provided for opening Education Guarantee Scheme schools in unserved habitations where there are no schools within a radius of 1 km. EGS & AIE will support diversified strategies for out of school children including bridge courses, back to school camps, seasonal hostels, summer camps, mobile teachers and remedial coaching. The investment cost per child per year has been increased from Rs 375 to Rs 845 at the primary level centre and from Rs 580 to Rs 1200 at upper primary level.

JANSHALA (GOI-UN) PROGRAMME

Janshala (GOI-UN) Programme is a collaborative effort of the Government of India and five UN agencies - UNDP, UNICEF, UNESCO, ILO and UNFPA to provide programme support to the on-going efforts towards achieving UEE. Janshala, a community based primary education programme, aims to make primary education more accessible and effective, especially for girls and children in deprived communities, marginalized groups, SC/ST minorities, working children and children with special needs.

A unique feature of the Janshala is that it is a block-based decentralized programme with emphasis on community participation. UNDP, UNICEF and UNFPA have committed to contribute $ 20 million for the programme while UNESCO and ILO have offered technical know-how.

The programme covers 129 blocks in nine States - Andhra Pradesh, Jharkhand, Karnataka, Madhya Pradesh, Chhattisgarh, Maharashtra, Orissa, Rajasthan and Uttar Pradesh - with a total project outlay of Rs 98.29 crore. Janshala programe is to run for five years, from 1998-2002.

At the State level, the programme is implemented through existing structures of educational administration. Janshala has started a large number of alternative schools in small and remote habitations in the programme areas, besides evolving strategies and setting up schools in urban slums of Jaipur, Hyderabad, Ajmer, Bharatpur, Puri and Lucknow with community participation. Other major areas of achievement are in teacher training, multi-grade teaching, intervention for education of the disabled, setting up of block and cluster resources centers and strengthening capacities at State, district and block level.

SARVA SHIKSHA ABHIYAN (SSA)

Sarva Shiksha Abhiyan is a significant step towards achieving the long cherished goal of universalization of elementary education through a time-bound integrated approach, in partnership with States. The SSA which promises to change the face of elementary education aims to provide useful and quality elementary education to all children in the 6-14 age group by 2010.

The SSA is an effort to improve the performance of the school system and provide community owned quality elementary education in the mission mode. It also envisages bridging of gender and social disparities of elementary level of education. SSA has special focus on educational needs of girls, SCs and STs and other children in difficult circumstances.

The objectives of SSA are:

i. All children in schools, Education Guarantee Centres, Alternate Schools, 'Back to School' Camps by 2003;
ii. All children complete five years of primary schooling by 2007;
iii. All children complete eight years of schooling by 2010;
iv. Focus on elementary education of satisfactory quality with emphasis on education for life;
v. Bridge all gender and social disparities at primary stage by 2007 and at elementary education level by 2010; and
vi. Universal retention by 2010.

The planning in SSA will be decentralized, participative and consultative. Habitation plans prepared after micro-planning, household survey, school mapping and diagnostic studies will form the basis for the District Elementary Education Plans (DEEP). Funds released to States would be channelized to registered societies at State level. Sarva Shiksha Abhiyan shall accord the highest priority to community monitoring, transparency in programme planning and implementation of capacity building at all levels as also to the adoption of a mission approach by the mainstream Education Department functionaries, to achieve UEE in a given time-frame.

A National Mission for Sarva Shiksha Abhiyan with Prime Minister as the Chairman and the Minister for HRD as Vice-Chairman has been approved. SSA will totally subsume all existing programmes including externally aided programmes within its overall framework with district as the unit of programme implementation. To make the approach totally holistic and convergent, efforts would be made to dovetail programme implementation at the district level with all other departments. This would include, programmes for children in the 0-6 age group under the department of Women and Child Development, sports-related interventions of the Ministry of Sports and Youth Affairs, establishment of Public Libraries under the Department of Culture and programmes of the Ministry of Health with regard to nutrition and school health.

ACHIEVEMENTS

As a result of the interventions mentioned above, in terms of access, as revealed by Sixth All-India Education Survey, 1993, 94% of the rural population living in 8.26 lakh habitations has now a school within a walking distance of one km. and 84% of this population has now an upper primary school within a walking distance of 3 kms. The situation has improved significantly thereafter as these figures relate to the year 1993. During the first three years of the Ninth Five Year Plan (1997-2000), over 43,000 new schools were opened and 1.3 lakh new teachers were added in the primary schools as against more than 21,000 new schools and 1.02 lakh new teachers in the upper primary schools. Gross enrolment ratio in primary level increased from 90.6 % in 1996-97 to 94.9 % in 1999-2000 while at upper primary level it declined from 62.4 % to 58.8 % during the same period.

Dropout rate at primary level declined from 42.4 % in 1998-99 to 40.3 % in 1999-2000, while in elementary stage it reduced from 56.8 % to 54.5 % during the period of one year. Despite the significant improvement in access to elementary education, the achievement so far in the Ninth Five Year Plan is short of the target as the Plan had envisaged additional enrolment of 250 lakh children in primary and 160 lakh in upper primary besides construction of 75,000 school buildings/ additional classrooms at the elementary stage. The Plan also targets appointment of 2.36 lakh teachers at primary level and 1.75 lakh teachers at upper primary level.

While Adult Education efforts in the pre-independence period were modest, there was a considerable degree of awareness of the importance of adult education, and gradual emergence, at the policy level, of the view that the state must shoulder the primary responsibility in this regard. Report of the Adult Education Committee of the CABE in 1939 showed, there was an awareness of the crucial role of primary education in eliminating illiteracy and that primary education is the only effective and permanent solution of the problem of illiteracy. In the period immediately after the Independence and through the successive Five Year Plans, the strategy formulated to provide education to the masses made a distinction between UEE and adult education and attached over-riding priority to primary education on the assumption that the expansion of primary education would automatically take care of the problems of illiteracy.

However, the first Five Tear Plan document recognized that in a country where 80% of the population is illiterate, democracy will not take roots without a nation-wide programme of primary education. But, at the same time, even such a programme would be considerably handicapped without a corresponding programme of adult education. In the Second Five Year Plan only Rs. 4 crore out of Rs. 273 crore was allocated to adult literacy. In the Third Plan, the figure came down to Rs. 2 crore out of Rs. 589 crore, which amounted to only 0.3 per cent of the budget? The Fourth Plan reflected the Kothari Commission report on education and yet adult education received only 0.6 per cent of the expenditure. In the Fifth Plan, the share for adult literacy was Rs.32 crore out of Rs.1286 crores, which amounted to only 2.48 per cent of the total budget.

It was only in 1977-78 that the Government decided to accord due weightage to adult education along with the programme of UEE and a programme "National Adult Education Programme (NAEP)" was launched on October 2, 1978. For the first time, adult education was put on educational agenda of the nation and thereby made central to the development approach that was pursued. Accordingly, an allocation of Rs. 200 crore was made in the Sixth Plan which was more than six-fold increase over the Fifth Plan provision. However, the NAEP did not work out because it was traditional, honorarium based, hierarchical and government-funded and controlled. With launching of the National Policy on Education, 1986, a thorough review of the strengths and weaknesses of past programmes of adult education was undertaken and wide ranging consultations organized. As a result, the Government initiated a move to start a number of "missions", most of them for application of modern science and technology to developmental issues concerning the disadvantaged social groups. The National Literacy Mission (NLM) started in 1988 was one such mission with the following aims:

- Increase motivation - the central issue in literacy;
- Secure participation through positive environment creation and mass mobilization;
- Increase Voluntary Agencies involvement; enhance quality of existing programmes with improved techno-pedagogic inputs;
- Launch mass movement for expanding Mass Functional Literacy Programme (MFLP), hitherto confined to university, college and Secondary/Hr. Secondary schools, to include different sections of society;
- Ensure availability of quality learning materials, aligned to mission goals;
- Universalise outreach of literacy learning facilities to all parts of the country by 1990; and establish Mission Management System for monitoring and concurrent correctives.

Creating a need for literacy among people was the major issue facing NLM when it set out in 1988 on the task of making 80 million literate. The Total Literacy Campaign (TLC) and Post Literacy Campaign (PLC) continued to be the dominant strategies of NLM during the Eighth Plan period for creating a mass upsurge of need and demand for literacy. The salient features of the basic strategy adopted in the Eighth Plan were as under:

- Full Literacy for India by 2005 A.D., with 100 million persons in 15-35 age-groups to be covered by 1998-99, as part of the Common Minimum Programme.
- The ratio of funding the Tribal Sub-Plan to be raised to 4:1 instead of the usual ratio of 2:1 and the enhanced ratio to be shared between the Centre and State Governments.
- Launching of Operation Restoration in those areas where the TLC had not taken off well due to natural calamities and other causes.
- Funding of Voluntary Agencies on 100% basis and decentralization of funding; through leading VAs or State Resource Centres, by setting up a VE Cell.
- Funding of State Resource Centres (SRCs) on 100% basis by the Centre.
- Devolution of the sanctioning powers to the States as soon as 50% of the population in half the districts in the State achieves NLM norms.
- It was proposed to continue the NLM during the Ninth Plan (1997-2002).
- A revised scheme of Continuing Education for Neo-literates was approved replacing the earlier scheme of Post Literacy and Continuing Education.

The scheme had provision for establishment of CE centres. The emphasis during the Ninth Plan was on restoring the lost momentum of the programme and to make it more effective by clarifying the administrative and financing roles of the Centre, the States, Zila Saksharata Samities, PRIs, other local bodies and NGOs. Therefore, an impetus was given to decentralized and disaggregated planning and implementation of literacy, post-literacy and continuing education programmes. The proposed measures were devolution of power from National Literacy Mission Authority (NLMA) to the State Literacy Mission Authority

(SLMA) for financial sanction to projects under TLC/PLC; empowerment of PRIs and Urban local bodies to achieve universal literacy; increasing the range and depth of NGO involvement in literacy campaigns; meeting special needs of SCs/STs; reducing rural-urban and male-female disparities in literacy through the strategies in campaign mode.

A remarkable feature of the Mission's work is that local initiative is clearly visible in the inter-sectoral committee called the Zila Saksharta Samiti, involving the administration, voluntary agencies, opinion leaders, professionals from the region as well as members of the community, in the process of imparting functional literacy. After the activities of environment building in which the community is informed, sensitized, motivated and mobilized through *kala jathas*, rallies, wall writings, posters, *melas* and the use of a variety of locally relevant traditional folk forms, the identification of learners and volunteers is undertaken.

The strategies of NLM have, however, been faced with difficulties in the low literacy States mainly due to the absence of voluntary organizations and other socio-cultural barriers, some of which are mentioned below:

- Lack of proper planning, weak and inadequate training;
- Training needs are not properly identified. Same training model is followed in low and high literacy areas;
- Lack of relevant training materials on specific aspects of TLC. Primers should be in local language/ dialect as far as possible;
- Lack of proper monitoring, evaluation and documentation;
- Fragile literacy - may lead to relapse. The programme was revamped in 1999 in view of some lacunae found in the working of the scheme. While increasing the scope, the parameters and norms of financial assistance of schemes under NLM were substantially enhanced. The main features of the revised scheme were.
- An integrated 'Literacy Campaign' amalgamating all the features of earlier Total Literacy and Post literacy phases.

- Full freedom given to District Literacy Societies to synergise their strength with those of local youth clubs, Mahila Mandals, voluntary agencies, Panchayati Raj institutions, small scale industries, cooperative societies, etc.
- Schemes of Continuing Education encompassing removal of residual illiteracy, individual interest programmes, skill development, rural libraries, etc., would allow for opening of Continuing Education Centres in every major village.
- Major role for NGOs.
- Strengthening of State Resource Centres.
- Enlarging the activities of Jan Shikshan Sansthan to enable them to function as district repository of vocational/ technical skills both in urban and rural areas.

LITERACY CAMPAIGNS AND OPERATION RESTORATION

Under the revised scheme, an integrated approach to literacy is being followed since April 2000. The new approach envisaged the integration of the activities of basic teaching learning with the post-literacy activities to ensure a smooth transition between Total Literacy Campaigns (TLC) and Post-Literacy Programmes (PLP). Now, it would be possible to take up TLC and PLP activities concurrently as two operational stages of the learning continuum drawing their financial sustenance from a single budgetary provision. The integrated approach seeks to effectively bring the activities of literacy campaigns under the umbrella of a single 'Literacy Project' in order to achieve continuity, efficiency and convergence and also to minimize unnecessary time lag between the two stages.

Districts, while submitting their initial Literacy project, would also submit their strategy for post-literacy on the basis of their anticipated targets and projections. In cases where, for reasons beyond the control of the local ZSS, such as natural calamities, absence of political will, transfer of collector, and lack of grass-root mobilization etc., TLC has stagnated, it would be possible to formulate strategies for restoration of these campaigns. For this purpose, ZSS would prepare a detailed work plan and the status of the campaign will be evaluated by experts nominated by NLM. Upon approval of the work plan for campaign restoration by NLM, an additional of up to 40-50% of the original TLC budget, if required, can be approved.

The existing funding pattern of literacy campaigns is 2:1 between Centre and State Government for normal districts, whereas for districts under Tribal Sub-Plan the ratio is 4:1. The per learner cost for a TLC and PLP has been revised upward with effect from 1st April 2000 and it now falls in the range of Rs 90-180 for TLC, and that for a PLP is Rs 90-130 for one year. The normal time span of TLC would be 18 months and that of PLP would be 12 months. It is expected that districts would complete the basic literacy and post-literacy activities within a period of 30 months and establish the necessary infrastructure. The Scheme of Rural Functional Literacy Projects is subsumed with the scheme of Literacy Campaigns and Operation Restoration. From the Tenth Plan onwards, this scheme will cease to exist and States will be asked to convert RFLP centers as CE centers.

SCHEME OF CONTINUING EDUCATION

It provides a learning continuum to the efforts of Total Literacy and Post-Literacy Programmes presently being implemented in 561 districts, out of 588 districts in the country. Under the scheme, the main thrust is given to setting up Continuing Education Centres (CECs) and Nodal Continuing Education Centres (NCECs) which function as a focal point for providing learning opportunities such as library, reading room, learning centers, sports centers, cultural centers and other individual interest promotion programmes. In accordance with the existing guidelines, Continuing Education Centres are set up to serve a population of 2000-2500 with a relaxation in the population criteria in sparsely populated areas. A Nodal Continuing Education Centre is set up for a cluster of 8-10 CECs to oversee and monitor their activities.

An important element of the Scheme of Continuing Education is the programme component under which opportunities are provided in the Continuing Education Centres for undertaking diverse activities such as Equivalency Programmes, Quality of Life Improvement Programmes, Income Generating Programmes and Individual Interest Promotion Programmes involving alternative and innovative approaches to cater to the need of the learners.

In order that the CECs perform these functions properly, it is important to ensure that community involvement and a feeling of ownership of the centre gets inculcated among the community. It is therefore proposed that the expenditure on activities under the programme components may be contributed by the user community of the CE centers. In accordance with the existing funding pattern of central financial assistance, the Central Government provides 100% funding for implementation of Continuing Education scheme for the first three years of implementation of the project.

For the remaining two years, the Central and State Governments share the cost of the project equally in the ratio of 1:1. The Department has proposed that the scheme is required to be fully funded by the Central Government at least for the initial period of five years. Planning Commission after due deliberations has decided that Centre-State ratio of contribution to financing may be 80:20 instead of existing 50:50 for two more years except for tribal sub-plan areas where Central assistance may continue at 100 per cent. Thereafter, the State Governments are expected to take over total responsibility of the projects. The norms of financial assistance under this scheme have been revised upwards with effect from 1st April 2000. In accordance with the revised norms of financial assistance, the NCEC and the CEC are provided non-recurring assistance of Rs. 45,000/- and Rs. 25,000/- per annum. Besides the non-recurring and recurring assistance, 10% of the recurring assistance is provided as administrative cost for each Centre.

The Scheme of Continuing Education has been sanctioned to 105 districts in 18 States and Union Territories till 31st

March, 2001. 260 districts are under the Post-Literacy Programme and a large number of them would be ripe for being sanctioned a Continuing Education project. By the 3rd year of CE, the districts currently under PLP+RFLP (290) also will be ready for CE. During the Tenth Plan, it is proposed to cover 80 districts each year, which would mean coverage of 400 districts during the Plan period, to ensure continuity in Literacy Programmes.

SUPPORT TO NON-GOVERNMENTAL ORGANISATIONS

Under the scheme, funds are released to NGOs under two broad categories:

i. To State Resource Centres.
ii. To NGOs for projects regarding Adult Education.

The scheme was revised for the Ninth Plan and the following major changes were incorporated:

i. Financial support to State Resource Centres has been enhanced.
ii. Provision has been made for one time grant for infrastructure to the State resource centers.
iii. Provision has been made for NGOs to undertake area-specific Continuing Education projects as well.

Under the scheme of support to NGOs, voluntary agencies are encouraged and financial assistance is provided for activities such as:

i. Running post-literacy and continuing education programmes with the objective of total eradication of illiteracy in well-defined areas;
ii. Undertaking resource development activities through establishment of State Resource Centres (SRCs) and District Resource Units (DRUs);
iii. Organising vocational and technical education programmes for neo-literates;
iv. Promoting innovation, experimentation and action research;

v. Conducting evaluation and impact studies; and
vi. Organising symposia and conferences, publication of relevant books and periodicals and production of mass media support aids.

JANA SHIKSHAN SANSTHAN

The scheme of Jan Shiksan Sansthan (JSS) or Institute of People's Education (formerly known as Shramik Vidyapeeth) is a polyvalent or multi-faceted adult education programme aimed at improving the vocational skill and quality of life of its beneficiaries. The objective of the scheme is educational, vocational and occupational development of literates, neo-literates, semi-literates and un-lettered persons. Though the scheme does not target any specific group or areas, it concentrates on the socio-economically backward and educationally disadvantaged groups of urban/rural population, such as neo-literates, semi-literates, SCs/STs, women and girls, slum dwellers, migrant workers, etc.

Now, with the emergence of millions of neo-literates, due to the total literacy campaigns launched across the length and breadth of the country and the transformation that has taken place in the economic and social set up over the years, the role and scope of these polyvalent educational institutes have widened manifold. In view of this, during the Ninth Five Year Plan, the scheme has been further strengthened with enhanced funding and widened scope and area of operation.

In the changed scenario, the focus of JSS is now shifting from industrial workers in urban areas to the numerous neo-literates and unskilled and unemployed youth both in urban and rural areas through the country. Ninety-two Jan Shikshan Sansthans have been sanctioned till the end of 2000-2001 including the 19 sanctioned during 1999-2000 and the 15 sanctioned during 2000-2001. Sixteen more Jan Shikshan Sansthans are proposed to be set up during the last year of the Ninth Five Year Plan i.e., 2001-2002. With this the total number of JSS set up during the Ninth Plan will go up to 50 and the total number of Jan Shikshan Sansthans in the country will be 108. It is proposed to open 100 more JSSs during the Tenth Five Year Plan at the rate of 20 per year. Ultimately, it is proposed to have at least one JSS in each district.

PARTNERSHIP BETWEEN PUBLIC AND PRIVATE SECTORS

Even though private initiative has always been a part of the school education endeavor, it is often felt that the country has not been able to fully exploit the potential of the private sector. Possibilities in this regard should be actively explored. It should be noted that private sector could contribute not only in monetary terms but also in the form of expertise for quality improvement through effective management of the system and development of locally relevant teaching-learning material. More collaborative efforts at institutional levels as well as programme implementation level should be designed in order to expand the profile of private initiative in elementary education.

7

Curriculum Framework for Quality Education

Teacher education is an integral component of the educational system. It is intimately connected with society and is conditioned by the ethos, culture and character of a nation. The constitutional goals, the directive principles of the state policy, the socio-economic problems and the growth of knowledge, the emerging expectations and the changes operating in education, etc. call for an appropriate response from a futuristic education system and provide the perspective within which teacher education programmes need to be viewed. When India attained freedom, the then existing educational system was accepted as such because it was thought that an abrupt departure from the same would be disturbing and destabilising. Thus a predisposition to retain the system acquired preponderance and all that was envisaged by way of changes was its rearrangement.

Consequently, education including teacher education largely remained isolated from the needs and aspirations of the people. During the last five decades certain efforts have been made to indigenize the system. The gaps, however, are still wide and visible. The imperatives for building the bridges may be as follows:

- To build a national system of teacher education based on India's cultural ethos, its unity and diversity synchronising with change and continuity.

- To facilitate the realization of the constitutional goals and emergence of the new social order.
- To prepare professionally competent teachers to perform their roles effectively as per needs of the society.
- To upgrade the standard of teacher education, enhance the professional and social status of teachers and develop amongst them a sense of commitment.

These are but a few of the major concerns which call for an immediate action. A comprehensive, dynamic and responsive system of teacher education needs to be continually evolved keeping the overall scenario in view.

SCENARIO OF TEACHER EDUCATION

The need for improved levels of educational participation for overall progress is well recognised. The key role of educational institutions in realising it is reflected in a variety of initiatives taken to transform the nature and function of education — both formal as well as non-formal. Universal accessibility to quality education is considered essential for development. This has necessitated improvement in the system of teacher education so as to prepare quality teachers.

Various Commissions and Committees appointed by the Central and the State Governments in recent decades have invariably emphasised the need for quality teacher education suited to the needs of the educational system. The Secondary Education Commission (1953) observed that a major factor responsible for the educational reconstruction at the secondary stage is teachers' professional training. The Education Commission (1964-66) stressed that 'in a world based on science and technology it is education that determines the level of prosperity, welfare and security of the people' and that 'a sound programme of professional education of teachers is essential for the qualitative improvement of education.'

India has a large system of education. There are nearly 5.98 lakh Primary Schools, 1.76 lakh Elementary Schools and 98 thousand High/ Higher Secondary Schools in the country, about 1300 teacher education institutions for elementary teachers and nearly 700 colleges of education/ university departments preparing teachers for secondary and higher secondary schools. Out of about 4.52 million teachers in the country nearly 3 million are teaching at the primary/ elementary level. A sizeable number of them are untrained or under-trained. In certain regions, like the North-East, there are even under-qualified teachers. As far as in-service education is concerned the situation is not very encouraging. It is estimated that on an average 40% of the teachers are provided in-service teacher education once over a period of five years.

Regarding non-formal education, though a number of models are in vogue in various states in the country, much more needs to be done to prepare teachers and other functionaries for the system. The Programme of Action (POA 1992) has emphasised teacher education as a continuous process, its pre-service and in-service components being inseparable. The POA, among others, has pointed out the following in respect of teacher education:

a. Professional commitment and overall competencies of teachers leave much to be desired;
b. The quality of pre-service education has not only improved with recent developments in pedagogical science, but has actually shown signs of deterioration;
c. Teacher education programmes consist mainly of pre-service teacher training, with practically no systematic programmes of in-service training, facilities for which are lacking.
d. There has been an increase in sub-standard institutions of teacher education and there are numerous reports of gross malpractices; and
e. The support system provided by the State Councils of Educational Research and Training (SCERTs) and the University Departments of Education has been insufficient and there is no support system below the state level.

In pursuance of the NPE 1986 a major step was taken by the Central Government to enhance the professional capacity of a large number of teacher education institutions. Nearly 430 District Institutes of Education and Training (DIETs) have already been established by 1997-98.

The DIETs are charged with the responsibility of organising pre-service and in-service programmes in addition to being the nodal resource centres for elementary education at district level. Likewise, Colleges of Teacher Education (CTEs) and Institutions of Advanced Study in Education (IASEs) have been given the responsibility of introducing innovations in teacher education programmes at the secondary and higher secondary stages and in vocational education.

The National Council for Teacher Education (NCTE) as a non-statutory body (1973-1993) took several steps as regards quality improvement in teacher education. Its major contribution was to prepare Teacher Education Curriculum Framework in 1978. Consequently, teacher education curricula witnessed changes in teacher preparation programmes in various universities and boards in the country. A similar effort was made in 1988.

During the last decade, new thrusts have been posed due to rapid changes in the educational, political, social and economic contexts at the national and international levels. Curriculum reconstruction has also become imperative in the light of some perceptible gaps in teacher education. Teacher education by and large, is conventional in its nature and purpose. The integration of theory and practice and consequent curricular response to the requirements of the school system still remains inadequate.

Teachers are prepared in competencies and skills which do not necessarily equip them for becoming professionally effective. Their familiarity with latest educational developments remains insufficient. Organised and stipulatory learning experiences whenever available, rarely contribute to enhancing teachers' capacities for self-directed life long learning. The system still prepares teachers who do not necessarily become professionally competent and committed at the completion of initial teacher preparation programmes. A large number of teacher training institutions do not practice what they preach. Several of the skills acquired and methodologies learnt are seldom practiced in actual school system. This highlights the need to bring realism and dynamism in the curriculum.

CONSTITUTIONAL GOALS

The Constitution of India solemnly resolves "to constitute India into a sovereign, socialist, secular and democratic republic and secure to all its citizens: justice-social, economic and political; liberty of thought, expression, faith, belief and worship; equality of status and of opportunity; and to promote among them all fraternity assuring the dignity of the individual and the integrity of the nation." These are the main goals which the nation expects to be realised through education. Teacher preparation must not lose sight of this basic thrust so as to empower teachers to inculcate the same among the students.

In order to reinforce faith in democratic socialism, secularism, justice, liberty, freedom etc. the role of education needs to be understood in its true perspective. Democracy is a process of building consensus among the citizens on matters of common concern. It expects high morality from them protects the interest and preserves their uniqueness, dignity and individuality. Quality of democracy depends on its citizens willing to discharge their responsibilities towards the self, the family, the community, the nation and humanity at large. Democracy is a way of life and its values need to be imbibed through education and practised in the day-to-day life. Democratic socialism attempts to achieve a synthesis between individual freedom and social compulsion and combines liberty with responsibility and authority with accountability. The Indian situation demands citizens capable of making conscious and purposive efforts directed towards social cohesion and living together harmoniously. Indian Society is plural and heterogeneous with an underlying current of unity. The imposition of a homogeneous and uniform curriculum of teacher education may prove counter productive under this situation. Except for identifying certain basics and essentials, regional autonomy must be exercised for developing region/culture specific curriculum of teacher education. Indian reality demands that plurality should be used for strengthening national solidarity and social cohesion. The Indian state is secular. The Indian society, however, is religious. To resolve this dichotomy between the state and polity, the principle of equal respect for all the religions has been accepted.

This is the essence of Indian secularism. The teachers themselves have to internalise the imperatives of secularism in national context and interpret the same effectively to the learners. That alone would develop the right attitudes among all citizens irrespective of their own backgrounds. In India religion is also the source of value and morality. The teachers have to develop values and morality in a different context. Teacher education has to respond to this reality. Justice, liberty, equality of status and of opportunity and promoting fraternity constitute another set of inter-related goals. Justice protects the rights of the weak and ensures impartiality. To ensure justice and fulfill the constitutional commitments in this regard, certain positive and legal provisions have been made by the state.

Special measures such as reservation in educational institutions, financial support, scholarships, hostel facilities, etc. have been extended to the under-privileged groups like Scheduled Castes, Scheduled Tribes, and Other Backward Classes etc. It implies change in attitudes and values through education, in which the role of teachers needs to be stressed. Liberty of thought, expression, faith, belief and worship is another constitutional goal which education is expected to help realise. Indian Constitution ensures equality of status and opportunity to all its citizens.

The objective is to minimise social and economic disparities, inequality of power and life chances by positive discrimination in favour of the weak. The education of teachers should equip them with the competencies needed to deal with discrimination, disparities and inequalities. Fraternity stands for acceptance of universal brotherhood, respect for human personality and feeling of oneness irrespective of linguistic, racial, cultural and religious diversities.

TEACHER EDUCATION AND PROBLEMS OF THE NATION

It is universally acknowledged that education is an effective means for social reconstruction and to a great extent it offers solutions to the problems a society is faced with. These problems may be economic, social, cultural, political, moral, ecological and educational. Since the teachers play a major role in education of children, their own education becomes a matter of vital concern. Teacher education must, therefore, create necessary awareness among teachers about their new roles and responsibilities. Education of teachers needs to strengthen and stress upon the main attributes of a profession, such as, the systematic theory, rigorous training over a specified duration, authority, community sanction, ethical code and culture, generating knowledge through research and specialisation. It is acknowledged that formal professional training on continuous basis is necessary for becoming a good teacher as it caters to the development of one's personality and sharpening of communication skills and commitment to a code of conduct.

Economic Problems

Poverty, unemployment, and low rate of growth and productivity are some of the major economic problems of the country which have led to the compulsions of the backward economy. These problems seek immediate solution and demand a realistic co-ordination between economic planning and manpower planning. Education can help find solutions if it is properly coordinated with manpower needs. Introduction of work education and vocationalisation of education in secondary schools will have to be given a modern and meaningful direction.

The attitude towards the work culture needs a transformation. The Indian society needs education with special emphasis on science and technology, vocational inputs and realistic work experiences.

Teacher education curriculum, therefore, has to promote such attitudes as are necessary for the emergence of a new economic order. Along with the vocational competencies and skills a new work culture will have to be created which necessarily involves the inculcation of dignity of work, the spirit of self-reliance and scientific temper among students. The courses of teacher education need to be enriched to enable teachers to understand the attributes of modernity and development.

Social Problems

Casteism, communalism and regionalism are some of the problems in the body politic of the society which misguide the youth. Increasing delinquency, violence, terrorism and fissiparous tendencies and use of inappropriate means to get one's ends served are threats to the national integration and social cohesion. Democracy, violence and terrorism cannot coexist. Education has to develop a peace loving personality and the programme of teacher education has to contribute in this regard.

The explosion of population with all its allied disturbing trends is not only neutralising the economic gains but also creating many problems for the country. Indian society still suffers from evils like child labour, child marriage, untouchability, and discriminatory treatment to women, violation of human rights, etc. and most of the people are unaware of their legal rights.

Modern model of development which puts man against nature by making it an object of exploitation has disturbed the harmony and equilibrium between the two. Its consequences are visible in serious environmental degradation, pollution and ecological imbalances. Strengthening national and social cohesion in a diverse and plural society, accelerating the process of economic growth, improving the life of the downtrodden and the people living below the poverty line, removing the widely prevalent ignorance, superstition and prejudices from the masses, inculcating scientific temper and developing a critical awareness about the social realities of Indian life are some of the issues which call for immediate attention. Teachers and the teacher educators have a special role to play in such efforts.

Problems of Cultural Reconstruction

Education is the process of transmission of dynamic and responsive components of cultural heritage and its continuous enrichment. There is a need to reinterpret the Indian culture in its distinct identity and composite strength. Its capacity to absorb the sublime from the other cultures needs to be highlighted. The teachers will have to play their role in cultural transmission and reconstruction.

Crises of Values and Morality

There has been a persistent erosion of values in the society. In the present day context certain values need to be redefined and reinstalled. There are situations when the values imparted and inculcated in schools are not generally practised in society. Value education demands a planned and purposive approach. It is through education and as of necessity through teacher education programmes that the task of inculcating values can be substantially accomplished. Whereas values are emotive, the other related significant dimension is that of moral education which is essentially conative in character. Morals are situation-specific and demand immediate decision and action and yet there are morals which are considered to be eternal and universal. Through committed teachers, the art of ensuring moral development in a secular, multi-religious and multi-ethnic society needs to be cultivated.

PROBLEMS WITHIN EDUCATION SYSTEM

The nation has yet to fulfill the constitutional commitment to provide free and compulsory education to all children till they attain 14 years of age. India is also a party to the global commitment for achieving the goal of Education for All by the year 2000. The education system however, has to respond to several major issues and problems which have hindered the progress in this regard. Maintenance of educational standards against the pressure of increasing enrolment, relevance and quality of school education, efficacy of school functioning under the decentralized role of political power through the enactment of Panchayati Raj Act are some of the pertinent issues.

In addition, specific requirements and need of social and economical groups of the society and of the minority communities, vocationalisation of education, scientific and technological literacy, alienation of youth, rush for urbanisation, perceived urban orientation of educational system and its inflexibility to respond to rural, tribal and regional requirements are some of the dominant issues. These would determine the nature and shape of teacher education programmes and the efficacy and functioning of teachers in their new and emerging multifaceted roles.

ISOLATION OF TEACHER EDUCATION

Teacher education institutions which were considered 'islands of isolation' have gradually developed linkages with schools, peer institutions, universities and other institutions of higher learning as also the community. However, much remains to be done in this direction. The curriculum of the school, its actual transactional modalities, examination system, management processes and its ethos need to be the main thrust areas of teacher education programmes.

To achieve these ends, teacher educators need to be made conversant with various aspects of school experiences. It is observed in day-to-day functioning that teacher educators often tend to lose contact with content areas relevant to their own disciplines resulting into gaps in communication and latest information. It is, therefore, a felt need in the present-day context that teacher education institutions keep in continuous touch with institutions of higher learning and peer institutions for effective transmission of knowledge and its upgradation.

The breaking of isolation from the community is essential for enabling teachers and teacher educators to reconstruct pedagogical and educational principles and practices in the light of experiences gained from mutually beneficial community interactions. Teacher as a professional and intellectual cannot remain indifferent to the events that are taking place in society. The academic and social issues are inter-related and inter-dependent. In contemporary context, the role of the teacher is no longer confined to teaching alone. The teachers are expected to play an active role in the developmental activities responding to progress of the community.

EXPANDING SCOPE OF TEACHER EDUCATION

Education of teachers is not an end in itself. Its target is the school. Any change in the nature, purpose, quality and character of the school demands a concomitant change in teacher education, especially in its curriculum. The implementation of the 10 + 2 scheme at the school level has transformed the complexion of education to a considerable extent from the pre-primary to the + 2 stage. There has been an increase not only in the quantum of knowledge, but also in its nature and purpose. In addition, new transactional techniques and strategies have also been evolved. Certain new subjects have replaced the old ones whereas some others have changed their context, content, orientation, theme and philosophy. These changes at the school level, out of necessity, demand a new pedagogy and evaluation techniques. But the changes at the level of teacher education have not adequately responded to the emerging realities at the school level.

All that the teachers are expected to do in their work places need to be reflected in the teacher education activities and programmes. The teaching community has to face the challenges thrown by science and technology. There has been an explosion not only of scientific and technological knowledge but also in the means and techniques of acquiring knowledge. The scientific researches and developments related to theories of heredity, learning, mental health, neurology, attention, motivation etc. can no longer be treated alien to teacher education programmes.

Evolving a Culture-Specific Pedagogy

Every region and state has its typical cultural identity, and there is a need to utilise the same as a basis for developing meaningful, relevant pedagogies. Since there is no one universal way in which the children learn, there is a strong need for looking into the cultural context in which a child is placed. A child in a tribal society may process information in an altogether different manner as compared to the one from the urban area and high socio-economic stratum. Pedagogy, therefore, should be culture-specific. Cultural practices such as story-telling, dramatics, puppetry, folk-play, community living, etc. should become a strong basis of pedagogy instead of using one uniform, mechanistic way of student learning. Cultural specificity should get embedded in the pedagogical practices which should be evolved for tribal, rural, urban communities and other ethnic groups.

INSEPARABILITY OF PRE-SERVICE AND IN-SERVICE EDUCATION

A learning society visualises education as a continuing activity. This is equally applicable to teacher education. The policy stipulation on inseparability of the pre-service and in-service education of teachers and the emphasis on continuing education needs to be given pragmatic shape at the implementation stage. The curriculum of pre-service and in-service teacher education has to be redesigned to maintain continuity between the two. Teachers who are being educated today will have to devote major part of their life to education during the twenty-first century. If the present rate of explosion of knowledge continues, in a few years the teachers will find themselves in a world where their present knowledge and teaching skills to an extent would become obsolete. They will have to face the challenge of electronic media and information technology.

RESEARCH AND INNOVATION

One of the major inputs towards enhancing the quality of teaching and learning in schools as well as the teacher education institutions would be the extent to which research outputs and the outcomes of innovations are utilized by the system. Researches on teacher education have been and are being conducted in universities, national level institutions and other establishments but their utility for the teacher educator or the classroom teacher remains rather low. Majority of the researches are undertaken to obtain a degree and hence the focus on its possible utility and relevance gets misplaced. The situation is compounded by non-availability of appropriate dissemination mechanisms, like journals, publication of findings in different forms and opportunities to the target group to get an access to these. Institutional capabilities and resources need to be augmented, enabling them to undertake relevant researches.

There is a definite requirement of bringing in research methods and methodologies in appropriate form in teacher education at pre-service and in-service programmes. To an extent, it finds a place in master level courses in education though in some universities the same is not insisted upon. The structure and design of future courses and programmes need to take this aspect into account. Preparation of teacher educators can no longer be completed without adequate grounding in various aspects of research. Researches must respond to policy issues, curriculum issues, evaluative procedures and practices, training strategies, classroom practices, etc.

The areas of teacher preparation for children with special needs, gifted children and children from groups with specific cultural, social and economic needs can no longer be ignored. Surveys and studies also need to be encouraged. These may be exploratory or diagnostic in nature. The new initiatives and innovations need to be encouraged and studied. Wherever considered appropriate, these could be brought into the system of teacher education for wider and gainful use.

The concept of field interaction and laboratory area approach in the context of establishment of DIETs is indeed timely. Researches, innovations and surveys must become an integral part of the training programmes of teacher education institutions irrespective of the stages. The trainees need to be familiarised with innovations in general and innovative practices in teacher education in particular.

Other Critical Concerns

The factors and forces influencing teacher education are many, some of which have been discussed in the preceding sections, and certain others are being mentioned hereunder:

- Gradual change-over from conventional programmes of teacher education to integrated courses to ensure greater professionalism.
- Increased duration of teacher education programmes to accommodate for proper assimilation of emerging professional inputs.
- stage-specific theoretical and practical components, transactional strategies and evaluation
- Plans and programmes of teacher education to respond to the expected role performance of teacher.
- Flexible and pragmatic approach to plans and programmes of teacher education.
- Proper planning and orientation of education of teacher educators.

SPECTRUM OF INSTITUTIONAL FUNCTIONS

In the light of context and concerns teacher education institutions will acquire a wider spectrum of functions and greater responsibilities. Resolution of specific functions from the spectrum will have to be made depending upon the institutional capabilities. It is visualised that the following institutional functions will have to be undertaken by different institutions according to availability of resources:-

- Develop capability to provide for both pre-service and

in-service education.

- Provide training and orientation programmes to the functionaries of alternative educational strategies aimed at achieving universal elementary education and eradication of illiteracy.
- Organise programmes for heads of schools and school complexes and supervisory staff.
- Offer courses for community leaders, voluntary agencies and parents.
- Provide academic support to schools and other agencies engaged in education of children and adults.
- Undertake research and experiments with innovative educational ideas.
- Act as a resource centre for education for a specific area.
- Offer counselling and guidance services.
- Organise need-based programmes for educational administrators, planners, curriculum designers, evaluators etc.
- Impart training for other areas of education, like physical education and special education.
- Act as a link between the school and the university system.

COMMITMENT AND PERFORMANCE IN TEACHER EDUCATION

A major concern in school education is the quality and relevance of education being imparted to young learners. Every learner is supposed to acquire mastery level learning in identified competency areas. NCTE has analysed the existing curriculum of teacher education from the point of view of competency areas.

It has emerged that to enhance the quality of school education equal emphasis needs to be given to competencies, commitment and willingness to perform. A curriculum framework based upon competencies, commitments and performance has been developed. Competency areas namely, contextual competencies, conceptual, content, transactional, related to other educational activities, developing teaching learning material, evaluation, management, working with parents and working with community and other agencies, have been identified as critical to teacher preparation at elementary stage.

Acquisition of competencies alone will not be sufficient until and unless the teacher is fully committed. Teacher commitment areas identified include commitment to the learner, commitment to the society, commitment to the profession, commitment to attaining excellence for professional actions and commitment to basic values. Along with competency and commitment areas, performance areas have also been identified. These include classroom performance, school level performance, performance in the out-of school educational activities, parents related performance and community related performance.

Teacher education institutions could identify details in each of the three major categories. For each competency, commitment and performance area, the existing curriculum needs to be analyzed. Whenever certain unit of curriculum is taken up for transaction, its relationship to commitment and performance has to be examined. Such an approach would provide an opportunity to the training institutions to prepare teachers who are not only competent but also committed and both these aspects are reflected in their performance leading to higher learning attainments by all children.

BREAKING THE BARRIERS

The critical analyses of the context and concerns presented in the preceding sections help in developing a vision for teacher education in future. In the Indian situation basic character of the framework must provide for adequate and inbuilt flexibility for incorporating the regional and local specificities. Total trust in the capabilities of institutions and organisations to develop an indigenous, comparable and area specific curriculum has to be the guiding principle. Teacher education has to be conceived as an integral part of educational and social system and must primarily respond to the requirements of the school system. It can no longer remain conventional and static but should transform itself to a progressive dynamic and responsive system.

National values and goals need to be meaningfully reflected and their inculcation attempted with care and caution. The theoretical and practical components need to be balanced appropriately. The theory and practice of education has to be enriched with the latest research findings not only in the field of education but also in the allied disciplines and areas. While it is essential to develop identified competencies to prepare effective teachers it is equally necessary to develop commitment and build capacity to perform as integral part of teacher preparation. The teachers have to keep abreast of the latest developments not only in their field of specialisation but also in areas of educational developments and social and cultural issues through continuous in-service orientation. Emphasis on continuing life-long learning has to become an essential concern of teacher education.

A nation concerned with erosion of values needs teachers who are professionally committed and prepared to present a value-based model of interaction with their learners. The basic tenets identified in the national basic education scheme - Head, Heart and Hand need now to be linked to another 'H' - highways. Information highways, websites and internet are going to become terms of common usage in teacher education. For sound mind we need strong hand and a vibrant heart. Areas like physical education and vocational education will continue to gain greater emphasis in years to come and will serve as the basis for developing competencies and skills in addition to commitments and values.

A comprehensive theoretical base is essential for a teacher to assume professional role and develop capacity to conceptualise inputs from other disciplines as well and evolve strategies to utilise them. A true professional is capable of perceiving complexities and uncertainties in the society, has a thorough grasp of the subject, possesses skills to make critical diagnosis, takes decisions and has courage and conviction to implement such decisions.

PRE-SERVICE TEACHER EDUCATION

Teacher education by its very nature is interdisciplinary. The major areas of inter-disciplinarity implicit in teacher education programmes include philosophy, psychology, sociology, anthropology, economics, history and culture. Recent researches in medical and life sciences are opening new avenues of knowledge which are relevant to education. Besides, teacher education has an essential and inalienable component of practical work including student teaching, internship, field work, working with the community, work education, etc. The country needs teachers with different orientation and specialisations to manage educational programmes. In addition, the teachers are also needed for physical education, music, art, painting, dance, work education and vocational subjects and for the non-formal stream, distance education, adult education, and open learning system. The scope of teacher education curriculum, therefore, gets enlarged.

The curriculum for teacher preparation, in future has to encompass the broader canvas which is consistently emerging before the teachers and shall continue to change at a much faster pace in times ahead. Teachers shall have to take a global view of the new trends, strategies and practices, and focus on indigenous heritage and thoughts which could fit in the local and national situations. Transplantation of alien educational ideas and practices has not been found rewarding in developing countries. Consequently, the emerging structures and designs of the curriculum shall lay greater emphasis on the ideas, practices and experiences that have emerged in India through the contributions of thinkers like Mahatma Gandhi, Vivekanand, Rabindra Nath Tagore, Zakir Hussain, Sri Aurobindo, Giju Bhai and many others. The teacher education programmes shall focus on competencies and commitment in much greater magnitude in future. Such a transformation in teacher preparation strategies would emerge only after due familiarity and adequate appreciation of indigenous thoughts developed over decades in India. Gradually an indigenous approach and strategy would emanate and replace the alien practices that have remained in vogue in teacher education over the decades.

Teacher Profile

The profile of a teacher which emanates from the contexts and concerns necessarily implies additional roles besides the conventional ones. The following capabilities and competencies need to be highlighted:

- Inculcating the intrinsic and extrinsic values of professional competency, professional commitment and professional ethics
- Creating and reconstructing knowledge
- Selecting, organising and using learning resources
- Effectively transacting curriculum, selecting and organising educational activities and programmes for learners with special needs
- Using media and appropriate instructional technologies
- Communicating effectively and responding to the challenges of continuity and change
- Counselling students for personality development, adjustment and learning attainment
- Conducting research, especially action research and initiating innovative practices
- Organising student-activities
- Inculcating a sense of value judgement, value commitment and value transmission
- Understanding the import of inter-relationship between culture and education and 'culture and personality'
- Fostering interest in life-long learning
- Understanding the aspirations and expectations of the community and establishing mutually supportive linkages between school and community
- Acting as a change agent for modernisation and development

The educational programmes for prospective teachers, therefore, need to be so designed as to develop in them the requisite potential and capabilities.

General Objectives

The general objectives of teacher education derived from the contexts, concerns and issues of education, teacher education and the perceived profile of the teacher could include the following:

- To promote capabilities for inculcating national values and goals as enshrined in the Constitution of India.
- To enable teachers to act as agents of modernisation and social change.
- To sensitize teachers towards the promotion of social cohesion, international understanding and protection of human rights and rights of the child.
- To transform student-teachers into competent and committed professionals willing to perform the identified tasks.
- To develop competencies and skills needed for becoming an effective teacher.
- To sensitize teachers and teacher educators about emerging issues, such as environment, ecology, population, gender equality, legal literacy, etc.
- To empower teachers to cultivate rational thinking and scientific temper among students.
- To develop critical awareness about the social realities.
- To develop managerial and organisational skills.

CHARACTERISTICS OF CURRICULUM FRAMEWORK

An overview of the context and concerns as discussed earlier, teacher's profile and general and specific objectives would define the boundaries of a curriculum framework. The perceived characteristics of the envisaged curriculum framework would include the following:

- Reflects the Indian heritage, acts as an instrument in the realisation of national goals and fulfills aspirations of people.

- Responds to the latest developments in the field of education.
- Establishes integration of theory and practice of education.
- Provides multiple educational experiences to teachers.
- Enables teachers to experiment with new ideas.
- Ensures inseparability of pre-service and in-service education of teachers.
- Sets achievable goals for various stages of teacher education provides for use of communication technology.

TEACHER EDUCATION FOR EARLY CHILDHOOD STAGE

The need for early childhood education has long been emphasised on the argument that it would lead to providing healthy and wholesome learning environment. It is also considered as a preparatory stage for the realisation of Universalisation of Elementary Education. In order to provide healthy and enriched childhood to young learners, a new type of teacher specifically sensitized about the perspectives of child development will be required. The enrichment programmes for early childhood education have been launched under Integrated Child Development Scheme through Anganwadis, Day Care Centres, Balwadies, Pre-primary Schools run by the State Governments, Municipal Corporations, Voluntary Agencies and Private Agencies.

All such efforts, though not adequately provided for, are continuing with diverse approaches without making a synergic impact. Concerted efforts are needed for organising early childhood education in a planned manner. It presupposes pooling of resources by the community as well as the concerned agencies. In order that early childhood education becomes a reality, in terms of its organisation and accessibility, one of the significant inputs in making a success story of it is that of a professionally trained and committed teacher. The professional preparation of teachers for this stage, hitherto unplanned and uncared for, calls for thoughtful planning of training sequences relevant to the developmental needs of early childhood interwoven with commonalities and specificities.

Specific Objectives

The objectives of teacher education specific to early childhood include the following:

- To prepare teachers for facilitating physical, mental, moral, social, aesthetic and linguistic development of children
- To acquaint them with the knowledge of child psychology
- To cultivate social sensitivity, affection for children and respect for their uniqueness
- To acquaint them with techniques of caring for children and enable them to identify their needs
- To provide experiences and organise activities that promote children's self-concept, creativity and inventiveness
- To enable them to select, prepare and use different kinds of resource materials
- to develop a sense of involvement with and appreciation of local resources (human and material) and their utilization
- To develop an acquaintance with basics of Scientific and Technological Literacy
- To develop a repertoire of children's games, songs and literature
- To empower student-teachers towards creating learning readiness among young learners

CURRICULUM FRAMEWORK

The framework given here is suggestive and not a prescriptive one. It has considerable space for flexibility, innovation and use of locally available community resources. The following curriculum framework is suggested for formulating a Plan of

Action for developing programmes and activities, devising strategies of negotiating the curricular inputs and methods of obtaining feedback. These are pre-requisites for improving the interaction processes directed towards the realisation of optimum enrichment of experiences at the early childhood stage.

Inclusion of the following components of theory and practice are suggested:

Theory

- Emerging Indian Society
- Early Childhood Education: Scope, Nature, Status, Problems and Issues.
- Psychology of the Child and Learning during early years (implementing developmentally appropriate curriculum).
- Planning, management and administration of ECCE programmes
- Methods and Materials for facilitating the growth and development of pre-school child through activities for:
  - Physical development
  - Mental development
  - Emotional development
  - Aesthetic development
  - Language development
  - Social development
  - Moral development
  - Neuro-muscular co-ordination
  - Self-expression
  - Health and Hygiene
  - Habit formation
  - Observation
  - Sensory-Motor Training

Practical Work

- Drawing and Painting
- Music
- Creative activities
- Story telling
- Dance and Drama
- Games and Physical Activity
- Plays
- Field trips
- Block making and related games
- Activities for children with special needs
- Practicum: Teaching, placement and internship

RATIONALE

The current areas suggested in this framework have been specially designed for understanding early childhood care and education in its realistic perspective. No formal teaching is visualised at early childhood stage. It is not a stage for introducing three R's.

In the preparation of teachers for this stage, therefore, the main thrust will be on sensitizing prospective teachers about change and its implications - cultural, social, economic, etc. as also with the change in the learner through motivation and learning. Future need will be to empower the teacher to observe change, interpret it and adopt, adapt, modify, consolidate accelerate or reject the same. It is not intended here to suggest details of programmes and theoretical content.

It is, however, expected that the course on Emerging Indian Society' will enable the intending teachers to know about the rights of child, human rights, legal literacy, community dynamics, knowledge of national and local festivals, emerging trends in community life and social living, prominent personalities in various walks of life, familiarity with factors and forces affecting environmental and population equilibirium, knowledge and appreciation of places of historical and cultural significance and landmarks and trends of development.

Another theoretical input which is intended to be given to the prospective teachers is regarding knowledge of nature and scope, status, problems and issues concerning early childhood education in India. These need to be understood in terms of Indian reality and perspective, foundations of child behaviour etc. In addition, it may include, among others, progress of early childhood education, its historical development, problems, need for looking at it from the point of view of diversity, flexibility, local relevance and specificities, and the agencies involved in the process of promoting early childhood education.

Basic to designing programmes and activities for children at this stage is a thorough understanding of various aspects of growth and development of the child which the prospective teachers will be required to internalise. Since, it is being recommended for intending teachers of pre-schoolers, it will be necessary to know about the fundamentals of early childhood care and education. Most of the training programmes of teachers for this stage will have major concentration on organisation and activities as mentioned above. In addition, the teachers will be required to have a practical training at early childhood education centres and the like. At this stage, greater emphasis will be given on propagation of early childhood care.

Transacting Curriculum

India is a conglomeration of diversities with a variety of manifestations and yet bound by a thread of commonality. Teacher is expected to recognise commonalities and specificities in order to shape the personality of children for living together in a perpetually changing complex society. The suggested theoretical components included in the framework are essentially, meant for broadening the intellectual horizons of intending teachers who will become conversant with the culture and traditions of the country with due appreciation of the diversities. The seeds of democratic living are sown from the beginning of childhood and education needs to be regarded as a vehicle for maintaining equilibirium in the growth of individuals from childhood to adulthood.

It would be worth experimenting with modular approach of teaching combined with interventions of realistic nature by way of field trips, visit to museums, zoo, educational excursions, visit to mountains, forests, intermediary interventions with real life situations and through audio-video devices, wherever possible. Teaching in teacher training institutions be directed towards empowering prospective teachers to enable to use their experiences in actual work places for enhancing growth and development of young children. There is to be a planned amalgam of theory and practice in a way that these two constitute a continuum of experiences. The teaching of theoretical components, in addition to what has been elaborated above, will combine various methods and approaches like lecturing, tutorials, seminars, term-papers, discussion groups, gaming, role planning, etc.

The teachers at this stage are being initiated into and introduced to the art of teaching. Teaching to them is romance with innovativeness and inventiveness. It is love for children. It is caring for children. It is seeking for optimum enrichment of experiences of children. It is providing happiness to children. It is making their stay joyful in schools. The early childhood education includes transacting developmentally appropriate curriculum which includes within its fold concept development, convergent and divergent thinking, creative activities, language acquisition, etc. It is an arduous task of equipping prospective teachers with competencies and skills needed for making the learning experiences of a child joyful and memorable. It must be admitted that the training of pre-school teachers is complex and full of challenges. The pedagogical aspects of training will be planned around activities and programmes for children, attending to their needs, identifying interests of learners by gender and their background, identifying children with special needs and devising strategies for their optimum growth and development, organising games, recreational activities, plays, etc.

Theory and practicum have to be linked and integrated in the training process. Much of what goes by way of practicals is intrinsically related with pedagogy and much of the essence of pedagogy lies in the practical work. The practical work may include comprehensive case studies of children including children with special needs, gifted children, children coming from different socio-economic and cultural backgrounds, etc. Development and use of schedules, assessment checklists and other evaluation tools and techniques will form an important aspect of practicum. The maximum utilisation of environmental and community resources can be done only when the teacher is thoroughly conversant with environmental resources. Community survey, therefore, is one of the several activities of practical work which requires systematic exploration.

The practical work of the prospective teachers will centre on evolving and devising programmes and activities for physical, psychomotor, cognitive, emotional and other aspects of development. Health and hygiene, habit formation, are certain other areas which require practical work. In addition, art, drawing and painting, using clay/plasticin, music, dance, recreation, story telling, games, and physical activity are a variety of examples of other practical experiences which a student teacher will be required to undertake for creative expression of children.

Evaluation for the theoretical component may include assessment of sessional work, term-papers, participation in seminars, discussion groups, etc. besides semester examinations which can be oral, written, practical and objective type. The written tests have to be reliable, valid and representative of the totality of experiences. Different tools and techniques of evaluation can be used for assessing the pupils' growth. Visits to and partcipation in activities of Anganwadis, Balwadis, Day Care Centres will make a part of training towards understanding the dynamics of working with children and educating them. The evaluation of this component is will be in the form of a cumulative record of the performance of the intending teachers. External evaluation of practical activities will defeat the purpose as the practical work is, by and large, activity-based. It is essentially sessional work, day-to-day internal assessment, feed back and monitoring. A record of some of the activities is all that may be suggested for purposes of evaluation in this regard.

Elementary Teacher Education Curriculum Framework

The constitutional provision of providing free and compulsory education to all children upto 14 years of age includes both the lower primary and upper primary classes, that is from class I to class VIII. There seems to be a compelling need for having multiple models for preparing teachers - for primary and upper primary classes. Incidentally, in a number of Elementary Teacher Education Institutions (ETEIs) in the country, the nomenclature of the training programme from pre-service training of primary school teachers has been changed to pre-service training of elementary school teachers. But in actuality, the transformation in programmes has yet to take place effectively.

There are three distinct possibilities of designing courses in teacher education for elementary stage:

- Teacher education programme exclusively for primary school stage (Classes I to V).
- Teacher education programme for elementary school stage (Classes I to VIII).
- Teacher education programme exclusively for upper primary school stage (Classes VI to VIII).

In view of the requirements of Universal Primary Education and Universal Elementary Education, only the first two alternatives are being recommended. However, the third suggested above, could be attempted by offering credit oriented modular courses after successful completion of primary teacher education programmes. It is significant to note that we have nearly 5.98 lakh primary schools which are mostly in rural areas as compared to upper primary schools numbering about 1.76 lakhs only.

TEACHER EDUCATION FOR PRIMARY STAGE

The formulation of curriculum framework for this stage (classes I to V) has been guided by general and specific objectives of the teacher's education and perceived characteristics of curriculum development. The specific objectives of primary teacher education may include the following:

- To develop understanding of the psychological and sociological foundations relevant to the primary stage.
- To enable teachers to manage appropriate resources for organising learning experiences of children.
- To acquaint them with methods and techniques of caring for children with special needs.
- To enable them to acquire necessary skills so as to develop curiosity, imagination and creativity.
- To develop in them the capacity to understand and analyse the social and emotional problems.
- To develop communication skills
- To enable them to establish mutually supportive linkages with the community focussing on the objective of UPE/ UEE.
- To enable them to understand implications of research for teaching-learning and undertake action research and use innovative practices.
- To enable them to organise games, sports, physical activities and other co-curriculur activities.

Keeping in view the teacher profile particularly the facilitative and resource management aspects, general and specific objectives of teacher education, the following framework which is flexible with ample scope for adaptation and for making it relevant to local environment is being suggested:

Curriculum Framework

Theory:

- Emerging Indian Society
- Primary Education in India: status, problems and issues
- Psychology of Teaching and Learning with special

reference to children of age group 6-11 years

- Assessment, Evaluation and remedial teaching
- Health and Physical Education
- School Management
- Education of Children with Special Needs
- Guidance and Counselling
- Content Areas for Primary Schools
- Action Research

Practice Teaching:

- Pedagogical Analysis of Primary School Subjects
- Practice Teaching in Schools
- Observation of Model Lessons

Practical Work:

- School Experience inclusive of Internship
- Work Education
- School-Community Interaction
- Action Research Studies (planning and execution)
- Organisation of relevant Educational Activities

The teacher needs to be empowered through training inputs to gain greater insights into the complexities of the society and the historical perspective of the developmental process. The paper on Emerging Indian Society is being introduced at this stage with a purpose of making the teacher aware of the contextual realities in which he or she has to work. The paper would take into account rights of children, human rights education, values and their broad features, perspectives of educational, social, economic and political development in the country, significant landmarks in the process of development in various fields including science and technology, etc.

Theoretical component is essential for understanding the learner, community and the society, the internal and external forces impinging upon the school and the internal and external variables operating upon the learner. The inclusion of Courses on Psychology of Teaching and Learning, Health and Physical

Education, Education of Children with Special Needs has been made for accommodating this point of view in the Framework. In the proposed training programmes, the prospective teachers would be imparted training in a manner that theory and practice are organically integrated. Correlation within the curricular areas of learning and external environment is established.

Psychology of Teaching and Learning, School Organisation and Pedagogical Analysis of primary school subjects will provide a sound base for the adoption of integrated approach to teaching and learning and for establishing meaningful and interactive bonds between theory and practice. The intent of including Action Research and Education of Children with Special Needs is guided by the fact that every student-teacher is expected to know the elements of action research, surveys, community services etc and is capable of educating children with special needs. Additional areas may be included for making the course content relevant and region specific.

TRANSACTING CURRICULUM

Transactional strategies invariably need to emphasise interactive, partcipative and activity-oriented approach. The transaction of curriculum will have place to place and intra- and inter-content variations. The theoretical component of the curriculum can be transacted by lecture-discussion, self-study approach, seminars, media supported teaching wherever possible, tutorials and through practical activities. It is expected that the intending teachers during the course of training acquire mastery of competencies and skills that are basic to making an effective, reflective and committed teacher.

Practice teaching remains to be a weak link of curriculum transaction. This point of view has been substantiated and re-inforced by field surveys conducted by NCTE at different places throughout the country. In this framework, pedagogical analysis of school teaching subjects has been thought of as an essential component of practice teaching. By way of pedagogical analysis a student teacher becomes conversant with the objectives of teaching a unit, the entry behaviour of pupils, classroom management and evaluation strategies.

With this background of having looked into the pedagogical aspects of school teaching subjects, the student teacher is likely to become more effective and confident in his/her interventions in the classroom. As a necessary part of the training of primary school teachers, knowledge of content is given due importance during the course of training. Mastery of subject matter, the insight gained through pedagogical analysis and the foundation courses when thoughtfully integrated and used for classroom instruction will lead to improving the quality of education.

Practical work is an essential component for internalising the theoretical concepts. Thus it will have to be planned on each aspect of theoretical inputs. In addition, practical activities centring on different school experiences, work education, school community interaction, action research projects and other educational activities directed towards development of personality of students will also be undertaken by intending teachers. It needs continuous planning, analysing, monitoring and evaluation throughout the duration of the course which will necessitate the involvement of teacher educators more vigorously than what it is presently.

It is expedient to employ the formative evaluation for obtaining continuous feedback, motivating students and guiding their efforts. There is an increasing felt need to replace external examinations by internal continuous and comprehensive examination system. External system of evaluation, until such times it is replaced, may be perceived as a corrective, moderating and balancing factor. It, therefore, needs to be carefully planned and testing tools made valid and reliable. In different situations evaluation of theoretical component may be based on essay questions, short answer type questions, objective type questions, objective-based questions, oral examinations, participation in discussion groups etc.

Evaluation of practice teaching can be done internally, externally or through judicious combination of both. Gradual transition to continuous and comprehensive internal evaluation of practice teaching and assigning grades instead of marks would be a professionally sound step. Evaluation of practical work would also be done internally.

TEACHER EDUCATION FOR ELEMENTARY STAGE

The justification for suggesting a separate model of teacher education curriculum for the elementary stage in addition to the one suggested for primary stage is given below:

- There is a constitutional commitment for providing compulsory education upto 14 years of age.
- The gradual transition of the teaching and learning processes from concrete operational stage of development to abstract reasoning process and change over of teaching-learning strategies from one stage to another needs to be ingrained in the minds of teachers for ensuring a continuum of learning experiences from class I to class VIII and matching the learning experiences with the maturity of learners. The present status does not reflect the gradual transition implicit in the development of thought processes from one stage to another.

The formulation of the curriculum framework for the elementary stage will also be guided by general and specific objectives of teacher education and characteristics of curriculum development.

The specific objectives relevant to the stage may include the following:

- To develop understanding of the psychological and sociological principles relevant to elementary stage of education.
- To enable teachers to select, prepare and use appropriate resources for organising learning experiences.
- To acquaint them with methods and materials of teaching

children with special needs

- To develop among them the capacity to solve the social and emotional problems of children.
- To enable them acquire necessary skills so as to develop curiosity, imagination and self-confidence among children.
- To develop communication skills
- To enable them to mobilise and utilise community resources as educational inputs.
- To enable them to organise supplementry educational activities
- To undertake action research projects
- To enable them to establish mutually supportive linkages with the community
- To enable them to organise games, sports, physical activities and other co-curricular activities.

Curriculum Framework

Theory:

- Emerging Indian Society
- Elementary Education in India - status, problems and issues
- Psychology of Teaching and Learning with special reference to learners of age group 6-14 years
- Health and Physical Education
- School Management
- Education of Children with Special Needs
- Assessment, Evaluation and Remediation
- Guidance and Counselling
- Action Research

It is expected that detailed curriculum plan would adequately provide for aesthetics, culture, arts, music, dance, drama, value inculcation, etc. The course on Emerging Indian Society will enable the prospective teachers to understand the demands that society expects education to fulfil. Similarly, proposed course on 'Elementary Education in India - status, problems and issues' will promote the capacity to examine if these expectations can really be met. The course on Psychology of Teaching and Learning will teach them how to formulate their teaching strategies to promote learning among children. Health and Physical Education will enable them to plan exercises for development of sound physiques of formative evaluation. They will be able to deal with children with special needs and adopting problem solving approach, a capacity built by Action Research.

The course on counselling and guidance will enable them to help children when they are confronted with problem of any kind. The pedagogical analysis will provide the prospective teachers an understanding of the complexity involved in the teaching of the subjects at the elementary level. This will enable them to plan their educational strategies. A critical observation of model lessons and practice teaching in the actual class room situation will make them effective and competent teachers. Internship in a school will offer the prospective teachers the varied experiences needed for working in a school. They will internalise educational value of the work and experience the dignity of manual work. The school community interaction would not only promote the interactive support between both but also enable them to evolve suitable pedagogy for children.

The organization of education activities will develop the capacity for planning and undertaking such activities as are essential for the development of personalty of the student. The theoretical and practical courses suggested in this frame are capable of preparing a competent elementary school teacher. The prospective teachers are to be prepared as to enable them to perform successfully in the pre-instructional, instructional and post-instructional phases of teaching. For this, several well-designed approaches like lecture discussion cooperative study, self-study and project methods, etc. may be adopted. Depending on the nature of the subject, the teachers may combine different strategies and instructional aids, utilize media supported teaching, organise field trips and practicals and demonstration techniques.

In this process due attention be given to children with special needs. The curriculum transaction will have to be adjusted with the needs of students and locally available resources. During the process of teaching and learning, the existing transactional strategies marginally promote the capacity for independent study, self discovery and self study and rarely seek prospective teachers' participation and remain one way traffic with the result that the subject matter communicated is partially assimilated and not fully utilized. Teacher education has to inculcate professional commitment, develop competencies and make teacher reflective to deal with specific situations.

Practice teaching, the weakest link of teacher education, possesses the potentiality of converting itself into a strong component if properly organized. The process of curriculum transaction needs improvement and enrichment. Pedagogical analysis of teaching subjects is sure to refine teaching and learning as it will transform the teachers' performance and develop competencies not covered by the method-cum-content approach. With the background of pedagogical analysis and model and demonstration lessons given by the teacher educator, the class room performance is sure to improve if it is supervised in detail by the subject specialist.

Work education is an important component of practical work and its potentiality has to be utilized by teacher education for developing certain qualities of character. Community surveys helps to formulate a proper social perspective. The mutually supported school and community interaction helps the teachers to evolve suitable teaching strategies. The teachers will be required to organise educational activities in school. They have to learn to plan and organize such activities as are essential to provide opportunities for self-expression and lead to development of personality of students. They have to be trained for utilizing supplementary materials essential for accelerating and promoting learning among students.

The teachers will be required to facilitate physical, social, emotional and aesthetic development of students. Their creative and constructive potentialities have to be fostered. Practical activities suggested in the document will help to achieve these ends. It is, therefore, necessary to organize these activities on continuing basis. The influence of teachers' personality and behaviour has lasting impact on students. In the selection and adoption of transactional strategies the teacher has to ensure that teaching becomes participatory, cooperative, activity-centred and joyful.

The success or failure of the curriculum transaction is ascertained by evaluation done by means of valid and reliable tools. At this stage, evaluation has to be continuous, formative and comprehensive to bring improvement in teaching learning process. Systematic evaluation will enable a teacher to select proper teaching strategies and effect suitable changes in the curriculum process. The evaluation of the pupil teachers at the elementary stage will not differ much from the primary stage and the same principles and similar practices which have been adopted at the primary level may be utilized at this stage.

TEACHER EDUCATION FOR SECONDARY STAGE

For teaching at secondary stage, the qualification most sought after is one year B.Ed. which is in fact B.Ed. for secondary stage. However, at present, there are several variations for first degree level qualification which are also available. These include B.Ed. (Elementary); B.Ed. (Special Education); which too are programmes of one year duration; B.Ed. through correspondence or distance education mode which is now of two years duration. There are certain other variations in the form of vacation courses or part-time courses which were available before NCTE norms came into force. In addition, there are four-year integrated courses for elementary stage and also for secondary stage.

Teacher education programme at this stage, like at all other stages, will include the theory, practice teaching in schools, and practical work in the light of contexts, concerns, profile of teachers and general and specific objectives. The specific objectives at this stage may include the following:

]h research in education including action research

A teacher helps in improving the quality of human life in the context of multiple internal and external forces impinging on man and the society. The course on 'Emerging Indian Society' would develop an insight into the nature of Indian society, its variety and complexities and making teacher education programme relevant to the community. Ingenuity of teachers lies in first understanding national ethos and then planning for teaching within this framework as a professional. A professionally trained teacher is expected to identify the strengths and weaknesses of secondary education in India and after having gained insights into the status, problems and issues concerning education at this stage, develop a mental make-up of evaluating the system and utilising the same for promoting excellence in education.

A teacher in the classroom has to make adjustments in teaching strategy according to the nature and scope of the curriculum and evaluate the success of teaching in terms of students' growth. The foundations of curriculum, pedagogy, evaluation and remediation need to be laid down firmly during the course of professional preparation of teachers. What kind of pedagogical strategy will give optimum results in specific units of curriculum and in what ways the outcomes need to be evaluated will be the main thrust? Distinct departure from the existing programme is noticeable in including a course on psychology of teaching and learning. The teaching of educational psychology to the B.Ed. trainees was done extensively even earlier but without establishing linkages with actual teaching and learning. The attempt to put teaching and learning together does not in any way undermine the importance of educational psychology.

Now the basic thrust will be on teaching - learning processes, group dynamics, learners' background, the internal and external forces of the institution and the community. Psychology of teaching and learning would require adjustments at different levels of schooling and for different grade levels. Foundation courses lend support to refining the education processes implicit in teaching and learning. Comparative perspective of educational systems in developing and developed countries would enable teachers to acquire a global vision of contemporary context and gain greater insight into ways of improving the quality of education.

The understanding of some specific areas of education in detail and in depth is needed for becoming an effective teacher. Guided by this consideration and having been supported through field interactions with different target groups, courses on pre-school education and elementary school education have been included as optionals. Teachers will also be required to get in depth understanding of areas like non-formal alternatives to school education. Similarly avenues for in depth studies in emerging areas of concern like vocational education, environmental education, population education etc. have also been suggested. The message of educational technology has to reach the classrooms in the form of its application. Prospective teacher has to be so equipped in the course of training as to enable him to think of using appropriate educational technology for improving the quality of instruction and for obtaining optimum results in terms of the students' growth.

Physical education has been considered as an integral part of education. In each system of schooling tremendous amount of emphasis is laid upon building up the cognitive base of students and the affective and psychomotor dimensions of human personality, do not receive adequate attention. A teacher fashioned in the culture of physical education would be conscious of catering to the physical dimension of human personality with concern. The inclusion of this course, however, may not be taken as an alternative to preparing teachers for teaching Physical Education. The impact of teacher training programmes has not been perceptible over the years in terms of transacting curriculum in schools. Lecture method, mostly taken recourse to by teacher educators, is generally not supplemented by using instructional materials. Interactive teaching, co-operative teaching-learning, self-discovery approaches seldom find place in the day-to-day teaching practices.

What is of importance and calls for top priority in the training programme, is to lay appropriately proportioned emphasis on 'why to teach', 'how to teach' and 'what to teach' aspects of teaching. It has to be reflected in the teaching-learning situations planned by teacher educators. Education as a field of specialised studies is inter-disciplinary in its nature. Since different branches of learning are involved in understanding the presage, process and product variables of education, it is essential that formulation of teacher education programmes adopts a holistic approach in order to promote proper understanding, insight and thinking on matters pertaining to this field. The complimentary character of theory and practice needs to be emphasised at every step.

The prospective teachers are encouraged to organise, express and communicate their ideas clearly in the class. It has to be accepted as a communicative process of an intensive teacher-learner dialogue and renewal of a two-way process as opposed to 'the banking concept' of teaching. The emphasis must be laid on cultivation, formation and development of power of mind in contrast to the prevalent tendency of aiming at the success in examination alone. Student teachers, it is hoped, in classroom transactions, will employ the use of divergent thinking and problem solving strategy. The teacher educators will be required to have clarity of thought in respect of components of a course, objectives of teaching, and their relevance to educational and social goals. One of the approaches may be the modular approach. Each module, though a complete teaching unit, remains a part of the total syllabus with built-in linkages and feedback mechanisms. Learning through this approach can be reinforced by library work, seminar readings, tutorials and small group discussions.

Self-study and self-motivated learning become an integral part of the curriculum transaction. The outcomes would result in better understanding of concepts better leading to mastery learning. The interdisciplinary approach in teaching has to be accepted and implemented for developing comprehensive understanding and vision of educational studies. Learning outcomes have to be assessed continuously, which is the basic tenet of the modular approach. This would help in modifying, adjusting and improving transaction strategies for better acquisition of knowledge. Universities have options to evolve their own examination system. Too much reliance on external examinations, however, would inhibit the progress of moving in the direction of quality education. There is no denying the fact that practice of education is as important as its theory.

Each good theory leads to a good practice and vice-versa. To strike a balance between theory and the practice of education, therefore, is a matter of judicious planning and scheduling in order to give proper direction to teacher education. Changes in the pattern and practices of student teaching have been only peripheral. The content-cum-method approach, wherever attempted, remained limited to the introduction of an additional component of content without fully achieving the objective of integration. The problem-solving approach, discovery method, competency based teaching learning and the indigenous contributions, like those of Gandhi, Tagore, Aurobindo, Zakir Hussain and several others have the potential for bringing in innovative ideas in teacher education. The applications of educational technology, informatics, telematics, cybernetics etc. have yet to make a discernible headway. The learning resources wherever available in the training institutions and the community as also in the schools have not been optimally utilised.

Prerequisite to preparing a prospective teacher can be thought of in terms of providing certain inputs such as, induction programme, an exposure of school experiences with special focus on the educational environment of the school, socio-economic and cultural background of the community constituting the catchment area, observation of classroom teaching and other related activities etc. Induction programme might include acquainting the intending teachers with the school settings, the school programmes - curricular and co-curricular. In addition, they will be prepared for actual classroom teaching and the roles they are expected to assume during the course of practice teaching/internship by way of focussed discussions, demonstration lessons, and preparation of lesson plans in a way as to encompass teaching for cognitive, affective and psychomotor development.

Practice teaching is essentially a joint responsibility of teacher training institution and the school involving teacher educators, prospective teachers and school teachers. Teacher educators will help in facilitating and guiding the activities as implied by the pre-instructional, instructional and post-instructional phases through which a student teacher has to progress. The role of a school teacher in this joint effort lies in extending cooperation to the teacher educator and the intending teacher. Various aspects as referred to above will have to be suitably adapted to varying structures and designs at different stages of teacher education. Practical work other than classroom instruction can be viewed in terms of school and community experiences and activities related to personality and leadership development.

Efforts need to be directed towards developing in a teacher trainee certain competencies and skills which would be helpful in the shaping of a teacher for effective role play. It is essentially directed towards capacity building which may embrace, among other competencies, managerial skills, organisational efficiency, leadership skills, democratic attitudes, innovative and creative abilities etc. The teachers' role, which they will be required to play in the school situation other than classroom teaching, may extend to a variety of activities, such as, maintenance of school records and registers, management of laboratories and library, preparation, repair and selection of instructional aids and equipments, selection and preparation of textual materials, preparation of tests and assignments, admission and selection of students, maintenance of progress reports of students, preparation of school budget and development plans, beautification of school and classroom management etc. The institutional activities within the school environs may include dramatic clubs, stage activities, literary activities, inter-house activities and sports and games, organisation of educational tours, etc.

Interaction between the institution and community is gaining importance in the modern context. One can think of several activities promoting school-community relationship, such as, celebration of birthdays of children, celebration of parents day, activating parent- teacher association for the welfare of the schools, organisation of school and community games, sports and other functions, utilization of community resources for education, understanding the background of children, celebration of national days in collaboration with the community, environmental education, adult literacy, plantation and social forestry. Likewise, community involvement and school development activities may lead to community awareness generating competency through community - institution interaction activities; mobilizing community resources for organising literacy programmes, environmental education, work education programme, health awareness programmes, etc. It is expected that organisation of such activities would lead to developing self confidence and initiative among student teachers and also develop among them positive attitude towards plurality of cultures.

The modalities to be employed for organising activities other than teaching for all round capacity building and empowerment of a teacher-trainee will involve joint supervision by the teacher educator and a school teacher. The transaction modes, for example, for motivating adults for making them literate can be through mass participation, folk songs, street plays etc. The identification of various sports and a variety of activities for cleanliness in the community, collecting success stories and disseminating them in the community, preparing simple write-ups of all the activities undertaken; utilizing community resources for the developmental needs of library building, students scholarships, awards, student aid funds, celebration of festivals etc; student-parent-community contact programmes and organisation of welfare shows for better institution-community participation are certain other strategies of transaction of practical work.

It is expected that a student-teacher undertakes several practical activities which facilitate instruction as also those that relate to management. Relevant to teaching and learning, the intending teacher develops competencies, like identification of support material, skills in preparation of indigenous and low-cost materials, judicious choice and utilisation of material for enhancing the learning and use of community resources for education. The likely activities may include preparation of an inventory of community resources, instructional material, and development of software and use of hardware. The teacher-trainee also gets acquainted with the techniques of diagnosis, remediation, guidance and counselling, classroom interaction inclusive of understanding of context variables implicit in the process of teaching and learning, knowledge of educational rules and regulations/laws, in addition to maintenance of cumulative and comprehensive evaluation records, maintenance of school records and is conscious of professional accountability and ethics. It is hoped that most of the activities will be undertaken by the teacher trainee during the internship period of a reasonable duration. Some of these activities will have to be integrated with practice teaching.

For meaningful organisation of practical work pre-internship stage may be utilised for demonstration lessons, lectures, simulation, role-playing, micro-teaching etc. The transactional mode of community related practical work may include interaction between school teacher and intending teacher and members of the community representing parents, panchayats, senior citizens, voluntary organisations, etc. Student-teachers may undertake a case study of a school (generally a practising school) for identifying its strengths and weaknesses, needs and problems, specific learning problems, such as, drop-outs, drug abuse, behavioural problems, learning difficulties etc. Street plays can be organised by the student teachers to sensitize the community in the ways in which community resources could be utilised and also motivate the community members for greater participation in the school welfare activities.

To come to its present form, work education has undertaken a long journey. From Marx's 'combination of productive labour and learning' to Abbot Wood's 'vocationalisation', it came to Gandhi's 'handicraft as the medium of education' and again took the form of Kothari's 'work experience' which Ishwar Bhai Patel thought to be devoid of 'social value' and coined the term 'Socially Useful Productive Work' (SUPW). Its central purpose is to shift the centrality of education from excessive verbalism to practicality. It has raised certain academic questions apart from the availability of teachers and other resources.

Work education is a powerful medium for personality development. There can be a variety of activities which are necessarily school based and which may be included under work education like maintenance of the school plant including its playgrounds, cleanliness, repair of furniture and production of material to be used as instructional aids. It will be a great educational experience if community visit, field work, nature study, school co-operatives saving bank, games and sports and other co-curricular activities are carefully organised as part of the programmes leading to development of qualities needed for the success of work education.

The rapid erosion of values in the society is causing concern, necessitating imparting of value education. It is generally agreed that cognition is basic to volition which by implication would mean that prospective teachers are expected to understand critical issues regarding values—concept, types, and problems involved in imbibing the values. It is also expected of them to be well-versed with the values enshrined in our Constitution and the values that have the cultural contexts and can be derived from our heritage. In the process of capacity building of intending teachers, what is of importance is to ensure that they become capable of understanding the import of value education, interpreting values in the contemporary contexts and evolving strategies of imbibing these by their students.

An overview of the preceding details would bring in focus the duration required to transact the curriculum and ensure achievement of objectives of teacher preparation at this stage. Through the national consultations initiated by the NCTE, a strong consensus emerged in favour of enhancing the duration of B.Ed. programme from one year to two years.

The new curriculum frame not only transforms the nature and content of the traditional foundation courses but also includes several additional components. Emerging Indian Society will deal with factors and forces operating in the Indian society leading to the emergence of a new social order. The psychology of teaching and learning has been given a new thrust. It will also include findings of researches in life sciences, medicine, neurology, genetics and communication technology having their relevance for teaching and learning. A new course on Secondary Education has been included to provide deeper understanding of issues related to secondary education. Likewise, Guidance and Counselling has been incorporated to make teachers more functional in their jobs.

The course on Curriculum Design and Development will promote the capacity of curriculum development evaluation and transaction. A component of Assessment, Evaluation and Remediation has been added. The school management has been incorporated as a compulsory course because all the teachers must possess its knowledge and acquire its techniques. A new component of action research has been included to develop the problem solving approach. Comparative education has been added to broaden outlook of student teachers and to develop their insight into educational problems and issues. A number of optional subjects out of which the students will select only two have been suggested in the frame. These optionals are intended to develop certain additional competencies among the prospective teachers. The whole spectrum of theoretical courses has therefore not only been enriched but also given a professional shape and outlook which cannot be achieved within the short period of one year.

The practice teaching is now not merely confined to the

teaching of certain subjects. Pedagogical analysis of the subjects offered for practice teaching has been made compulsory. The prospective teacher will analyse the subject before going to class and evolve a need-based pedagogy and transactional strategy. The teacher educators will now deliver model lessons of different types in actual classroom situation and the prospective teachers will not only learn the techniques but make its critical appraisal and evaluation to be subsequently discussed with the teachers. Teacher educators supervising the classroom performance, pupil teachers will discuss their observations with them for providing proper feedback to improve their performance. The practice teaching will, thus, require thorough preparation, detailed supervision and adequate time. Its gain would be acquisition of higher level of teaching competencies.

The practical work has been made comprehensive and meaningful. Internship programme shall be enriched to provide all the experience that a teacher needs. After completion of the period of internship the prospective teacher will acquire necessary experiences for working in school and the training received would be complete as against the partial one at present. The implementation of internship in this format will also need increased duration. The field work, community interaction, school community relationship and similar programme will enable the pupil teacher to develop need based pedagogy. The organisation of physical education and the educational activities, work education, sessional and practical work related to practice teaching and optional, the formulation of programmes for the development of personality, creativity and aesthetic sensibility and action research will lead to the promotion of skills and competencies needed for a teacher, The practical activities mentioned above will enhance the competence of the teachers. The duration of the B.Ed. pogramme will therefore have to be increased. Besides these, a perceptible change in the pedagogy of teacher education itself has been suggested. Its centrality has shifted from the training colleges to schools and its transactional strategies have been transformed.

The teacher educators have to make pedagogical analysis of the subjects to be taught and achieve integration between the theory and practice and also the methodology of teaching. They are expected to evolve a culture-specific and need-based pedagogy and develop the potentiality needed for independent learning and self study for which a number of suggestions have been made. The lessons will have to be supervised intensively and formative approach has to be adopted.

The teacher educator has now to devote more time in the preparation and planning of his own activities for the professional uplift of the prospective teachers by developing certain additional competencies. All these demand more rigour and need more time. Professionalism involves its own compulsion and pressure. It needs a change in attitudes and value systems of the teachers. They have to earn social sanction from the community by improving the quality of their work. The scope of teacher education has been enlarged. Teachers have to perform many additional roles in society. Apart from teaching, they have to act as the agent of change and modernisation, cultural reconstruction and social development to earn recognition as a professional from the society by acquiring new competencies and commitment. They have to become effective and result oriented to enhance their knowledge and develop skills for its communication. These are not possible to be achieved within the short span of one year. Hence the need to increase the duration of the present B.Ed. programme from one year to two years. Existing programmes of two years duration leading to Bachelor's degree in education like B.P.Ed. may continue to be of the same duration. Two years B.Ed. programme will provide a strong base for pursuing M.Ed. course duration for which may continue to be the same as at present.

TEACHER EDUCATION FOR SENIOR SECONDARY STAGE

Teacher education programmes have to respond to three major determinants: the stage-specific developmental characteristics of the students, the courses of study they pursue and the academic qualifications the prospective teachers possess. At the Senior Secondary stage all the three become distinctly different from that of the secondary schools which offer a common curriculum upto class ten.

IN-SERVICE TEACHER EDUCATION

In service teacher education within the overall framework of teacher development has a crucial role to play. It is no cliché but a reality that those who teach should never cease to learn. The National Policy on Education, 1986 stipulates that teacher education is a continuous process and its pre-service and in-service components are inseparable. The initiatives taken in setting up District Institutes of Education and Training (DIETs), Colleges of Teacher Education (CTEs), and Institutions of Advanced Study in Education (IASEs) are some of the major developments in this regard.

Professional development of teachers begins with pre-service and gets renewed through in-service programmes. It, however, does not mean that there is a simple linearity between the two. There are elements of 'change' and 'continuity' in teacher education system which necessitates renewal and upgradation of skills and competencies. The in-service programmes are also organised to sustain the 'survival competencies' which the teachers acquired years ago, during pre-service education.

In the professional updating of teachers, changes in the societal goals, educational structure, curriculum framework, transactional strategies, evaluation techniques and management processes play a significant role. New advances emerging on the educational horizon have to be addressed to and teachers made aware of the same as well. Teacher development is a complex process. Teachers update themselves by putting in various efforts of self-learning, peer learning and interactions with the community. Other alternatives to professional development are participation in recurrent programmes, extension activities and continuing education programmes.

In service teacher education programmes are essential in view of obsolescence as well as explosion of knowledge and are necessitated on account of changes in educational and social realities. Whenever teachers are required to execute new and different roles or get promoted to a position that requires new set of competencies, participation in appropriately designed in-service programmes is called for. Advancements in the fields of curriculum, evaluation, audio-visual aids and telecommunication, etc. demand updating and orientation of teachers. Innovations both at macro and micro levels, would fail if teachers are not equipped and properly oriented to implement. In the Indian context, the developments, such as the 10+2+3 pattern, the making of science compulsory upto class X, new practices in evaluation like internal assessment, question banks, continuous and comprehensive evaluation, scaling and grading, introduction of new areas like environmental education, population education, computer education, AIDS education, gender sensitivity, etc. demand in-service training of teachers.

In-service training programmes are offered in various ways. Resource institutions at the national level offer orientation programmes of varying duration for different target groups. Besides this modality there are others like attachments, visits, national exchange programmes and international study visits; which form a significant component of in-service programmes. Pre-service and initial teacher education is reinforced by self-initiated learning, in-service teacher education programmes and recurrent and continuing education. Self-initiated learning involves study on one's own for professional development. Recurrent and continuing programmes are organised through seminars, workshops, and orientation courses etc. as per the professional requirements.

In the changing context of globalisation, liberalisation and advances in tele-communication, teachers and teacher educators need to become conversant with international trends, internationalism, multi-culturalism, multi-racialism and other pluralities. Both pre-service and in-service teacher education programmes should be receptive to new thinking and new changes. However, reforms and innovations in education can reach schools in large magnitude and expeditiously through in-service education programmes.

MEDIA BASED DISTANCE EDUCATION MODEL

With the advent of satellite technology and computers many training programmes are imparted using electronic media. Audio-conferencing and tele-conferencing are already being used. In these the electronic media play the key role and print material play a supportive role. The advantage of this model is that training objectives can be achieved within limited time period. The constraint of this approach is the limited availability of the technology itself, and its high initial investment. Besides the above three models, some other important considerations contribute to effectiveness of an in-service training programme.

i. *Locale:* Training institutions at the national, state and district level organise training programmes generally at their respective institutions. These institution based trainings have their own strengths in terms of availability of resources. Their limitations are that they dislodge participants from their work place. This approach is often known as off-site approach. On the other hand using on-site approach many institutions organise training programmes at the school site itself. Thus participants are not dislodged from their work place. Extension programmes and on-site programmes take training to the doorsteps of schools/institutions.

ii. *Target Groups:* At present in-service programmes are organised largely for teachers. A few programmes are also organised for headmasters, principals and other supervisory staff. This net has to be widened and many more categories of personnel brought into the fold. In-service teacher education programmes ought to be offered to all teachers working at pre-primary, primary, elementary, secondary and senior secondary levels. These could cater to teachers working in formal schools, non-formal centres, open and distance teaching institutions and institutions of physical education, adult education, special education, etc.

Teacher educators, in general, have limited exposure to in-service education. There is a need to train teacher educators at all levels. In fact, an apex institution needs to be set up for training of teacher educators. Alternatively some selected institutions may develop special expertise in training of teacher educators. Such institutions would have to develop relevant support material and undertake critical research studies relevant to in-service programmes of teacher educators. Besides teachers, supervisors and administrators, there are other categories like Zila Pramukh, Pradhan, Sarpanch etc. connected with Panchayat Raj System who have the responsibility to look after primary level education. Depending upon the resources available staff of the support system, including librarians, hostel wardens, etc. should also be exposed to various programmes to enhance their professional competence.

iii. *Transactional Strategies:* An effective in-service education and training programme would use various transactional strategies like case study method, brain storming sessions, panel discussions, seminars, symposia, small group techniques, project work, library work and lecture-cum-discussion sessions.

The organisers and the resource persons can make an in-service teacher education programme more effective and interesting if the age, experience and background of participants are appropriately used at the planning phase. Since in-service participants bring a lot of experience and way of looking at educational events, they can significantly contribute to the design and development of programmes.

iv. *Content:* Content of in-service programmes would depend upon objectives of each programme which could be grouped under the following major categories:

- School subjects.
- Pedagogy and methodology.

- Emerging issues.
- Teacher's new role.

The focus of in-service programmes is on developing competencies and commitments. The overall aim of in-service programmes is to enable teachers to improve their classroom activities, out-of-the-classroom activities, school activities and community activities.

v. *Evaluation and follow-up:* Evaluation is a weak link in many in-service training programmes. In most of the cases in-service programmes are evaluated, if at all, on an *ad hoc* basis. Each in-service teacher education programme should have monitoring as an integral component so that effectiveness of a programme can be properly assessed and appraised. Programme evaluation should assess whether the required inputs were provided to the programme on time, the logistics properly looked after and coordinated, the reading materials provided to participants etc. Another aspect of programme evaluation should be to assess the gains of each participant. The other subtle aspect is the impact evaluation to assess the impact of the programme at the grassroot level and in the field situation.

Success of an in-service teacher education programme may be assessed by collecting perceptions of trainees and of resource persons.

POINTERS FOR FUTUREP

Education and training programmes become more productive and effective when programme planning is participative and transactional strategies are interactive. The need of all in-service teacher education programmes must emerge from the grassroots.

For example, under the centrally sponsored teacher education programme, District Institutes of Education and Training are expected to organise programmes for teachers in such a way that every elementary teacher gets a chance to participate in the programme of his or her choice at least once every five years. In this venture state level coordinating agency like SCERT can play a facilitative and co-ordinating role to ensure that need based in service programmes are launched.

In some states due to certain reasons and other considerations, untrained and under-qualified teachers get recruited. These untrained and underqualified teachers need training and content upgradation. The backlog of untrained and underqualified teachers has to be cleared at the earliest. Whenever teachers are promoted from elementary level to secondary level or from secondary level to senior secondary level, intensive in-service training programmes should be designed and offered to them. Whenever a teacher takes up new educational assignments (headmastership or principalship), he/she would require task oriented in-service training. There is a need to make a shift in organising programmes from training institutions to schools and school clusters. Concerted efforts may be made in this direction.

Development of support material is very important for in-service education. Unless quality support materials are developed, face-to-face training alone may not be enough. Good quality support material in the form of print, video cassette and computer programmes have to be designed developed and disseminated.

Some in-service programmes are made credit oriented. On successful completion of specified programmes, participants may be considered for professional mobility. Participation in in-service programmes within a stipulated period should be made obligatory and appropriate incentives thought of. Organising in-service training porgramme using mobile training teams may also be thought of.

ALTERNATIVE SYSTEMS/ APPROACHES IN EDUCATION

Global upsurge for universal education, explosion of knowledge, expectation and aspirations for better quality of life have led to the exploration of alternatives to formal system which suffers from inherent inadequacies of rigidity and structural deficiencies.

These alternatives include non-formal education, adult education, distance education, etc. While a good deal of work has been undertaken to spread and improve education through various alternatives, a major problem has been lack of trained functionaries. However, these functionaries cannot be prepared on the formal models of teacher preparation. Since they are required to perform functions of different nature, their training has essentially to be job-specific. Developing skills, competencies and commitments in the personnel involved in alternative strategies demand preparation and use of teaching and learning materials to be specifically designed for the programmes.

NON-FORMAL EDUCATION

Non-formal education consists of an organised systematic and planned educational activity, essentially characterised by inbuilt flexibility and carried on outside the framework of the formal system. It provides learning experiences to children in the age group of 6-14 years who are not able to avail of the facilities of formal schooling. Children from the non-formal system are eligible to appear in the examinations leading to certification to join the formal stream.

In certain respects formal and non-formal education are similar as both are organised to augment, promote and facilitate learning. They differ in their institutional management and the organisation of the course content. The training of the functionaries at different levels including instructors, supervisors, material writers, project officers and managers is significant.

ADULT EDUCATION

To achieve its present status, adult education has undertaken a long journey. Literacy campaigns during the thirties led to strengthening of social education. In sixties, it took the shape of functional literacy programme which was further reinforced to include functional literacy, numeracy and technocracy. It is now seen as an integral part of life-long learning. It duplicates certain functions of non-formal and continuing education. Adult education is expected to provide the skills needed to survive in the modern world for leading an effective and 'good life'. It includes adults of all ages.

National literacy programmes focus specifically on those in the age group of 15-35 years in Indian context. It aims at developing the capacity of 'learning to learn' with or without the help of adult educator. Adult education concerns those who are not full time learners and have not been exposed to formal education. The knowledge gained and skills developed from it are utilised in a variety of situations. Thus, it has become need-based.

DISTANCE EDUCATION

Distance education is emerging as an alternative to the formal education system. The emphasis on education for all, explosion of population along with the desire for education, limitation of the formal system in providing greater accessibility and the rising expectations from education are some of the factors for its increasing demand. The new communication technology has brought it within the reach of all. Originally designed to provide alternative educational avenues to the poor and the working people for higher education, it has now developed as a parallel system in India from the primary to tertiary levels and covers not only liberal but scientific and professional studies as well.

Distance education implies the provision of educational opportunity at the place of learner from a distance by means of multiple media such as self-learning materials, audio-visual gadgets and short-term personal contact programmes. Information technology and cybernetics are simultaneously being utilised for upgrading the knowledge and skills.

STUDENTS WITH SPECIAL NEEDS

Democracy intrinsically implies provision of equality of educational opportunity to all according to the learner's age, ability, and aptitude. It envisages equality not only in terms of access, but also in achievement and the life chances. Every child in the classroom is unique and therefore, deserves individual attention. There are also children having mild or moderate disabilities who can be served by the general classroom teachers only if they are properly sensitised to the needs of such children. Similarly, gifted and talented children also need to be identified and provided necessary educational inputs. In addition, there may be children lagging behind due to specific learning difficulties which may have remained unidentified.

Teachers for the Gifted

In every society or school one can find children who are much above the average and possess certain special abilities. They are referred to as the gifted or talented children. It has been observed that generally teachers are not properly trained to nurture the talent of such children. Every society needs the gifted and the talented for its progress. It is, therefore, necessary that proper provisions are made for their education.

In India certain schools have been started for the education of the gifted and the talented children. In these schools as well as in the general schools the teachers are appointed from the general pool of trained teachers whose training, by and large, is not oriented towards meeting the educational requirements of such children. Since giftedness and talent, like disability, have different shades and colours, the preparation of teachers should also be multi-dimensional.

EDUCATION OF TEACHERS FOR PHYSICAL EDUCATION

Physical education is an integral part of the education system. It aims at building a sound body, a sharp mind and wholesome personality. It is essential for the cultivation of vitality, courage, self-confidence, cooperativeness, leadership, obedience, discipline and positive attitude towards life and the world. Development of physical fitness and health of students is not the responsibility of the teachers of physical education alone. In fact, every teacher has a role to play in this direction, especially at the elementary stage and must have substantial exposure to physical education and health education. The teachers other than physical education teachers also need to take interest in games and sports and physical activities.

Every prospective teacher irrespective of the level needs to be made conversant with the basics of physical education. In addition, every trainee is required to participate in at least one major group game and two items of sports. It needs to be provided for in the curriculum with a view to enabling them to generate a climate for promotion of physical activities.

EDUCATION OF TEACHER EDUCATORS

The role of teacher educator is of prime importance for effective implementation of teacher education curriculum. Education and training of teacher educators is a pre-requisite for effective changes in the training and orientation of teachers. India has a large system of teacher education. There are more than 2000 elementary teacher education institutions, Colleges of Education and University Departments of Education. Nearly 30,000 teacher educators are engaged in the preparation of school teachers. In addition, there are teacher educators working in pre-primary training schools as well as institutions concerned with the preparation of teachers for the education of children with special needs and alternative education such as non-formal education, distance education, etc.

It is well recognised that the overall quality in education mainly depends on the quality of teachers and a sound programme of professional preparation of teachers is essential for imparting quality education. However, Teacher educators' own education leaves much to be desired. Teaching is an art which can be inculcated through a series of well designed activities in respect of education and training of teachers and is equally valid for professional preparation of teacher educators. The teacher educators would not only be training pre-service and in-service trainees but would also be associating themselves with several other activities. New strategies and techniques of material development, the changing approach to evaluation, intensive interactions with the community, creating an activity-based environment in the training institutions, acquiring skills for resource mobilisation and several other such competencies at mastery level would be essential for professionals to function as teacher educators.

Changes in the school curricula would be faster in the near future. Corresponding changes in training pro-grammes and strategies shall have to be perceived and given a shape by the teacher educators. In the context of universalisation of elementary education, teacher educators will be expected to display a deeper understanding of the issues pertaining to access, participation and attainment in their specific regions or areas. They need adequate professional competence to conduct such surveys and studies would reveal the region specific and area specific issues and problems which would help the functionaries of the education department and the community.

They will prepare the trainees in responding to these issues during the training period and also in schools subsequently. The professional quality of teacher educator will determine the quality of the training of teachers, both pre-service as well as in-service. The professional level at which teachers are prepared would, in turn, determine the quality of school education. Again, teacher educators have to be fully familiar with the school realities, social environment and community expectations to realistically perform the challenging tasks before them. On the professional side, teacher educators need to be actively associated with policy formulations, implementation strategies and monitoring of programmes.

Existing System

At present, the only programme which is often treated as preparing teacher educators is that of M.Ed. Scrutiny of the curriculum of most of the M.Ed. programmes would reveal that these have not been specifically designed to prepare teacher educators. There are some M.Ed. programmes where provisions do not exist for writing a dissertation. The products of these programmes would certainly not be in a position to conduct research, initiate innovation on their own and induct teacher trainees in these areas which are essential functions of teacher educators. Prior to the establishment of the NCTE as a statutory body, NCERT acted as its secretariat and organised several professional development programmes for teacher educators in areas like micro-teaching and simulation, student teaching and evaluation, preparing research proposals, improvement of teacher education curricula and so on. The University Grants Commission (UGC) has been organising national and regional level workshops for improvement of the teacher education programmes.

Through various schemes it offers financial support for seminars, workshops and research projects for teacher educators for such themes as higher education, educational technology, non-formal education, population education, environmental education, research methodology, etc. The National Institute of Educational Planning and Administration (NIEPA) organises programmes for Principals of Colleges of Education, Heads of University Departments of Education and other administrators concerned with teacher education. The SCERTs and State Boards of Teacher Education organise continuing education programmes for teacher educators on teaching methodologies for new subject areas and on innovations in education.

Some University Departments of Education organise seminars, workshops, and orientation programmes for teacher educators on teaching, development of instructional skills, interaction analysis, teaching behaviour, educational technology, guidance and counselling and research methodology. Certain Colleges of Education and University Departments of Education have been upgraded as Colleges of Teacher Education (CTEs) and Institutions of Advanced Study in Education (IASEs) for taking up innovations in teacher education. NCTE after its establishment in 1995 as a statutory body, has initiated several programmes aimed at enhancing professional competence of teacher educators. These include seminars and workshops in the area of human rights and national values, indigenous thoughts in education, indigenous approach to teacher preparation, institutional networking and capacity enhancement and production of good quality enrichment materials for teacher educators.

These institutions have considerable experiences in organising training and development activities. Based upon the experience gained they will have to evolve programmes of sequential nature with in-built mechanism for assessment and impact evaluation. In the absence of an appropriate policy of recruitment, especially at the pre-primary, primary and elementary stages of teacher preparation, the manpower in the institutions of teacher education does not necessarily possess the professionally required qualifications for the preliminary stages. At the pre-primary stage one comes across teacher educators who have passed high school or higher secondary examination and possess a certificate in teacher training, not necessarily meant for the pre-primary stage; graduates or those with higher qualification with absolutely no training background or with the background not appropriate for that stage or level.

As regards the primary and elementary stages, the teacher educators, generally, possess graduate or higher qualification with teacher training mostly at the B.Ed. level. There are serious lacunae in the recruitment policies in as much as the professional qualifications prescribed are not stage-specific and mostly not suited to the education of teachers for the stage or level concerned. This situation calls for fresh thinking regarding recruitment policies for teacher educators and well-planned programmes of education for teacher educators.

Education and training of teacher educators has to focus its attention on the new role of teacher educators on the problems which reflect the emerging global trends in education and the overall needs and aspirations of the people in India. It has also to deal with specific problems confronting teacher education institutions and to make teacher education more responsible and responsive. It also has to encourage teacher educators' continuing professional growth. In addition, there are certain practical problems as well. For instance, what would be the basic qualifications of teacher educators at various stages of teacher preparation? What would be the requirements in respect of the core education courses and for the organisation of procedures and practices in the institutions?

EVOLVING MODELS OF PRE-SERVICE EDUCATION

The present system of pre-service education of teacher educators is characterised by lack of perspective in terms both of contents as well as qualifications. For instance, while it is well accepted that the B.Ed. qualification entitles a person to teach at secondary stage, it is doubtful if the M.Ed. programme adequately prepares a person to become teacher of secondary school teachers.

The existing M.Ed. programme has little provision of training in and working out teaching and evaluation strategies suited to the needs of teacher trainees. And yet one finds M.Ed. degree holders entrusted with the responsibility of teacher preparation not only at secondary stage but also at the pre-primary, primary and elementary stages of teacher preparation. Likewise, while the B.Ed. qualification legitimately entitles a person to teach at the secondary stage, it cannot, at the same time, be accepted as a good enough qualification for being a teacher educator at the primary stage.

The existing B.Ed. programme is designed mainly to teach high school students and not for preparing primary school teacher educators. Thus, it is imperative that the professional qualification of teacher educators is made stage-specific suited to the needs of teacher trainees of different categories. It is time for seriously considering designing of definite programmes to prepare teacher educators rather than depend on the conventional B.Ed. or/and M.Ed. course. Education of teacher educators has necessarily to correspond to teacher preparation programmes. It is nonetheless necessary to consider alternatives and institute programmes like M.Ed. (Teacher

Education) catering to the needs of stage-specific and category-specific preparation of teacher educators alongside general M.Ed. programmes.

Strengthening the Programmes

An altogether fresh look is necessary for first developing need-based programmes for the preparation of teacher educators and then working out well planned strategies for implementing these programmes. Needless to say that the preparations of teacher educators would concern itself with the relevant theoretical courses as well as the consonant practicum. At the theoretical level, the choice of pedagogical inputs has to be guided by various contexts and their educational and professional concerns. In addition to theory courses, specialisation courses with reference to teacher education have to be included. The theoretical courses will have a bearing on the practice of teacher education. It will be necessary to develop competencies and skills in prospective teacher educators relating to their work situations.

What goes on in teacher training institutions by way of educational programmes and activities has to be reflected in the education and training of teacher educators. It essentially implies that the preparation of teacher educators has to be made an integral part of the system of teacher education. It will be pertinent to evolve pedagogy relevant to the stage or category specific programmes. It will lay due emphasis on societal goals, values specially those enshrined in the Indian Constitution, higher order learning processes, curriculum development and theory and practice of educational research including action research. Competence to carry out research and innovations needs to be acquired by all. Training in curriculum development and preparation of learning materials is inalienable aspect of entire process of teacher education. Similarly, development of evaluation materials would result into more effective utilisation of evaluation in teacher education institutions.

The practical work has among other things necessarily to include internship programme by way of attachment to the stage-specific and category-specific teacher education institutions. This will give the prospective teacher educators an adequate knowledge of the total functioning of teacher education institution, the improvements needed and also provide insights into the problems and issues concerning maintenance of institutional plant, classroom management, organisational climate of the institution etc. As for practice teaching, the main thrust has to be on a variety of techniques such as team teaching, micro-teaching, panel discussion, seminar, demonstration, etc. as integral part of classroom-teaching-learning-evaluation procedures. Practical work other than internship and practice teaching has to develop competencies and skills in organising activities concerning work education and working with community as per the practical work requirements in the teacher education institutions.

THRUSTS IN IN-SERVICE AND CONTINUING EDUCATION

The present provision for continuing education of teachér educators is inadequate in respect of both quality and content. Planning in respect of in-service education of teacher educators needs to be evolved for different stages and levels. The major thrusts in respect of programmes for teacher educators among others may be as follows:

- Designing short-term programmes for those who are already placed in these institutions.
- Specific short-term induction programmes for those who do not have the experience for the stage they are supposed to be working at.
- Identification of certain university departments of education and Institutions of Advanced Study in Education as institutions which may work mainly for teacher educators. They may focus on induction training, recurrent training, orientation programmes, research studies and surveys, curriculum development, preparation of training materials, evaluation strategies and techniques, use of educational technology, media and others.

- Establishment of institutions for preparation of teacher educators for special education at different stages. These may be open to primary and secondary trained graduates willing to become teacher educators. Such programmes need to be designed with particular focus on the practicum that would familiarize the trainees with school situations in totality.
- Networking of various institutions and organisations for designing and carrying out collaborative programmes by pooling and sharing of resources.

The fact that our education system has inadequate facilities for preparation and orientation of teacher educators has been a major factor for not taking due care of the education and training of teacher educators in several respects. With the policy focus changing to quality and relevance of education; it is necessary that only those, who are professionally competent, committed and willing, are charged with the responsibility of preparing teachers for the nation. Teachers for various stages, levels and categories are prepared professionally by teacher educators. The quality and character of teachers therefore, would largely depend on the professional education of teacher educators. Towards this, It is necessary, therefore, that their education should be given a new orientation and improved qualitatively and adjusted properly with the demands of the new curriculum.

MANAGING THE SYSTEM

This Curriculum Framework is characterised, by among other things, ample measure of flexibility and responsiveness to the needs of teacher education system in the country. Teacher education institutions and organisations at various levels will initiate the process of development of curriculum after in depth perusal of this document. The exercise has to be need-based and in tune with demands and directions of the National Policy on Education. The extent of success in implementation would largely depend on the support and assistance provided by the management system. Imposition of a rigid and uniform management system ignoring the regional variations and cultural diversity of Indian society may not be conducive to achieving the targets of teacher education.

Consultative in policy planning and decentralised implementation are bound to be more acceptable and productive. Institutional autonomy for the experimentation of innovative ideas and practices needs to be assured. This, however, would be possible only if autonomy and corresponding accountability are blended together. Accountability within the system is to be transparently reflected and judged to the extent to which it responds to the regional expectations and requirements. The system need not merely be concerned with the needs of the present but also be dynamic and forward looking.

While developing the curriculum of teacher education, disciplinary and professional components need to be interwoven to improve the quality. An attempt of this kind will give it a more meaningful direction. The research findings in the areas of life sciences, anthropology, etc., when included in the curriculum of teacher education, will increase its relevance and make it more functional. The use of indigenous educational thought will enhance its relevance to Indian situation. Various types of dichotomies and misconceptions need to be carefully identified and subsequently weeded out from the content of studies. The increased duration of the programme of teacher education may be properly utilised for the professional development of teachers. It would also require inclusion of additional inputs of theoretical, pedagogical and practical components and proper allocation of time and resources for improving the quality of teacher education.

Any sudden and abrupt departure from the prevailing practices would only destabilise the existing programme and may prove to be counter-productive. The teachers must be fully exposed to philosophy and purpose of this curriculum framework. A time bound programme for its implementation should be prepared, its priorities be fixed and strategies evolved after careful planning. The gaps of the existing system be identified and removed. In this document certain alternative models of teacher education have been proposed. It will depend on the concerned organisation/institutions to select one or the other for implementation after due consideration of its possible professional gains and availability of resources and expertise.

A favourable climate at the national level needs to be created for implementation of the recommendations. Seminars and meetings of teachers, teacher educators, and administrative functionaries at the state level will have to be arranged. The regional language versions of this document will be widely circulated. The NGOs working in the field of education and other welfare activities may be involved. The meetings of Education Secretaries, DPIs, Principals of DIETs, Principals of CTEs/IASEs, Directors of SCERTs, Chairmen of Faculties of Education, Heads of Departments of Education and conveners of the Boards of studies may be arranged. Short term training programme in the form of seminars, workshops, summer schools and orientation courses may be organised.

These exercises of awareness generation will prepare institutions, universities, state Govts. bodies and others to evolve a specific plans of implementation in their own areas. The NCTE should take the responsibility of assisting in preparation of relevant materials. The professional association of teachers and teacher educators will have to come forward and play a constructive role for upgrading the quality of teacher education. For putting the suggestions into actual practice supplementary materials will be required in the form of teachers' guides, handbooks, etc.

8

Population Education

Population Education is an educational programme which aims at making learners aware of the inter-relation-ships between population and sustainable development since it also aims at inculcating in them rational attitude and responsible behaviour towards population and development issues, co-curricular activities can play a very important role in achieving this. It is widely agreed that the purpose of education is that students shall be trained not only to know the right things but also to behave in the right way. A close relationship between right knowledge and right action is sought for – Here the former is mostly taken care by the Curricular Activities and the latter part is taken care mostly by the Co-curricular Activities.

The Curricular Activities are mainly cognitive in nature and concentrate on intellectual development of the students. However, the objective of education is not confined to intellectual development only but also an all round development of personality, i.e., besides intellectual growth, education shall also cater to the emotional, physical, psychological ad social development.

The development in these areas may take place if curricular activities are supplemented with the co-curricular activities. Thus CCA may be defined as – The Activities undertaken to strengthen the classroom learning as well as other activities, both inside and outside the classroom to develop the personality of the child.

Historically this is not a new field for we know that such activities were common places in Greek and Roman times as well. Our Modem Olympic Games are based on early Greek athletic contests. In India, there is ample evidence from of ancient scriptures, like Upnishads, Mahabharata, etc. which reveal that in the ancient Gurukuls and Ashrams of the Vedic Rishis and Gurus, the pupils were expected to participate in a number of co-curricular activities, such as taking the cows to pastures, milking the cows, cleaning and decorating Ashrams or Gurukuls, cooking, wrestling, arching, singing, dancing, etc. All our great philosophers/educators, right from Plato and Aristotle to Herbert Spencer and John Dewey, have stressed the importance of providing opportunities in schools to organizing activities which are known as Co-curricular Activities.

It was during British rule that Indian education system suffered a great drawback that it became too literary or bookish. The Co-curricular activities regained its original importance when many of our national leaders focussed upon its need. Dr. Zakir Hussain, then Vice Chancellor of Jamia Millia Islamia, Delhi has been credited with giving co-curricular activities their due place in the form of physical and socio-cultural activities when he prepared the Basic Education Curriculum on the lines suggested by Gandhiji. Later, in the post independent India, all Education Commissions/Committees set up from time to time and the National Policy on Education also have promoted the importance of involving children in schools in all kinds of co-curricular activities.

Importance of co-curricular activities regained socio-psychological perspective. The importance of activities lies in the fact that there had been an attempt to find a more satisfactory term like CCA instead of earlier being known an Extra-Curricular Activities - which made it appear as something outside of the real function of the school and consequently, as non-essential. The co-curricular activity, as already mentioned earlier is very important for realizing the goals of Education. Further they also have certain social and psychological implications. For instance, students who participate in drama or any cultural activity, come in contact with various people, like organizers, fellow participants, teachers, etc. This contact or interaction with various persons satisfies the need of socialization, self-identification and self-assessment - these in turn satisfy the need of belongingness.

Similarly, out door activities like tours, rock-climbing, camping, etc. provide ample opportunities where the students develop the spirit of fellow-feeling, sympathy, co-operation, sacrifice etc. Human beings have a psychological tendency to influence their fellow beings by their achievements. Activities like sports and games provide the children many such occasions when they can display their qualities and attain appreciation. At the same time in the course of their participation, they learn how to develop sportsmanship and how to behave when they win or lose an event.

ACTIVITIES FOR ADOLESCENTS

Adolescence is a very crucial period in the life of an individual. It neither is a twilight zone in which society, neither accords them full adult responsibility and roles nor considers them children. During this period children move from a period of sheltered, cared and dependent life towards independent and responsible life of adulthood. The adolescents tend to assert their identity, start taking their own decisions, distancing from their parents, depending more on their peer groups and demonstrating strong preference for privacy. Though these are normal developments among them that occur because of hormonal changes, the achievements and adjustments in life depend to a great extent on the experiences and behaviour patterns acquired during this period. Since all kinds of developments - physical, social, emotional and psychological are taking place almost simultaneously and the effect of development of one aspect has a bearing on the development of other aspect, it becomes pertinent to ensure the all round development of the adolescent child and hence the need of co-curricular activities. Further, these activities channel their energies to proper direction. Also, these activities give adolescents a feeling of competence and self-confidence and help them develop useful and enjoyable skills. It may be music, sports, rock-climbing or any other hobby that may interest them.

RELEVANCE OF CCA IN POPULATION EDUCATION

The National Population Education Programme was launched in India in 1980 in almost all the states with an overarching objective of institutionalising Population Education in formal and non-formal education although the text-books continue to be the mainstay of the teaching- learning process in schools for various reasons. It was realised right from the inception of this Programme that the CCA will have to play a significant role in conveying the elements of Population Education not only to the students but also to the community at large.

As we are aware that it takes a rather long time for any new educational concern to become an integral part of school syllabus and textbooks, and hence in view of the urgency to make students aware of the new components like adolescent reproductive health, etc. which have been lately included in the reconceptualised Population Education, there is a need to adopt an approach that extends beyond prescribed courses, because of its very vide scope. The reason being - as it is not all the components of Population Education could be integrated in the textbooks of various subjects at all school stages because of the limitation, of subjects concerned.

For the transaction of those 'leftover' components, the CCA has been an effective medium. Secondly, even those components, which are there in the textbooks, can be communicated much more effectively if reinforced through CCA. Finally, for any educational innovation like Population Education programmes to be successful, it is essential that it interest the target group and CCA help in generating that interest among the target group. The Project Evaluation study conducted by IIPS, Bombay has revealed that students who participated in Population Education related activities show better awareness of and more positive attitudes towards population issues.

TYPE OF ACTIVITIES

The school has a strategic role to play in planning and organising within its scope a wide range of co-curricular activities. Major objective is to promote learning through creative self-expression and at the same time offering enjoyment, relaxation, satisfaction and recreation to the students. There are a number of ways in which learning through CCA can be planned. A suggestive list of activities in 6 broad categories viz. literary, art and craft, dramatics and music, social action, specific projects and celebration of special events, for example Days/Weeks are given in the tabular form.

Some of important CCA which can be undertaken to make the teaching of Population Education effective are discussed below:

- *Village Adoption:* In this activity, schools are encouraged to adopt villages for intensive work relating to all aspects of Population Education. Messages related to the themes of Population Education may be communicated in several ways. The approach, in general is that of integration with community development in which messages related to various themes under P.E. are transmitted to the people.
- *Population Education Laboratories/Club:* Through Population Education Laboratories as set up in schools, ways and means of transmitting Population Education messages may be evolved and innovative materials and programmes for the same may be developed. In general, the activities organised in Population Education Laboratories and in Village Adoption Programme are organising Quiz, Group Singing, Lectures, Celebration of P.E. Day, etc.
- *Celebration of Important Days/Weeks/Events:* Generally, the schools celebrate special Days/Events/Weeks by organising relevant activities. With a view to make Population Education an integral part of the school programme, celebration of special events/days/weeks

related to population issues and themes like World Population Day, World AIDS Day, Women's Day, Environment Day, Population Education Week etc. are encouraged. On such occasions, Population Education activities are organised which convey the messages in a subtle manner.

- *Debate:* Under debate, opposing points of view are presented and defended by the members of two teams. It is an effective technique for probing into controversial issues. The advantages and disadvantages of an issue are presented in the debate. It helps students in taking rational position on any issue. Debate is useful when we wish to explore a topic from several point of view. The issue to be debated should have positive and negative aspects that can be argued for and against by students. The students may be asked to form two teams. One team may be in favour of the motion and the other against the motion.

The task of each team is to identify the supporting arguments and assemble the relevant evidence for an assigned position. Each team may then select three or four speakers to represent their group's views in the debate. The teacher may chair the debate. When all the speakers have presented their views, the chairperson may then sum up the points made by students during the debate. Alternatively, a panel of judges may be formed for evaluation and selection of best speakers from both the teams.

Painting Competition

The objective behind this activity is to involve the students in this competition so that they give some thought to the topic of painting and then are able to manifest their thoughts in the form of their art work. This is one of the most popular activities in schools. The topic for the painting may be given to the students well in advance so that they are able to gather information and support material on population issues (the topic of painting) as reference for authentic depiction in their art work.

Alternatively, the topic for painting competition may be given on the spot. In that case the teacher may initiate some discussion on the given topic and indicate possibilities of population related issues and ideas which can be expressed suitably in the form of visuals. The advantage of holding this activity is that children of all ages can participate. In fact, the competition must be organized separately for Secondary/ Higher Secondary, Upper Primary and Primary stages) in schools. The students may be asked to bring with them the art related materials like colours, brushes, paper etc. and allow them to prepare their art composition. A panel of judges may be invited for evaluation and selection of best paintings from each school stage. The selected paintings may be exhibited at appropriate places in the school premises.

Role Play

Role play means presenting small spontaneous plays which describe possible real life situations. A situation is given to the group and they take on the roles of the people involved. The role play amounts to initiating someone else's character. It is an important activity as it allows students to practice such situations before they may meet them in their real life. It also provides them an opportunity to practice skills that are significant for protecting themselves from risky or adverse situations. For organizing this activity, the teacher may discuss population related issues on the basis of which either the students themselves prepare a small play, or the teacher gives a play. The students may volunteer for enacting the roles of the character involved in the play. They should be encouraged to expand on their roles. After the role play, the teacher may discuss the appropriate actions needed with respect to the action taken under each role in the play.

Essay Competition

The Essay competition can also make a significant contribution in creating awareness regarding population issues. This is because it provides opportunity to students to gather information from various sources on the topic of Essay. At the same time, while writing the essay students understand and appreciate various aspects of the given topic as exercise which develops in them the competence of logical and rational thinking which is very important for a curricular area like population education. For organizing Essay competition, the students may be given one hour to write their essay on the topic given to them. A panel of judges may assess all the essays written by students. A few selected essays may be read out by students in the classroom. Also some good essays may be included in the school magazine.

Population education which emerged as an educational innovation in response to population problems about four decades ago, is now being experimented in over a hundred countries of the world in non-too-uniform a manner. It has been introduced in the education systems of different countries as an important component of the multi-pronged strategy employed to help nations attain the goals of population stabilisation and sustainable development. Very few educational programmes have matched its pace of expansion and adopted such varied conceptual frameworks and strategies of curriculum transaction. Perhaps no other educational concept has experienced such frequent changes in its framework and been subjected to so many misunderstandings as the concept of population education. This has been so because of not only the nature of the context in which it emerged but also its newness and its complex characteristics.

The concept of population education emerged in the context of population and development - the two most pressing issues before humankind today. Both are closely interrelated and both encompass a number of complex factors. Viewed as an epiphenomenon of the process of development, population issues have aroused widespread concern among almost all the members of the comity of nations. There have been undaunted endeavours to accelerate the pace of socioeconomic development through the instrumentalities of science and technology and to secure distributive justice for the people through different institutional mechanisms. But those are confronted with some basic population related questions of how many people are going to inhabit the earth, how they are to be supported and enabled to make their contributions to development efforts, what they are going to bequeath to posterity and how long they are going to be sustained by the natural and human resource base.

The rapid population growth and the concomitant problems of poverty, lack of adequate health and educational facilities, malnutrition, non-fulfilment of even the basic needs of a vast majority of the populace, paucity of employment opportunities, dwindling natural resources and consequent environmental degradation constitute critical dimensions of the present population and development phenomena. It is also pertinent to note that the population phenomenon today embraces issues beyond development. While the size, growth, composition and distribution of population have a close bearing on socioeconomic development, the population related issues also bring forth concerns for the "carrying capacity" of biological and ecological system and the future of mankind.

NEED FOR POPULATION EDUCATION

It has been gradually realized that since the interrelationship between population and development is highly complex and population problems are multidimensional, it will not yield to any single solution. It is basically related to the developmental needs of a nation and its people. Demographic trends influence, and are influenced by, the level of development and the quality of life of the people. The population situation of any nation largely depends on the demographic behaviour of its people. Changes in the demographic profile of a nation depend largely on attitudes and behaviours of individuals in respect of population and development issues. The demographic behaviour is to a great extent informed by population socialization, a process by which people acquire norms, values, attitudes and belief systems in respect of population related issues and which is embedded within the larger complexes of social practices reflecting the society's internal logical system.

This process is greatly influenced by education which enables the individual to know the phenomenon of population change and its consequences. It is commonly observed in many countries that the knowledge of the simple facts of population change, let alone the complex interrelationships with other parameters, is very low even among educated people. It is precisely because of these complexities that population education has emerged as an integral part of the multi-pronged strategy employed to solve contemporary population problems that face the nations.

The idea that population education can play a potential role in addressing population problems was first mooted in Sweden in 1935. The Population Commission of Sweden, which expressed its concern on the declining rates of birth in that country, recommended a comprehensive and truly vigorous educational campaign to clarify population related issues aimed at influencing the fertility behaviour of individuals. A similar view was expressed in the United States during 1937-38.

Since the birth rate continued to decline and population seemed to be dwindling, it was suggested that population studies be included as a content area in the school curriculum. However, nothing noteworthy happened during the next two decades.

It was in the 1960s that the matter was seriously reconsidered in the United States. Warren S. Thompson and Philip M. Hauser published papers in March 1962 issue of *Teachers College Record,* Columbia University reiterating the inclusion of population content in the school curriculum. Interestingly, they made such recommendations in a completely different context, as the perception of population problem had changed during 1960s and the concern had shifted from decline in growth rate to rapid population growth in both the industrialized and developing worlds. In the fifties and sixties, therefore, efforts were initiated in a number of countries to arrest population growth; and motivational activities for adults provided information about the consequences of high birth rate.

The information, education and communication "IEC" or information education and motivation "IEM' strategy was employed in family planning programmes to achieve the desired objectives. However, in the developing world the "IEC" activities of family planning programmes were not always as successful as had been expected. It was in this context that the potential of education was realised in order to overcome deeply entrenched traditional learning that influenced demographic behaviour of the people. The school education, in particular, was considered effective for achieving this objective. However, the nomenclature of population education was given to this educational innovation at a later date. Sloan Wayland was the first to use the term "population education".

The first national endeavour to evolve and concretise the concept of population education was made in India in 1969 and then in the Philippines and the Republic of Korea in 1970. The Workshop on Population and Family Education sponsored by the UNESCO Regional Office for Education in Asia held in September 1970 at Bangkok was a land-mark in the history of population education. It not only facilitated the identification of objectives of population education, the selection of suitable contents and the consideration of strategies for introduction of population education into formal and non-formal education systems but also resulted in the launching of national population education programmes by many countries in Asia. Similar activities were initiated by UNESCO Regional Offices in Santiago (Latin America and Caribbean) and Dakar (Africa South of the Sahara). The United Nations Population Fund (UNFPA), previously known as United Nations Fund for Population Activities, played a vital role in appreciating the potential of population education and providing funds for national programmes from the late sixties onwards.

Population education emerged as an educational innovation during 1970s and various countries initiated activities to introduce it into their ongoing education systems.

The recommendations of the World Population Plan of Action adopted at the 1974 World Population Conference held in Bucharest, also encouraged nations to adopt the strategy of population education. The Plan of Action recommended that "the Governments should consider making provision, in both the formal and non-formal educational programmes, for informing their people on the consequences of existing or alternative fertility behaviour for the well-being of the family, for the educational and psychological development of children and for the general welfare of society, so that an informed and responsible attitude to marriage and reproduction will be promoted".

In India, the Family Planning Association for the first time sent a Memorandum to the State Government of Maharashtra in 1968 recommending that education in population dynamics should be made a part of school curriculum. However, the idea of population education was crystallised in the National Seminar on Population Education organised in Bombay in August 1969. It recommended that population education should be introduced into curriculum of schools and colleges. The Seminar made an attempt to define population education in the context of Indian situation, but more importantly, expressed the national consensus for introducing this educational innovation in the education system of the country.

POPULATION EDUCATION AND OTHER CONCEPTS

In the initial phase of its evolution, there were several misconceptions regarding population education, and some of those still continue to affect its proper understanding. Population education was popularly equated with family planning or family planning education, primarily because of its emergence in close association with the "IEC" or "IEM' activities of the family planning programmes. It was also regarded as a euphemism for sex education and family life education, as in some countries the concerned programmes approached population issues in terms of sexuality.

Population education was also equated with population studies, and even now both the terms are sometimes used interchangeably, because the core of the knowledge base of population education, (the basic core content upon which the population education curriculum is developed), contained the elements of population studies. While population education is none of these "educations" in the true sense, it draws contents from all those educational areas the objectives of which are mutually supportive. It is necessary, therefore, to discuss the nature and objectives of certain related areas, as it may help in proper understanding of the distinction and complementarity between population education and them.

FAMILY PLANNING

In many countries population programmes were initiated as family planning programmes which had a special "IEC" or "IEM" component. This component came to be popularly known also as family planning education. In some countries this campaign was launched in a very narrow sense aimed at creating awareness about controlling birth by using contraceptives.

It helped in the supply and use of contraceptives to eligible couples. But over the years family planning also has adopted a broad orientation. It is now increasingly being regarded more than an intervention to promote the use of contraception. It is a means of caring for the health of mother and child, enhancing the quality of families by regulating and spacing child birth, raising the age at marriage and improving the position of girls and women, helping sub-fertile couples to beget children and providing counseling for parents and potential parents.

Despite these changes, the family planning education continues to address itself primarily to adults and youth, and its approach also remains predominantly prescriptive, explaining the oversimplified dogmatism of assertions like "small family is a happy family". Population education shares all the content of the family planning education and also focuses on its objectives. But the scheme of contents of population education is broader and its specific objectives are more varied than those of the family planning education. Both have basic differences in their approach. Population education does not follow prescriptive and didactic approaches. Whereas family planning education aims at conveying specific messages of family size and quality of life issues, population education focuses on influencing attitude and behaviour of individuals and developing basic thinking and decision-making skills in them.

Sex Education

Sex Education is an educational programme designed to provide learners with adequate and accurate knowledge about human sexuality in its biological, psychological, socio-cultural and moral dimensions. It largely, though not exclusively, focuses on the individual self-awareness, personal relationships, human sexual development, reproduction and sexual behaviour.

It also covers the anatomy and physiology of reproductive systems, physical, emotional and psychological changes during puberty and conception, pregnancy, and birth. It deals with sexual behaviour, sex roles and sexually transmitted diseases. Whereas population education deals with many of these contents, it focuses on their interrelationships with population issues and also on population processes other than fertility.

Family Life Education

Closely related to sex education, the family life education is an educational process designed to assist young people in their physical, social, emotional and moral development, as they prepare themselves for adulthood, marriage and parenthood. It deals with issues like ageing as well as social relationships in the sociocultural context of family and society. It provides an opportunity to the learners to study family relationships and peer relationships. It does not simply deal with physiology and anatomy of reproduction and human sexuality. While population education includes these concerns in its scheme of content, it also covers many other issues that are beyond the scope of the family life education.

Population Studies

Population studies is the body of knowledge, concepts and theories, which describe and attempt at explaining the dynamics of human populations and their relationships with social, cultural, economic, political and biological environments. It focuses on population issues related to the demographic processes of fertility, mortality and migration. It also covers components such as population size, age and sex composition, its spatial distribution and socioeconomic characteristics. Population studies as a general body of knowledge, therefore, has made substantial contribution to the knowledge base of population education.

During the initial years of the evolution of population education it was thought to be the be-all and end-all of population education, and the curriculum framers were expected to perform the simple task of including and hierarchically arranging the facts, theories and concepts of population studies into the scheme of content of population education. But over the years, the conceptual framework of population education has broadened to incorporate those components which do not belong to population studies but to other disciplines and professional fields, such as life sciences, medical sciences, social sciences, pedagogy, and psychology and so on. Moreover, population related attitudes, behaviour and decisions, rather than the internal logic of population studies are characteristically the major concerns of population education.

Population education differs from all the areas delineated above in that its need arose under special historical circumstances and some typical contemporary issues. Family planning education was initiated with a view to conveying specific messages focussed on the need to control population growth. Sex education originally developed in response to the concern for changing sexual mores and increasing incidence of deviant sexual behaviour, venereal diseases and out of wedlock pregnançies. Family life education grew out of recognition of the growing evidence of family instability and disintegration. Population studies evolved, not as a separate discipline but as an interdisciplinary body of knowledge by bringing together facts, theories and concepts based on the research studies conducted by the specialists of different disciplines and professional fields for explaining various facets of population phenomenon. Population education emerged as an educational response to the concern for population problems emanating from the changing inter-relationship between population and development.

It is primarily because of the context in which it emerged that population education, by its very nature, has been treated as a culture and region specific concept. Its definition in one country or region differs from that in the other. The numerosity of definitions is also the result of the constant changes being effected in the concept by including new areas of concern based on the experiences of international regional and national experimentation. Moreover, the definitions have been construed in various ways. Population education has been defined by describing the nature of activity or by stating objectives or contents or by spelling out behavioural outcomes. However, not all the definitions are actually different from one another; there is a substantial commonality among them with certain differences in the emphasis on some aspect or the other.

Population education is broadly defined as an educational intervention aimed at helping individuals in understanding the interrelationship between population and development, in appreciating the determinants and consequences of population processes and changes, in assessing the possible actions that they and their respective families and communities can take to modify these processes and in carrying out selected actions. It is a part of total social learning process and based on the premise that an educational intervention which helps the learners defines problems and search for solutions will have greater impact than the prescriptive programme that employs only assertions.

EVOLUTION OF THE CONCEPT IN INDIA

Since its inception the conceptual framework of population education has been changing quite frequently because of the changes in the perception of population phenomenon and its relationships with development variables. Every time when there was a change in the perception pattern of population issues, a need was felt to reconceptualise population education. Although the changes that have occurred in the conceptual framework of population education in different countries over the years have reflected the context-specific variations, there has been an overarching commonness in them. And hence, the understanding of the process of evolution of the concept of sometimes erroneously, population education in one country such as India will provide adequate insight into its evolution throughout the world.

Conceptualization of Population Education

The first attempt to conceptualise population education in India was made during late 1960s. The National Seminar on Population Education held in August 1969 made the following recommendations to define the concept:

- "The objective of population education should be to enable the students to understand that family size is controllable, that population limitation can facilitate the development of a higher quality of life.... It should also enable the students to appreciate the fact that for preserving the health and welfare of the members of the family, ensuring economic stability to the family... the Indian family of today should be small... with only two or three children."
- "Students at all levels have a right to accurate information about the effect of changes in family size and in national population on the individual, the family and the nation so that this body of knowledge is utilized to control family size and national population

- "Population should not be treated merely as a quantitative phenomenon.... It is the quality of the population that is most relevant both as a factor of growth and an end product of growth.

In pursuance of the recommendations of the National Seminar, a Population Education Syllabus was developed by National Council of Educational Research and Training (NCERT) in 1971. It defined population education as an educational intervention to make the target groups aware of the multi-faceted population phenomenon so that it leads them eventually to take rational decisions concerning population matters. The Syllabus contained a scheme of content which was developed by drawing contents from the six major content areas - population growth, population and economic development, population and social development, population health and nutrition, population, biological factors and family life and ecological considerations and population. Population education thus was treated as a demography-laden concept, predominantly as education in demography and population studies.

The need to reconceptualise population education was felt for the first time during the early part of 1980s because of certain specific reasons. Evaluation studies on various facets of the implementation of the National Population Education Project identified significant gaps in the integration of elements of population education in content and process of school education. It was realized that since population education had been treated as a demography-laden concept, its ambitious conceptual framework, with excessive elements of population dynamics, had hindered the process of effective integration of its elements into the school curriculum. The need for modification in the conceptual framework was also felt in the background of the recommendations adopted by the International Conference on Population held in Mexico City in 1984, which unfolded new dimensions of population phenomenon.

The initial step in reconceptualising population education was taken at the UNESCO Regional Seminar held in 1984, in which five major themes were identified as the core elements of the conceptual framework of population education. Those were: Family Size and Family Welfare, Delayed Marriage, Responsible Parenthood, Population Change and Resource Development, and Population related Beliefs and Values. The National Policy on Education 1986 which reflected the magnitude of the major causes and consequences of rapid population growth also specified "promotion of observance of small family norm" as one of the core curricular areas to be reflected in the national system of education. It provided an appropriate context to reconceptualise population education. Moreover, nearly half of the ten core curricular areas identified by the policy document such as equality of sexes, protection of environment, removal of social barriers, and inculcation of scientific temper were considered critical for realising population education objectives.

During the process of revision of the conceptual framework of population education in India, six major themes: family size and family welfare, delayed marriage, responsible parenthood, population change and resource development, population related values and beliefs, and status of women were identified. The scheme of content was prepared by drawing contents relating to these major themes from the following six content areas: economic development, social development, environment and resources, family life, health and nutrition, and demographic implications. The reconceptualised framework also emphasised the strategy of integrating maximum contents at minimum points in order to provide comprehensive treatment to contents to make the integration of population education elements in the textbooks more effective. The new conceptual framework defined population education as an education in the interrelationships among population, development, resources, environment and quality of life.

All concepts having an interactive relationship with social environment require reconsideration particularly after a perceptible change takes place in the context in which they were formulated. Sometimes, it is the odd fate of a concept to have too successful a rein. After it secures scientific acceptance, it may become so popular and fashionable that it is applied indiscriminately, leading to the dilution of its essential characteristics, generating a need to resuscitate it. The concept of population education has also undergone such a process. The need to reorient the conceptual framework of population education was reflected in the Istanbul Declaration and the Plan of Action adopted by the International Conference on Population Education and Development, 1993, which brought forth the limitations of the existing concept and recommended the inclusion of a number of emerging concerns in it.

But the reconceptualization of population education was necessitated by the latest and most striking development of a global consensus on population and development. In course of Population Debate since Malthus initiated it, population phenomenon has been analyzed in view of perceptions of its interrelationships with other variables of development and social environment. The present perceptions of the patterns of these interrelationships reflected in the Programme of Action (POA) adopted by the International Conference on Population and Development, held in Cairo in 1994, made it an imperative requirement for planned interventions addressed to population phenomenon to reorient, revitalize and rejuvenate them to realise the vision of the new paradigm of population and development.

The ICPD Programme of Action has effected what is being described as "Paradigm Shift" from number to conditions for population stabilization. It is considered essential now to focus on the individual needs instead of demographic targets and to integrate population concerns into development strategies rather than pursuing and providing sustenance to population control approach. Moreover, the ICPD for the first time has explicated two distinct roles of education:

a. Education as a key factor in population stabilization; and
b. Education as a means to promote greater responsibility and awareness of the interrelationships between

population and sustainable development. The need to shift from purely demographic or population control approach to a broader sustainable development approach has been advocated in other international conferences also.

The United Nations Conference on Environment and Development, Rio De Janeiro, 1992 focused on the linkages between population, natural resources, environment, development and quality of life in the Agenda-21: The Global Plan of Action adopted by it. The International Conference on Population Education and Development, 1993 and the Fourth World Conference on Women held in Beijing, 1995 that adopted Beijing Declaration and Platform for Action also emphasized these linkages. The experiences gained during the implementation of NPEP have also suggested the need to reconceptualise population education again.

The Population Education Framework even after the first reconceptualisation did not include elements relating to the process of growing up and HIV/AIDS, as these elements had been regarded very sensitive. But without these elements the Population Education Framework remained incomplete. In view of the problems that adolescents have been confronting for lack of authentic knowledge about the process of growing up from childhood to adulthood and the recently realized urgency to impart HIV/AIDS education, it was felt that the Population Education Framework must incorporate all the elements that had been considered crucial for attaining the objectives of population education.

Moreover, the Framework of Population Education being primarily influenced by the IEC approach had not been in consonance with the existing school curriculum framework, and hence the gaps in effective integration. Population education tended to be didactic making efforts to convey messages. But the existing school framework is open-ended and is considered a process during which messages are caught. Population education, therefore, needed to be reconceptualised as an educational endeavour that would make the learners aware of all possible dimensions of population - development interrelationships, promoting a general approach of supporting and empowering learners to take rational decisions regarding population and development issues; and also making them aware of the social consequences of their individual decisions. Accordingly, the population education framework was once again reconceptualised. It makes an attempt to focus on all possible variables that interact with population and development phenomena and to bring the concept of population education in tune with the existing school curriculum.

Bibliography

Ayyar, Vaidyanatha R.V., (1997), 'Educational Planning and Administration in India: Retrospect and Prospect', *Journal of Educational Planning and Administration,* Vol. XII, No.2, April 1997, pp.167-214.

Ayyar, Vaidyanatha R.V.,(1997), 'Basic Education and Human Rights', *Journal of Educational Planning and Administration,* Vol. XI, No. 1, January 1997, pp.67-87.

Basu, A.N., (1947), *Education in Modern India,* Orient Book Co., Calcutta.

Bhola, H.S., (1984), *Campaigning for Literacy,* UNESCO.

Dayal, Bhagwan (1955), *The Development of Modern Indian Education,* Orient Longman, Bombay.

Department of School Education, Government of Madhya Pradesh, Bhopal, *Annual Administrative Report* (1996-97).

Department of School Education, Government of Madhya Pradesh, Bhopal, *Annual Administrative Report* (1997-98).

Department of School Education, Government of Madhya Pradesh, Bhopal, *Annual Administrative Report* (1998-99).

Directorate of Public Instruction Madhya Pradesh, Bhopal, *Basic Educational Statistics* (1997).

Education and National Development Report of Education Commission, July 1996.

Education Policy in India 1968, Ministry of Education, Culture and Social Welfare, GOI, New Delhi, Aug. 1968.

Education for All - The Indian Scene, Department of Education, Ministry of Human Resource Development, GOI, Dec., 1993.

Gore, M.S., (1995), *Indian Education: Structure and Process*, Rawat Publication, Jaipur.

Govinda, R., (1997), *Decentralisation of Education Management: Experiences from South Asia*, International Institute for Educational Planning, Paris.

Haq, Ehsanul., (1997), *Education, Polity and Society*, Shipra Publications, Delhi.

Jolly, K.G., (1992), *Literacy for All by 2001: Strategies at District Level*, D.K. Publishers, New Delhi.

Limaye, P.M., (1945), *Education in India Today*, Deccan Education Society, Poona.

Mahajan Baldev and Others, (1994), *Education Administration in Madhya Pradesh (NIEPA)*, Vikas Publishing House, New Delhi.

Mehta, P.L. and Poonga, Rakhi (1997), *Free and Compulsory Education*, Deep and Deep Publications, New Delhi.

Naik, J.P., (1975), *Elementary Education in India: A Promise to Keep*, Allied Publishers, Bombay.

Naik, J.P., (1966), *Elementary Education in India - The 'Unfinished Business'*, Asia Publishing House, New Delhi.

National Policy on Education 1986, Ministry of Human Resource Development, GOI, New Delhi.

Premi, M.K., (1972), *Educational Planning in India*, Sterling Publishers, New Delhi.

Ramachandra, Vimala, (1996), *Women and Girls' Education in South Asia*. India Country Paper, (mimeo), 1996.

Rao, D. Pulla (1998), *Economics of Primary Education*, Rawat Publications, Jaipur.

Rao, Digumarti Bhaskara (1997), *Success story of a Primary Education Project*, APH Publishing Corporation, New Delhi.

Sen, Amartya and Dreze, Jean, (1995), 'Basic Education as a Political Issue', *Journal of Educational Planning and Administration*, Vol- IX, No. 1, January 1995, pp. 1-26.

Sharma Amita & Gopal Krishnan R., (1999), *A New Strategy for the Total Literacy Campaign* (Document 5, Rajiv Gandhi Mission, June 1999).

Sharma Amita and Gopal Krishnan R., (1996), *Bringing the People Back In: From Lok Sampark Abhiyan to Education Guarantee Scheme* (Document 3, Rajiv Gandhi Mission, October 1996).

Sharma Amita and Gopal Krishnan R., (1999), *Universal Primary Education and Total Literacy in Madhya Pradesh: A Proposal for Institutional Reform* (Document 4, Rajiv Gandhi Mission, March 1999).

Sharma Amita and Gopal Krishnan R., (1996), *Wanted, A New EGS: An Education Gaurantee Scheme* (Document 1, Rajiv Gandhi Mission, August 1996).

Sharma, S.N., (1995), *Elementary Education: Experience and Expectations*, Kanishka Publishers, New Delhi.

Singh, U.K., and Sudarshan, K.N., (1996), *Primary Education*, Discovery Publishing House, New Delhi.

Sinha, Amarjeet (1998), *Primary Schooling in India*, Vikas Publishing House, New Delhi.

Tilak, J.B.G., (1992), *Educational Planning at Grassroots*, Ashish Publishing House, New Delhi.

Tilak, J.B.G., (1995), 'Elementary Education in India in the 1990s, Problems and Perspectives', *Journal of Educational Planning and Administration*, Vol. 4, No.2, April, 1995, pp. 387-407.

Venkatesh, B. and Athreya, Sheela Rani Chunkath, (1996), *Literacy and Empowerment*, Sage Publishing.

Weiner, Myron, (1996), 'Child Labour in India: Putting Compulsory Primary Education on the Political Agenda', *Economic and Political Weekly*, Nov. 9-16.

Zellener, A. A. (1951), *Education in India*, Bookman Associates, New York.

Index

Q

R

S

T

U

W